Dedication

To dad and mom, for all the love!

About the Series

The African Humanities Series covers topics in African histories, languages, literatures, philosophies, politics and cultures and is intended to speak to scholars in Africa as well as in other world areas. Its core goal is to foreground the best research on the continent. The rigorous review process of submitted manuscripts, editorial vetting and, where warranted, involvement of a manuscript mentor to work with the author on their writing, assure that the best quality material is published.

The establishment of the African Humanities Association in Abuja in 2020 has allowed the Series to expand in scope and authorship beyond the original five participating countries of the African Humanities Program (Ghana, Nigeria, South Africa, Tanzania and Uganda), to include the entire continent. In addition, the African Humanities Series has broadened its coverage of topics and authorship to capture the work of scholars engaged in African Humanities research globally. The expanded scope encompasses two categories, each under its own imprint:

Reflections: A forum for African scholars as well as those in the diaspora to publish work on the state of the humanities on the continent. It will encourage especially senior scholars to reflect on their own experiences of past and current Humanities scholarship.

Cutting Edge: An outlet for innovative Humanities work which unsettles the boundaries of knowledge in ways which make us think anew about the abiding social problems across the continent.

The African Humanities Series is produced in collaboration with NISC (Pty) Ltd, established publishers of academic work on the continent, and is widely accessible in print and online formats from local and international sales outlets and aggregators of book content.

Series editors: Adigun Agbaje & Fred Hendricks

Published in the African Humanities Series

YABBING AND WORDING
The artistry of Nigerian stand-up comedy

IZUU NWANKWỌ

Published in South Africa on behalf of the African Humanities Association
by NISC (Pty) Ltd, PO Box 377, Makhanda, 6140, South Africa
www.nisc.co.za

First edition, first impression 2021
Publication © African Humanities Association 2021
Text © Izuu Nwankwọ 2021

ISBN: 978-1-920033-85-9 (softcover)
ISBN: 978-1-920033-86-6 (PDF)
ISBN: 978-1-920033-87-3 (ePub)

Project manager: Peter Lague
Indexer: Sanet le Roux
Cover design: Advanced Design Group
Cover photograph: © Fer Gregory/Shutterstock

Contents

Acknowledgements

I am grateful to God for the opportunity to have this work finally in print. Without the inspiration and direction You give, I would be nowhere near where I am today. Thank You! Much love to Nenye and our boys, Daniel and Dubem. The way you climb my back and your mom encouraging you with smiles is all the inspiration and motivation I need. You guys rock! A significant portion of my appreciation goes to the American Council for Learned Societies (ACLS), which has supported my research variously through its African Humanities Program (AHP). This publication's success is attributable to its unwavering support for humanities research in Africa. Through the AHP network, I have come to know great scholars who have, in no small measure, positively impacted my career. Special thanks to Ibukun Filani for his wealth of knowledge and commitment to the study of stand-up in Nigeria. I am also grateful to the Stellenbosch Institute for Advanced Studies (STIAS), the Alexander von Humboldt Foundation, and the Department of Anthropology and African Studies, Johannes Gutenberg University Mainz, for the several opportunities provided for researching, commencing and completing this book. Special thanks to my Alexander von Humboldt postdoctoral fellowship host, Professor Dr. Matthias Krings, for his trust, support, suggestions, and timely interventions. There are also individuals that I owe special thanks to, for this work – Rowland Amaefula for reading the first draft and making impactful suggestions, and Daria Tunca, Ifeyinwa Okolo, Laura S. Martin for their characteristic encouragement and nudgings.

Foreword

Today, Nollywood films and Afrobeats music are the two genres of popular culture for which Nigeria is best known beyond its borders, across the African continent and globally. Equally prolific, yet somewhat less known outside Nigeria, is a third genre: stand-up comedy. Like the other two, it originated during the 1990s, took off during the 2000s and has matured over the past decade. From its humble beginnings on radio and television and its evolution into multimedia variety live shows, staged not only in Nigeria but also in the diaspora, stand-up comedy has developed into Nigeria's third genre of popular culture to be reckoned with internationally.

Whereas the genre's name hints at inspirations taken from US models and elsewhere abroad, its very essence is uniquely Nigerian. It is rooted in the experience of the Nigerian everyday whose multiple challenges afford patience, witty workarounds and a personal approach that rather laughs about the inevitable than risk being dragged down by it. A wonderful expression of this attitude is to be found in the funny and often ironic 'translations' of acronyms almost every Nigerian is familiar with; during the 1980s, when the National Electric Power Authority (NEPA) failed to deliver a constant flow of electricity, its acronym thus came to stand for 'never expect power always'; also immortalised by a Tony Allen album of the same title in 1984. Creating their jokes mostly from the vantage point of the ordinary people, it is only consequential for comedians to perform in Nigerian Pidgin English, the lingua franca of the postcolonial Nigerian urban experience. In this sense, Fela Anikulapo Kuti, who decidedly crafted his lyrics in pidgin and was the first to take 'yabbing' – the satirical trading of insults – on stage needs to be mentioned as one of the forerunners of present-day stand-up comedians. Driven by Afrobeat music (not to be conflated with today's 'Afrobeats') his powerful, lyrical, sermon-like 'yabis' would last a whole night – as I was fortunate enough to experience during one of his shows in his Afrika Shrine back in 1991. Another precursor is to be found in Wale Adenuga, the founder of *Ikebe Super*, Nigeria's legendary tabloid-sized comic magazine. Before the first issue came out in 1976, Adenuga had been collecting jokes from the people's mouths for years which he then translated into his comic strips built around a cast of typical Nigerian stock characters he had created to engage an audience as diverse as possible; among them Papa Ajasco, a bald, womanising husband, Boy Alinco, an adventurous and somewhat self-loving lad with a signature coiffure and mode of walking, and Miss Pepeiye, a materialistic young lady. Quite comparable to the early Nigerian stand-up comedians who borrowed a generic form from elsewhere,

Adenuga did not invent the comic strip, the generic form he used for his artistry, but he thoroughly Nigerianised it. His comic characters became so successful that they survived the magazine's decline and soon after it went out of print took to a different medium. From 1997 onwards they have featured on television in a comedy series named "Papa Ajasco and Company" which has become very popular.

There are many others who need to be mentioned as precursors and early companions of Nigerian stand-up comedy, like radio and television comedy show hosts, masters of ceremonies, and Nollywood comedians. Since Izuu Nwankwọ introduces many of them in detail in this book, I restrict myself to singling out only one more here – the popular television and film actor, Nkem Owoh. As a comedian, he is most famous for acting the role of Osuofia, a somewhat stubborn but witty villager who travels to London to claim his long-lost brother's heritage. Owoh's hilarious performances have brought him a huge number of fans and I count myself among them. I might be wrong, but it seems to me that traces of Osuofia can still be found here and there in contemporary stand-up performances.

Some of the reasons for the immense popularity of stand-up comedy in Nigeria are not different from elsewhere: the performer's licence to violate social taboos that facilitates cathartic laughter caused by the delight in hearing the otherwise unspeakable on stage, the dialogic approach that brings the audience into the performance endowing them with agency by either laughing or refusing to laugh, or by 'heckling' to provoke an immediate response from the comedian, the chance to reflect on oneself and others or even society at large through the prism of parody, puns and other modes of what could be labelled a 'jocular anthropology'. In the Nigerian case, where live shows have very expensive VIP table seating segments in front of the stage, attending such events also serves the purpose of public self-presentation by means of conspicuous consumption. Those who cannot afford to buy even the cheaper tickets may at least follow by watching recordings sold on DVD, broadcast on television, or uploaded to the web. Other reasons for stand-up's popularity in Nigeria have been mentioned already: its ability to speak to the urban experience in the very medium of that experience, pidgin, and doing so mostly from the vantage point of the ordinary people. Despite this, stand-up performances cater to all strata of Nigerian society. What sounds like a paradox at first becomes less strange if one compares joking to eating. In Nigeria, as in many other African societies, one cannot distinguish class membership by what people eat but only by how often and how much they eat of certain (expensive) ingredients. In other words, as chief and commoner enjoy the same type of meal, they also tend to laugh at the same kind of jokes. Only in the past couple of years, have there been signs that this is beginning to change, and eating habits and joking preferences seem to gradually take on the significance of class markers. There is thus a growing sensibility among the educated middle class regarding gender issues and other sensitive topics. It will be interesting to observe how Nigerian stand-up comedians will accommodate these emerging differences in tastes of humour in the near future. Will individual performers begin to develop different sets for different class segments of society, something that, according to Izuu Nwankwọ, is taking place already as can be gleaned from comparing sets performed in Nigeria to those in the diaspora or elsewhere outside of Nigeria. Or will the entire comedy scene diversify, some catering for the middle classes, and others for those with a more robust sense of humour, as is the case in European societies?

While stand-up comedy has been male dominated in Nigeria for much of its existence, as is the case in most countries, there are now also a number of comediennes who have become very popular. As Izuu Nwankwọ explains, this has been facilitated by changing production formats and new distribution outlets such as social media platforms, webcasting and online streaming services. Whereas stand-up in Nigeria has long been associated mostly with live mega events that took on the character of variety shows aiming at 'total' entertainment by presenting a line-up of as many comedy performers and musical acts as possible, the forced move to online formats due to the COVID-19 pandemic has made the comedy 'industry', as it is often called, somewhat more accessible for newcomers, among them several female performers who have developed their own programmes.

In view of Nigeria's political geography, which divides the country (at least) into two parts, there is yet another peculiarity that needs pointing out when discussing the 'Nigerian-ness' of stand-up comedy in this country of over two hundred million: while it reflects the Nigerian everyday from a transethnic urban perspective, it clearly does so from a southern Nigerian viewpoint. Among the performers, northerners are literally missing. This is not because people in the northern parts would not know how to make others laugh – various social institutions point to the contrary, from formalised joking relationships between different ethnicities, professions, and generations, to royal court jesters, traditional travelling jokesters, and present-day video film comedians – all mentioned in this book. The absence of northerners on stand-up comedy stages rather mirrors the Nigerian cultural division between north and south, which has caused and continues to cause serious limitations to cultural exchange and rather fosters the doubling of cultural institutions catering to different audiences than the joining of forces. A good example of this is the two Nigerian film industries, Nollywood and Kannywood (the latter named after its northern production hub in the city of Kano) that exist side by side rather than collaborating. If northerners appear on southern comedy stages, it is by and large through impersonations by southern comedians, i.e., as figures to make fun of, such as the stereotypical 'aboki' – a patronising nickname given to northern migrants by southern city dwellers by, ironically, using the Hausa word for 'friend' – and not as performers in their own right. Despite this, or perhaps even because of it, Nigerian stand-up comedy is a shortcut to getting to know how Nigeria's urban population truly ticks. If you want to learn something about a people, turn to their joke(ster)s! By introducing his readers to Nigeria's dynamic comedy scene, Izuu Nwankwọ allows us to try this proposition for the case of Africa's most populous nation.

Professor Dr. Matthias Krings
Johannes Gutenberg University Mainz, Germany
September 2021

List of figures

.

Preamble

Yabbing comes from the Nigerian Pidgin English verb *yab*, and the verb *wording* (also a pidgin English expression) is a peculiar rendering of the noun *word*. The former denotes insulting or directly abusing someone, and it is a form of competitive exchange of spontaneously generated gags or outright ridicule. *Wording* also signifies the deployment of made-up funny yarns about one's opponent(s), but, in this case, it sometimes goes without outright ridicule. While both terms are used interchangeably to mean a war of wits, they are not the same, given that *wording* refers specifically to an exchange between two equally matched competitors. At the same time, *yabbing* means more of *talking down* at someone from a position of superiority or *punching up* in the manner of political satire. In this manner, when a comic is calling out the government for hypocrisy and corruption or hurling insults at individuals, groups or institutions, it is *yabbing* and not *wording*. Though scarcely studied as standalone humour traditions, these two are modern-day descendants of pre-colonial joking genres also found in various forms around Nigeria. They have permeated Nigerian stand-up practice in many ways, influencing how jokes are produced, dispensed, and received. Hence, although the nomenclature 'stand-up comedy' has a western origin, the present form of the stand-up art in Nigeria has a recognisable affinity with *yabbing* and *wording*, as well as many other pre-existing humour traditions.

Stand-up comedy's ancestry has a long-standing link with Jewish Americans before African Americans entered the genre in the 1960s (Auslander 2004, 107). The 1990s saw a resurgence of stand-up practice in the United States (US). This development had an overwhelming influence on the Nigerian entertainment scene through satellite television catalysing the emergence of professional joke performance in the country. However, the roots of what later turned out to be a vibrant stand-up tradition in Nigeria started to sprout from pre-colonial humour pieces presented by the comedic radio and TV pioneers of the early 1980s. The metamorphosis of Nigerian stand-up from these early acts to the boom era since the dawn of the twenty-first century parallels developments in the US. It is attributable to what Auslander identifies as the spread of stand-up comedy from its original space to being 'no longer confined to the cultural ghetto … (to) become a primary source of entertainment for a middle-class, cable-viewing, club-going audience' (1992, 196–197). Put more succinctly, before the emergence of professional stand-up practice in Nigeria in the 1990s and the successes that followed, jesters featured in social events as mere entertainers, principally as poorly remunerated masters of ceremony (MCs). Some comedians' accounts show how deeply ingrained the dislike for the performing arts was at that time. With an increased preference for less conventional forms of artistic expression, Nigerian stand-up artists transited from being mere MCs to becoming well-paid stage performers. Thus, the industry has grown from its humble beginnings to the present position of being one of the country's most lucrative and pervasive entertainment genres.

In considering Nigerian stand-up comedy and its various traits, one is reminded of the story of the seven blind people who went to *see* an elephant and how they each could only describe the enormous animal in terms of the part they could feel. Similarly, it is impossible to capture all dimensions of Nigerian stand-up practice, first because of the speed and expansiveness of its growth in the past three decades and, second, because it is still unfolding with the potential to undergo further changes. In addition, owing to the impact of the COVID-19 pandemic lockdown, further experimentations have emerged, especially with online performances and dramatic comedy. Currently, there is an assortment of performances, ranging from the glitzy mainstream practices to the less professional routines in formal and informal spaces. Mainstream jokesters control big money, feature in high-paying shows, corporate events, and official government/State functions, mainly in prestigious settings suitable for more privileged clientele. At the other end is the emergent, often unrecognised local practice, which occurs in small comedy clubs and at private and localised events like parties and church programmes. These are largely unknown, occurring on the fringes, because they are localised and restricted to in-group participants. They are, however, the training ground for most comics who eventually make it to the bigger league. They are also quite helpful and functional, pandering to the pockets of audiences, thereby keeping stand-up comedy alive for those who do not have the means to attend more expensive events.

This industry's success is a product of many factors, one of which is that at its inception, practitioners took advantage of stand-up's low-budget nature to fill the lacuna that the dearth of live theatrical performances had created. Its development as a cheaper stage art genre meant that artists could hold their events without first having to source funds, do a script, rent a venue, hire a cast and crew, commence rehearsals, engage publicity in order to get patronage and attend to all the capital-intensive requirements of theatre before the performance could take place. Initial performances were not entirely successful, but with the adoption of the Nollywood film distribution format to market the video recordings of live shows, further popularity came. New shows have emerged from the initial ones, thus providing vast opportunities for the burgeoning corpus of performers to showcase their talent. The proliferation of these humour gigs has also – in just three decades of professional stand-up practice – given rise to multiple 'generations' of Nigerian stage humourists in terms of joke forms, performance mechanics, themes and performers. Together, each of these specificities defines the Nigerian stand-up industry and underscores its position and relevance as a kind of popular creation aptly described as 'the unofficial' and 'non-canonical' cultural productions of everyday life that come from 'ordinary people' (Barber 2017, 1). Nigerian stand-up comedy fits into this category chiefly because it arose from the efforts of individual artists devoid of the support of government and corporate bodies. Interestingly, unlike other art forms such as Nollywood, which started in like manner, stand-up art in Nigeria has been largely ignored in scholarly considerations. Despite its successes on many fronts, it has received scant academic enquiry in Nigeria, thereby creating a massive gap between its practice and critical study.

One reason for the elision of stand-up comedy, especially in studies on present-day African arts, is that humour is viewed chiefly as a not-too-serious endeavour. This supposition is quite evident from orature wherein one sees that much of the extant cultural productions of humour in pre-colonial settings have been subsumed in other art categories. One way this has happened is through naming as evident in the statement that African languages have no 'specific words for theatre and drama' because they preferred 'terms that broadly encompass a host of performance activities' (Okagbue 2007, 1). As such, Nigerian languages, for example, do not have equivalent terms for generic compartmentalisations like comedy and tragedy, neither do they have separate words for music and drama or dance and acting. The three main languages use one word, which translates as *play* – *wasa* for the Hausa, *egwu* for the Igbo, and *mu sise* for the Yoruba. All forms of *play* – dancing, music, acting, jesting, masquerading – come under these terms, perhaps because there are no demarcations about the 'category' or 'genre' of play. Consequently, before now, in all its intrinsic varieties, *play* was communally viewed, appraised, and enjoyed. Thus, it is a composite word that denotes forms of entertainment that have now been compartmentalised according to western categorisations such as stand-up comedy, theatre, and so on. Furthermore, due to the largely oral nature of precolonial African performances, the transfer of most of its components into written form did not consider that in indigenous cultures such compartmentalisations were never used. Jocular enactments of all sorts are incorporated into others instead of becoming a standalone art form. Therefore, it is almost impossible to trace a direct link between pre-colonial joking relationships and modern-day variants like stand-up comedy.

Another challenge that African orature faced in its transfer into written form has been the inability to capture the entire gamut of enabling conditions of the original performances. This anomaly has negatively affected joke-telling, mainly because any joke's currency depends on the context and circumstances surrounding its telling. These environments make jokes more understandable and less offensive. It then follows that bereft of its accompanying milieu, the joke as a standalone artefact, is essentially mis(re)presented to succeeding generations and others who were not part of its original telling. The potential to portray jokes negatively outside its enabling surroundings is because the

> [u]nderstanding of oral works depends upon an appreciation of the totality of their historical essence: particular details such as spontaneous composition and performance, traditional pattern, textual contents rendered in vocal utterances, communal participation (e.g., narrator and the audience as in a folktale session), place and time of performance, costume, as well as social and supernatural essences... (Na'Allah and' الله. 1997, 125)

Consequently, since some original performance environments and social references of most orature have not survived, it is impossible to determine what purposes some of them served in the communities of their production. Specifically, satiric performances have been relegated to the background in the move from orality to written scripts because, due to their peculiar existence at the nexus of abuse and amusement, many of them have become unduly irreverent, offensive, and inappropriate. More so, those that survived have become somewhat absorbed as appendages to other forms to which they were formerly superior or equal. One evident example is that joke telling is more suited for oral transmission. As such, some of its basic elements cannot be truthfully presented in writing. For example, how does one record the response of the audience to the joke? It is undoubtedly an impossible task to recreate specifics like tonal quality, gestures, movement, use of songs, and other specific joke qualities expended in the moment of narration. None of these can faithfully be taken from one generation to another, and definitely not from spoken to written texts. Thus, it is evident that the nature of transference of orature, to no small extent, disfavoured performed comedy; hence, some of its elements have been absorbed into other genres. For these and other challenges, comedy has been considered a less serious art and, as such, much of what belonged to it in oral tradition has been attributed to other genres.

The third challenge is that traditional observances, especially the satiric ones, do not influence people as they used to. In the past, people would naturally avoid acts that would make them susceptible to being ridiculed by artists. Today, there is a sense of intolerance, and people who are offended by satire can seek redress in courts (Chima 2017, 136). Both Islam and Christianity, since their inception in Nigeria, have facilitated the loss of a substantial chunk of orature through their outright interdiction of various traditional observances and beliefs. Early Christian missionaries, for one, left no chance for any form of 'adulteration' of its 'pure religion' and, as such, sought to destroy every trace of indigenous beliefs, some of which have nothing to do with religion. In doing this, the accompanying *play* that followed festivities and religious celebrations was roundly demonised, condemned, and eventually lost. Therefore, devoid of the communality of traditional societies and the somewhat homogenous adherence to the same commonly held religious and socio-cultural rules, contemporary living conditions have become much more heterogeneous than they used to be. Thus, there is a more diverse view of satire, emboldening and rationalising opportunities for offence.

This book's geographical scope is Nigeria, explicitly focusing on the mainstream stand-up events and comedy clubs in the country's entertainment hubs of Lagos, Abuja, and Port Harcourt. Mentions of the influence of Nollywood on stand-up's development are made. The work discusses the origins and the personae of Nigerian stand-up comedy explicitly, examining the historical and social contexts of joke-telling within the country and the global outreaches of the practice. As such, it is expository, examining Nigerian stand-up comedy's procedures of enactment and appreciation, analysing and appraising its form, content, and personae, and laying bare its uniqueness and similarities to other art forms. Joke themes, individuals involved in making laughter, the artistry of it all, the mechanics of enactment, the contexts within which jokes are made humorous, and how this is achieved are all part of the book's discourses. There is also the analysis of language deployment and its particular uses within stand-up enactments, the types of audiences specific comedians play to, venues in which these exchanges happen, and the various ways in which stand-up comedy is staged and distributed in Nigeria. One of the closing chapters is dedicated to discussing diaspora artists to show the nation's contribution to stand-up comedy globally. Thus, the book provides a study of an art genre other than literature and video films, for which Nigeria has become renowned over the past couple of decades. It contributes to bridging the gap between the practice and the academic study of Nigerian stand-up comedy. It thus seeks to diversify attention and catalyse increased interest in emergent and marginal art forms, which have become more veritable yardsticks for measuring artistic preferences and contemporary urban tastes in Africa today. Furthermore, the book is an additional contribution to studies on how evolving popular art forms fill up spaces opened up by the escalating inability to sustain productions in hitherto more conventional forms due to depletion in funds and patronage. It further brings critical attention to an ongoing joke-telling tradition often occluded in global humour research.

The book does not argue in any way that stand-up comedy is theatre, nor does it strive to posit it as a replacement for theatre. However, it adduces a position that sees stand-up art as a kind of live performance that continues to flourish on the Nigerian stage in ways that theatre has not been able to do for over four decades now. Successes in stand-up practice have reactivated interests in theatre staging in parts of Nigeria. Discourses in the book take cognisance of the peculiarities of stand-up art, specifically seeing the art from a sympathetic view of the strenuous routes through which comedians entertain audiences via the evocation of laughter. Such sympathy is not borne out of a sense of pity, but from an appreciation of the eerily unsettling feeling of standing in front of a bunch of strangers who are there for just laughs, and not any kind, but that of seeing performers denigrate themselves. Also, given that the success of routines depends on the amount of laughter elicited in the audience, stand-up comedy places unequalled forms of demands on performers. Put more succinctly, no other artist is constrained to provide entertainment in this manner and to do so without recourse to insulating mechanisms such as the fictional characters of novelists, poets, and playwrights, or just working like painters, sculptors, and other artists who do not have to be present when their work is displayed. The directness of stand-up art – the comedian's stage presence and the confrontational nature of joke-telling – makes it an in-your-face kind of presentation. Even when what the jokester says is entirely made up, it appears to be personal opinions, part of the reason for the growing censure comedians have been receiving.

For audiences accustomed to games where insults and verbal abuses are exchanged, such as *yabbing* and *wording*, Nigerians are well inured to playing with offence. In this book, there are explorations of the use of various forms of subjects that are ordinarily divisive but very amusing when deployed on the stand-up stage. Fela Anikulapo-Kuti's song, "Shuffering and Shmiling," [Suffering and Smiling] underscores the capacity of Nigerians to find amusement, even in the direst of circumstances. Over the past two decades, with the dawn of multiparty democracy in 1999, Nigerians had been hoping for a better life under civilian rule after many torturous years of military dictatorship. The opposite has been the case, with every successive government becoming worse than its predecessor. Corruption has multiplied exponentially, and, in its midst, there is growing insecurity on several fronts with no sign of it abating any time soon. Government ineptitude and the inability to enact policies that would make life better for ordinary people have become the norm. The economy has taken hits as foreign debt once again rises to unmanageable heights. Amidst this, Nigerian audiences are finding succour in laughter. Comedians have become essential to the psychological well-being of the people as they navigate the many troubling experiences of contemporary Nigeria, ridiculing and speaking truths that others can only mutter in private and out of trepidation. Even with the End-SARS[1] protests in late 2020, which the Buhari government shut down with lethal force, Nigerian comedians and other artists were directly involved in mobilising people online and in-person at protest sites. This is one of the ways in which stand-up comedy has progressed from being merely a stage work to actual activism in bringing about social change.

Notes

1 SARS refers to the Special Anti-Robbery Squad of the Nigerian police which has been implicated in numerous human rights violations. Nigerian youths took to street protests to ask for its proscription. Instead of heeding their calls, the government sent soldiers and scores died, especially in Lagos.

1

Origins and influences

Pre-colonial joke performance genres

There are informal situations wherein community members are entertained by personae who unwittingly take up comic roles and exert the same through their actions. These characters do not engage in such acts out of their own volition. Hence, they are here considered 'unconscious' performers, because their acts result from 'deviant' behaviours inherent in drunkenness, exhibitions of cowardice, stereotypical attitudes that designate extreme poverty, being introverted and/or extroverted, and expressions of being frivolous or miserly with money. There are also the less salutary attitudinal derivatives from the mentally challenged, people with speech difficulties, autism, and other forms of physical challenges. These latter forms are pretty caustic and are prone to arousing a sense of repulsion and offence when exploited for the generation of humour. Where none of these persons aims to evoke laughter through their actions, it is wholly politically incorrect to consider their or anyone else's living conditions funny, given the overabundant ethical and moral transgressions that such depictions instantiate. Even though most characterisations of these aforementioned traits do not necessarily seek to mock the affected individuals, such representations are incontrovertibly insensitive, inappropriate, demeaning, and offensive.

Despite the high level of sensitivities that now surrounds these subjects, comedians often elicited many of the character traits noted above for humour-generation. Drunkards, mentally-challenged people, minorities, and people living on the margins of different communities were often made fun of and easily turned into objects for jokes and ridicule. These unconscious performers either evoked humour by their actions or were imitated by performers for the same purpose. One of the most common appropriations of unconscious performance in present-day stand-up is that of drunkenness. Often, the use of drunkenness by humourists is not to satirise those who drink excessively but to use their demeanour for other ends. For instance, in drunkenness, with the resultant loss of mental cognition, people become more loquacious than usual, thereby acquiring the ability to confront or speak to anyone in any manner they deem fit. A drunk person loses the capacity to be ashamed or scare easily, thus becoming fearless to the point of publicly deflating the egos of highly placed persons. Also, given that inebriated persons have peculiar speech and behavioural patterns – the slurred incoherent speech, droopy eyes, unsteady gait, and the like – their acts become humorous, especially when accurately mimicked by jokesters. This deviant role confers upon individuals a licence to criticise just about anybody and broach taboo subjects without any backlash. In fact, in certain instances, when a drunk person talks in this manner, and his (since most depictions of drunkenness are of men) victims cannot act against him, the natural thing they do is to dub the individual 'a mad person.' However, not being considered serious does not detract from the truthfulness of the statements; nor does it make them less humorous.

In several Nigerian communities, some children and adults have been known to provoke or incite drunk and sometimes mentally challenged people for fun. Some people also mimic character traits gleaned from everyday life to create laughter. Depictions of character eccentricities are garnered from careful observation of people and then kept only to be retold for private or public entertainment at a later date. Of course, such representations are hardly given in front of the individuals being referred to, but when they are known to the audience, laughter comes also from the performer's ability to accurately replicate the personalities and their demeanour. Comedians are usually successful when they are able to create believable circumstances on which to erect their joke work. On the professional Nigerian comedy stage, character traits – gait, manner of speaking, body movement, and the like – have been used to describe various public figures. For example, former presidents Olusegun Obasanjo and Goodluck Jonathan, while still in office, were described as being miserly and spendthrift, respectively. Some other characterisations of public figures are discussed in subsequent chapters. One bequest of forms of unconscious or 'abnormal' enactments of humour is that contemporary artists often adorn the garb of 'madness' to speak the truth without the fear of being victimised. Their personae have roots in Igbo culture since 'the Igbo perceive madness as a state in which an individual could condemn evil without fear of punishment' (Ezenwa-Ohaeto 1999, 122).

Imitations of drunkenness and madness by comedians are best seen as the adornment of 'the mask (or courage) of the madman to speak about the evils in his [or her] society' (Bodunde 2001, 65). Thus, comedians wear this mask to speak the truth fearlessly, not only to and about the government, but also to the ordinary people about shortcomings and eccentricities they naturally overlook. Bodunde puts it more directly by positing that artists question 'the actions of despots' through the momentary embellishment of the mask of 'madness' (2001, 95). Nigerian stand-up artists employ the cloak of madness to shroud their satire and criticism. For example, Ahamefula Igwemba (Klint da Drunk) plays the stock character of a drunk on Nigeria's stand-up stage. Using this persona, he counters hecklers and often insults members of the audience. One of his favourite neutralising statements is:

I am making a fool of myself. You paid to come and watch me make a fool of myself. Between two [sic] of us, who is mad?

Klint reserves this form of retort for his most persuasive hecklers, a statement that reverses the supposition of madness, placing it on the audience who pays to watch a 'mad man' rather than on the individual playing the 'mad man' to make money. The difference between Klint da Drunk and the wretched-looking village fool, drunk with palm wine, for instance, is imitation and actuality. Their similarity is in the gratification that they receive: Klint gets paid for his appearance on stage, the village fool gets more drink and sometimes food depending on who they are entertaining. In more precise terms, Klint da Drunk is a modern-day replica of the village fool; a professional who adorns the act of drunkenness rather than being one himself. Alongside Klint's depictions of inebriety, another Nigerian comedian, Jephthah Bowoto (Akpororo), has successfully created his brand of stand-up around imitations of madness. He affirms to the audience that he is mad and that his stage acts are products of his 'madness.' Even on his social media handles, Akpororo posts videos of his performances to promote his self-acclaimed madness. These enactments are made up of ridiculous dance steps, prancing around the stage in energetic movements, and vigorous shaking of his long dreadlock hairstyle. He sometimes rolls his eyes, opened wide to the point that they become scary, and makes gibberish utterances. Having established this form of background, Akpororo finds the pedestal to situate very satirical statements about government personnel interspersed with statements such as: 'my head de touch o,' 'na craze we dey,' among others.[1]

Apart from these less formal unconscious productions of humour, there are more conventional forms in several pre-colonial Nigerian communities. Among what has historically been considered as the major tribes out of the over two hundred and fifty others, the Yoruba *efe* or *yeye*, the Hausa *wawan sarki* (king's fool),' *yan kama* (literally, 'the catchers'), and its numerous variants, as well as the Igbo *njakiri* (literally means 'jest') and *ikoonu* (insult) are better known. Other tribes also have equivalents of these forms, with the *Kwagh-hir* of the Tivs, a puppet theatre still being practised, coming tops in terms of scholarly interrogation.[2] These enactments provided a licence for 'clowns, fools and jesters [...] not only to express things which are commonly unthought (and very often unthinkable) but to embody them, and [...] to act them out' (Grainger 2010, 23). Modern-day comedians have in various ways borrowed extensively from these pre-colonial humour-performance genres in building their acts, on the one hand, while local audiences have been conditioned to be more receptive to offence-prone jokes due to earlier experiences of these enactments.

For the Igbo, satire played essential roles in keeping people in check since there was no central government, meaning that people lived in independent communities administered by groups of elders and titled men.[3] Scholars rightly observe that '… the Igbo of all social cadres are encouraged from infancy to participate in events of jollity and conviviality often lodged in jokes, some of them quite biting' (Nwachukwu-Agbada 2014, 379). *Njakịrị*, defined as a 'joke or jest […] that has] a humbling tirade with a ticklish outcome in view' (Nwachukwu-Agbada 2006, 153), is one example of such satirical engagement. It is an exchange of ridicule, a teasing game among adult (mostly male) friends, family members and acquaintances. The nature of *njakịrị* informed this observation more than eight decades ago: 'one may often see two Igbo reviling each other in the strongest language for several minutes and then bursting into laughter as they walk away' (Meek 1937, 230), highlighting the playfulness and lightheartedness of the genre. Despite its regularity and funniness, *njakịrị* 'can [also] hurt, abuse, or humble the recipient' (Nwachukwu-Agbada 2014, 379), thereby causing not just offence but possibly an escalation into a brawl. The other variant, *ịkọọnụ*, is a more serious type of *njakịrị*, which comes close to cursing (*ịkpọiyi*). Though there are times when one becomes the other, *ịkpọiyi* seldom becomes a form of jesting because it is used in severe confrontations to inflict pain with words. Ebeogu refers to them as 'two shades of the rhetorical art' from which the 'njakiri context emerges' (1991, 29): an indication that *njakịrị* usually contains elements of other forms of abuse exchange within its cavernous and receptive corpus.

Nevertheless, it is worth noting that *njakịrị* is more laid back, mostly engaged by adult males amidst other more sombre discussions. In contrast, *ịkọọnụ* is more fast-paced and is primarily a game played by children or a serious quarrel between adult females, in which case it could spiral into *ịkpọiyi* or *ịdụikwu*.[4] Indubitably, most forms of verbalised abuse among the Igbo deploy 'mockery, noisy laughter, raillery, parody, exaggeration and understatement of image' (Nwachukwu-Agbada 2004, 153). Differences among various forms of Igbo rhetorical joking relationships come from levels of playfulness and seriousness, better summarised thus:

> Once a joke loses its njakiri flavour, it becomes *ikoonu*, a type of *nleda* (looking down on another person) and therefore outright *mkpari* (profound abuse). Thus, *njakiri*, is amusing if it merely generates hilarity, comicality, or jocular figuration. […] the Igbo poetic insult of similes (or *ikoonu*) calls for some type of description that may hurt. The verbal Igbo exchange of *ikoonu* is of two kinds—the playful type, usually among children, which is of interest to us here, and the caustic types, usually among adults. As already mentioned, among adults, *ikoonu* derives from *nleda*, and, as a result, it is *mkpari*. However, among children, it is the first lesson in the roughness of life. (Nwachukwu-Agbada 2014, 378–380)

Apart from noting the symbiotic relationships among the different forms of Igbo satire, it can be inferred from the foregoing that comedy for the average Igbo person is primarily shaped by ịkọọnụ at childhood, from where people hone their skills in preparation for the adult form, njakịrị. Among adults, ịkọọnụ becomes something else, and is generally not accepted as a form of play.

Besides these divisions of satirical performances among the Igbo, the night masquerades performed judicial and entertainment functions to shame, mock, and sometimes execute judgment on errant community members. Night masquerade performances featured in different forms in pre-colonial Igbo societies, mostly deploying satire as their basic operating mode. In most Igbo communities, the night masquerade group is exclusive to individuals who had passed through pre-set tests and learnt the strict rules of the responsible guild. Only members of the masking group could be about at night while every other community member remained indoors, with all lights put out.[5] With their guttural voice and esoteric riddle-laden language, night masquerades walk the length and breadth of the community in the dead of night, calling out evildoers. They sing, dance, and play amongst themselves while the rest of the village is under the blanket of darkness. However, amidst the playfulness, which is also a form of entertainment, the serious business of righting the wrong and punishing of offenders is carried out. The deeds of the night masqueraders will only be evident at dawn when people emerge from their homes. Ezenwa-Ohaeto captures the nature and essence of this form of masking in the introduction to his collection of poems titled, *The Voice of the Night Masquerade*, where he observes that,

> [...] it is the cultural tradition in my part of the world, that when abominations become unbearable, and the truth must be told with great courage, then the night masquerade appears [...] to set a senseless practice right; sometimes the night masquerade must confront the ruler and point out the nakedness of his utterances [...] this is the voice of the night masquerade, I am only the medium. (1996, 8)

Specifically, these night masquerades called *Achụkwụ* or *Onye-kulu-ya* are 'lampooning masks' that 'can publicise, ridicule and disgrace … criminals without challenge as a first step to social control' (Udoye 2011, 103), employing various satiric renditions to shame offenders. This form of masking was also prevalent among the Yoruba of southwestern Nigeria.

Unlike the Igbo, however, the Yoruba had a centralised administration before colonisation under the ancient city of Ife. Their night masquerade performance is known as *efe*, often performed by *gelede* made up of a group of masked female performers. *Efe* is more widespread among the Yoruba than the night masquerades are in Igboland. It is a joke performance in which performers have the licence to use songs and other artistic mediums to 'allude to misdemeanours and other indiscretions' (Apter 2007, 69) within the society. The aim is to shame culprits and possibly get them to change their ways. Lawal describes it precisely 'as a "play," "buffoonery," "sometimes to laugh at" [something with] numerous songs ridiculing or mocking foolish or antisocial behaviour' (1996, 38). Where the Igbo example is restricted, *efẹ* takes place at the central market with the whole community in attendance: 'men, women, children—all bringing with them lamps, mats, chairs, and food. They arrange themselves in a large circle, often sitting together in age group societies' (Drewal and Drewal 1983, 18). Sola Olorunyomi provides a cogent description of both the *gẹlẹdẹ* masks and their acts by averring that,

> *Efé* and *gelede* are intertwined. *Efé* is primarily a satirical form, and it is the high point of the *bolojo* season when the *gelede* masquerade makes an outing. [...] The term *efé* itself refers, first, to the mask; second, to the mask's songs, poems and actions; and third, to the entire concert. An additional contemporary usage of *efé* is to equate it with a joke. *Gelede*, on the other hand, is *essentially* a female mask primarily concerned with ethics of guaranteeing social peace and order. (2003a, 166)

As such, *efẹ* is often a review of communal activities by the women because they use the festival's opportunity to satirically evaluate all instances of antisocial and deviant attitudes in the past year. Against this backdrop, Drewal sees *gẹlẹdẹ* as a 'tribute to the special powers of women' (1974, 8) in compelling the menfolk and every other community member to be conscious of their actions.

The highpoint of *efẹ* is that 'the traditional artist gets a day off from seriousness and rationality and is empowered by the community to ridicule all forms of rules, individuals high and low, gods and systems' (Obafemi 1996, 56). The implication is that *efẹ* is a liminal period within communal festivals wherein comedians – masked and unmasked – are given leave to poke fun at any event, person, or institution of their choosing. These community-endorsed privileges are thus described as

> sanctioned obscenities [that] made social sense [because performers are allowed to channel] repressed desire and 'pent-up emotion' [...] into harmless 'palliatives' [...] and collective activities that were generally (but not exclusively) sanctified by [the] ceremonial. (Apter 1998, 68)

Put differently, the performers of *efẹ* 'devise a painless way of [...] making [humanity] laugh at its absurdity and defusing its pain, at least temporarily, by the creation of an alternative reality' (Grainger 2010, 23). This reversal of the profoundly serious to the less harmful within *efẹ* comes through sundry comic styles: 'ridicule (*yeye*), jokes (*awada*), and jest (*apara*)' (Lawal 1996, 130); and all these forms are identifiable in today's stand-up comedy.

The Hausa of northern Nigeria had a highly developed pre-colonial joke performance tradition most similar to stand-up comedy. The *dan kama*, a 'solo performer[,] addresses an audience, usually in a market, playing a range of character types' specifically to elicit laughter (Dan-Inna and Tandina 1997, 216). Like stand-up comedians, the *'yan kama* (mostly travelling artists who played both in public spaces and in royal courts) worked solely to instigate amusement with the use of an array of comedic devices.[6] They are described explicitly as 'burlesque artists' who 'perform in groups of two or three for money in markets and at social gatherings' and are 'perhaps the most overtly mimetic' of Hausa traditional performers (Furniss 1996, 86). *Yankamanci*, the art of the *'dan kama*, involved the use of 'satirical skits, songs and scurrilous surrealism' (Banham, Hill and Woodyard 1994, 70), whose practitioners are 'traditional clowns' (Khaleel 1996, 44).[7] Their artistry included engagement 'in social criticism, but deal[ing] less with serious issues of governance and administration,' they used a great deal of imitation while mostly directing their parodic statements at themselves (Kofoworola 2007, 106). Furthermore, as satirists and imitators, *'yan kama* employ *habaici*, described 'as a useful, albeit mean-spirited way … to mock someone indirectly,' using the 'the comedians' "skilful touches of humour"' to tone the satiric sting down (Gaudio 2009, 98). Hence, *'yankamanci* is very similar to contemporary stand-up except that it also involved the additional artistry of funny magic, tricks, and pranks adjoined to the performers' verbal exploits.

Wawan sarki (the king's fool) was another variant of joke performer in northern Nigeria. He served as an informal go-between for the king and his subjects, running uncensored commentaries on socio-political matters by relating the people's feelings to the king and, in turn, making the king's intentions clearer to his subjects. He could also ridicule, satirise, and amuse the king and his courtiers through the use of 'slapstick, parody and satiric burlesque', with which he communicated 'serious messages in the form of jokes without creating any form of embarrassment' (Kofoworola 2007, 105). Thus, the *wawan sarki* possessed 'verbal licence within the environment of a traditional court' (Furniss 1996, 86). In this manner, the *wawan sarki* was the 'jester-cum-adviser of the Chief,' and his 'free association with the *Sarki* earned him the title,' *abokin wasan Sarki* (the king's playmate) (Joe 1984, 22). Consequently, where the *'dan kama* owns the public spaces outside the palace with what Kofoworola identifies as his 'witticism and innuendoes' (2007, 103), the *wawan sarki* is a member of the king's court who goes mostly where the king goes, sometimes even being seen on horseback in public as the king (Joe 1984, 25). Certain characteristics of these joke traditions have in multiple ways condensed into present-day stand-up comedy, depicting the latter as a piebald genre of humour incorporating old and new forms of jesting.

Television and radio comedy

Hubert Ogunde (1916–1990) established a thriving theatre in southwestern Nigeria in the 1940s based on the pre-colonial Yoruba travelling theatre tradition before others like Duro Ladipo, Kola Ogunmola, Moses Olaiya, and Oyin Adejobi came on board. Ogunde's theatre was popular, syncretic, and exerted tremendous influence on the form of succeeding Nigerian theatre (Lindfors 1976; Clark 1980; Fiebach 2009; Ajayi-Soyinka 2011; Coates 2017). Comedic enactments were the speciality of Moses Olaiya, better known by his stage name Baba Sala. He was 'a carefree clown who cannot be linked to anything serious,' to the point that the name Baba Sala became synonymous with anyone who behaves 'in an unserious and clownish manner'(Onifade 2011). With an increase in the number of theatre groups came competition which led practitioners to explore other mediums and methods such as 'waxing their music and plays in discs [and] printing their plays as photo-plays and literature' (Adedeji and Ekwuazi 1998, 163). The establishment of Western Nigeria Television, Ibadan (WNTV) in 1959 also lured a couple of theatre companies into television specifically to fill in the need for local content (Olayiwola 2011, 187). Baba Sala and his Alawada Theatre group won a 'Talent Hunt' contest sponsored by NTA Ibadan station in 1965. This success enabled the group to get a weekly half-hour slot on prime-time television (Haynes 1994, 17), thereby birthing Nigerian television comedy.

Television made Baba Sala extremely popular, especially in southern Nigeria (Lakoju 1984, 39–40). His comedy brand, derived from *efe*, enabled him to create unparalleled dexterity in treating the 'excruciatingly funny, the farcical' (Obafemi 1996, 55). With his borrowings from Yoruba oral tradition, Olaiya emerged as a precursor to slapstick comedy in Nigeria. He managed his stage and TV presence so well that he equalled Hubert Ogunde and Duro Ladipo in the theatre while still being hailed as the father of Nigerian television comedy. The success of his work encouraged the emergence of such other talents on television and radio as Gbenga Adeboye, Papa Luwe, and Jaguar. They were equally outstanding in their outlandish portrayal of dramatic as well as verbal comedy. Gbenga Adeboye, for instance, took over radio and replicated Baba Sala's television successes. He had a large following in the southwestern part of Nigeria, with jokes in Yoruba. His presentations 'rendered through rich Yoruba poems, mythology and imagery on Lagos State Broadcasting Corporation in the 1980s, [earned] him the name "Funwontan" which translates as "no-holds-barred"' (Olonilua 2011).

The southeast region experienced its television and radio comedy in Mike Ori Ife Di Mma (literally, Mike who eats good things) and Uche Ogbuagu (Mr Talkingson). Mike, who lived in the commercial city of Onitsha and worked closely with film sellers at the Upper Iweka Road market in the late 1980s and early 1990s, is esteemed for his comedies on television which he eventually released on VHS videotapes titled "Ife na-eme n'Okpuru Anyanwụ" (literally, 'The things that take place under the sun').[8] Mike's work preceded *Living in Bondage* (Rapu 1992), an Igbo language film that kickstarted Nollywood. Mr Talkingson distributed his work mainly on audiotapes and through radio presentations. He performed on radio stations around

Aba and its environs and was popular in Igbo-speaking areas. He did not use video to circulate his work but eventually became part of professional stand-up comedy. Mike and Mr Talkingson told their jokes in Igbo language. The former used more recorded drama on video films while the latter used radio and audio cassette, moving on to add stage appearances as stand-up art became widely accepted by audiences in the southeast. There are more comedic emergences in other parts of Nigeria that are equally localised and well-suited to the humour needs of those communities which are too diverse and beyond the scope of this book to enumerate and discuss.

It was not until the 1980s that 'NTA in its typical "one-Nigeria"-wisdom, had three weekly comedy programmes from the three "cultural" regions: [*Village Headmaster*] from Lagos, [*Samanja*] from Kaduna, and [*The Masquerade*] from Enugu' (Fiofori 2010). *The Village Headmaster* was a serious drama with a couple of comic characters, created for NTA by Olusegun Olusola and produced by Dejumo Davis. It started as a radio before metamorphosing into a TV soap opera, running from 1968 to 1988 as Nigeria's longest running television drama series. The setting is mainly in the palace of Kabiyesi, the full titled ruler of a small community where the characters table, discuss and decide on several issues arising from the people's day-to-day lives. *Samanja Mazan Fama* featured the main character, Samanja, played by Usman Baba Pategi.[9] This television drama series started first in Hausa language on NTA Kaduna in the 1970s, but later migrated to the Network Service of the NTA, where it changed its language to Nigerian Pidgin English to accommodate a wider audience, in the 1980s and remained till the 1990s. The programme's story surrounds the living conditions and lifestyle of the rank and file of the military. It satirised soldiers and barrack life at a time the nation was under military rule. For its part, *The New Masquerade*, created by James Iroha and which aired on the NTA Network Service in the 1980s and 1990s, centres on a middle-class family's domestic life amidst the challenges of economic difficulties further compounded by oppressive fiscal policies of the government.[10] The principal character is Zebruddaya, played by Chika Okpala, who, through this TV drama, created a personality that has gone beyond its original setting to become almost a permanent identity for him. By way of summarising the contributions of these earlier television comedies and their eventual demise in the 1990s, Fiofori (2010) observes that,

> Somewhere along the line, these comedy programmes lost their fun-punch and became predictable. They degenerated into either trading long-winded insults in convoluted English as jokes or were thinly woven around obvious and obnoxious tribal and social-class jokes; including supposed jokes at the expense of physically challenged people. No wonder when Ken Saro Wiwa's Basi and Company hit the TV screens it was an instant well-deserved success for its intelligent play on words. Wiwa's show raised the bar, for good, in Nigerian English-language comedy!

Fiofori's statements capture the transition in television comedy in Nigeria, from the farcical, pidgin and broken Englishes low comedy of the older programmes mentioned above, to the more elitist, standard English high comedy of Ken Saro Wiwa's *Basi and Company*. It started in 1986 on the Network Service of the NTA and ran till 1990, captivating audiences nationwide, creating humour from the several mishaps of Basi and friends, who are hellbent on becoming millionaires by whatever means possible, and their landlady, known as Madam de Madam.[11] The drama showcased the get-rich-quick escapades of a group of individuals in the face of worsening living conditions under the military. These characters' escapades reflected the frustrations of ordinary Nigerians while bringing laughter into homes through their comedic renditions. The impact of Nigerian television dramas of the 1960s through to 1990s has been investigated in a handful of studies: Okigbo 1986, Umeh (1989), Timothy-Asobele (2003), Betiang (2013), and Haynes (2016).

MCs and events entertainers

In the 1980s, alongside the television drama explosion and amidst the doldrums of worsening socioeconomic conditions in the country, several comedians emerged, some of whom were TV personalities. These performers served primarily as masters of ceremonies (MCs) engaged mainly to anchor social events. Though not expected to make their audiences laugh, their ability to crack up attendees at functions turned out to make their services more sought after. Because people enjoyed the jokes more than the business side, their trade's funny side gradually became more explicit. Those who made their mark in this way include Patrick Doyle, Bisi Olatilo, Femi Segun, Femi Jarret, Leo Onmudi, and Smart Otemu. This crop of comedians never crossed the threshold to become stand-up comedians. Instead, they remained in their other jobs, especially journalism, basically because of the subsisting social label attached to comedians as unserious and somewhat wayward people. In addition, comedy business was not as successful as it had been in the previous decade. It would thus have been foolhardy for any of these individuals as MCs to venture into comedy full time and professionally, as many have more recently done.

Within the ranks of those already mentioned, there were other cohorts of theirs, like John Chukwu (popularly called 'John God'), Chimamkpam Anyamkpa, Yibo Koko, Basorge Tariah Jr., and Mohammed Danjuma, who became MCs with a difference. This second group went out of their way to develop their comedic acts even while they were involved in other forms of employment. Some of them eventually turned out to become fully-fledged stand-up comedians. What has evolved into professional stand-up comedy in Nigeria today began decades ago in the contributions of these older comedians, some of whom never became stand-up artists. John Chukwu, for instance, set up 'Klass Nite Club' in the heart of Ikeja, Lagos, in the 1980s and is said to have dedicated Fridays at the club to comedy while still working as a staff member at NTA (Olonilua 2011). One outstanding contribution of these performers is an identifiable link between what they did and the emergence of those who later became professionals in the industry. For instance, Chimamkpam Anyamkpa tells how he underwent tutelage under John Chukwu (Nnenyelike 2005), and Bisi Olatilo divulges how he 'discovered' Ali Baba. According to Olatilo's account,

> Alibaba was just a rookie, someone who just left school in 1988. I was in Radio Nigeria 2 then. I was heading the indigenous languages services of Radio Nigeria, which was called Radio 3 then. We used to have an early morning show which we called Another Day Don Break. It was a breakfast show that I anchored. And I had gone to an event at the University of Lagos. He [Alibaba] was engaged to handle the comedy aspect and I was one of those honoured. I looked at that young man and I saw some latent, natural talent. I mean he was very quick at it. And everybody liked what he did. So I just walked up to him and said: 'Can we start something? Because you are new in town, you need an avenue to be able to express yourself better and because people need to know you beyond the university.' He agreed. We worked a program out. Every morning, he would come to my show and do five minutes of jokes. And it started that way. It started catching on and before we knew it, it spread. (Odeh 2011)

Olatilo was a seasoned broadcaster and MC in the 1980s; Ali Baba, for his part, turned out to be one of the initiators of professional stand-up in Nigeria, as discussed in the next chapter. Other accounts detail initial bottlenecks performers encountered as they evolved as individual stand-up comics. Stories about how family members derided comedians before the industry's success have been used repeatedly by many. Ali Baba and and Gbenga Adeyinka have interesting tales about how family members looked down on them because they wanted to become comedians. Adeyinka narrates his own experience, thus:

> I was very lucky to have studied English. What I wanted to study initially was Theatre Arts and that was my passion as a student but my uncle then was like, 'Olorun maje' (God forbids). We sent you to the best schools, you now say you want to do Theatre Arts!' When I graduated and I started comedy, they were all complaining. They said, 'we sent you to school, you now say it is Baba Sala you want to do!' But for me, it was always acting, I think I started acting when I was in Form Three. (Ijalana 2010)

It is pertinent to note how Baba Sala's name is used derogatorily here, based on the assumption that individuals who take up full-time acting or comedy will turn out to be lowlifes providing cheap laughter. Apart from the fact that performing comedy was a low-paying engagement, Baba Sala and Hubert Ogunde, for instance, had almost all-female travelling troupes, and they were married to some of the women working for them (Lindfors 1976; Clark 1980; Jeyifo 1984; Haynes 1994). This condition was construed as a form of promiscuity that extended to all comedians and performers alike. In actuality, Ogunde and other actor/managers of his generation were trying to break even by minimising production costs and marrying members of their cast was one way through which they hoped to save money. Wives were not paid to participate in the theatre work of their husbands, hence having more wives meant having more unpaid performers. Baba Sala married eighteen women, and he affirms the centrality of his polygamous marriage to his art, thus: 'I married many women because I was into acting and I needed them to help me in acting' (Adesina 2011). Hubert Ogunde, for his part, married seventeen of his actresses for the same reason (Oyatogun 2017). However, this condition has changed considerably in recent times with the boom in stand-up comedy practice in Nigeria. Humour artists have now become highly sought after, and the industry has empowered many youths who have become employers of labour themselves. Nevertheless, there are three direct catalysts that have directly given rise to Nigerian stand-up comedy: the decline of theatre, the emergence of Nollywood, and the contributions of two individuals, Opa Williams and Ali Baba, who brought about the professionalisation of the industry.

The decline of theatre

Nigeria's rich theatrical nature is evidenced by the diverse and colourful festivals all year round among its constituent ethnic groups and cultures. Some of the pre-colonial festivals and observances variously discussed in Ogunbiyi (1981) formed part of the indigenous theatre forms of different communities. With the advent of colonialism came western performance forms, giving rise to a merger of indigenous and received theatre experimentations as exemplified by Hubert Ogunde, Duro Ladipo, Kola Ogunmola, and others. This fusion was followed by the scripted plays of James Ene Henshaw, which heralded academic drama. Ogunde and his contemporaries had emphasised the touring of various cities in the pre-colonial Alarinjo travelling theatre mode. Henshaw's contributions, often dwarfed by Wole Soyinka's, were scripted comedies that were easily accessible and easier to stage at schools. With independence in 1960 and for twenty years afterwards, many playwrights emerged. Femi Osofisan's socialist-minded generation emerged in the 1970s following Soyinka's. Their sharp social criticism and ridicule soon became acerbic and so trendy that Soyinka, in 1977, turned to political satire in his *Opera Wonyosi* from his often obscurantist dramas of the past. With the preponderance of scripted plays and growing interest in theatre performances, drama departments became hotbeds for nurturing talent and research in the stage arts at the dawn of the 1980s. Following a series of erroneous fiscal policies around this time, Nigeria found itself in the throes of financial hardship, exacerbated by a brain drain and capital flight. Coming on the heels of the oil boom of the 1970s, it was exceedingly difficult for even government to adjust to the day's economic realities. The arts became one of the earliest casualties due to significant drops in attendance, unsafe streets, depleting state funding, declining remuneration for performers, and then the evolution of low social esteem for artists.[12] The dwindling clientele and lack of funds made it difficult for professional companies to break even, forcing theatre productions to retreat from public life.

One primary factor that initial practitioners of stand-up comedy in Nigeria found attractive is its contemporaneous nature – where the performer talks ,about prevailing circumstances without first *doing* a script, sourcing funds, casting and rehearsing before the performance. It is improvisational, interactive, and oral, which imbues it with an immediacy that circumvents most conventional theatre production demands. It shares liveness, embodied (speech, body movement and mannerisms) and spatial (space movement and stage décor) modes of expression. It is thus an inexpensive way of making theatre. To further understand the relationship between the decline of live theatre in Nigeria and the concurrent rise of stand-up comedy, Ezechi Onyerionwu (2007) observes that,

> For those who have been disheartened by the continuous decline of the Nigerian theatre tradition, the advent of an avant-garde alternative in the emergent stand-up comedy culture has hugely compensated for a truly sad loss. This feeling of loss is completely understandable [...] But today as we have come to see, the only artistic medium that has undisputedly inherited [... the] laudable responsibilities of the theatre tradition is stand-up comedy. It is perhaps to the credit of the many characteristics which both genres share that an overlap-free transition has been guaranteed. First, like the core dramatic theatre, stand-up comedy is essentially a stage art.

Stand-up's relative cost-effectiveness (in terms of production costs compared to more conventional forms like theatre) gives it leverage over more capital-intensive genres because it is much easier for promoters to make gains on their investments. By circumventing the cumbrous and expensive demands of theatre productions, stand-up comedy naturally became a preferred choice, just like the video film is for cinema in Nigeria. In the words of Homi Bhabha, 'a state of emergency is also always a state of emergence' (2004, 41), which means that the 'state of emergency' of the Nigerian theatre catalysed 'an emergence,' namely the evolution of stand-up comedy. It is thus not theatre because it was *ab initio* designed to be one, but because it shares dramatic theatre's *liveness* and, most importantly (specifically for Nigeria), it has been an alternative live performance since the decline of theatre. It has also, in diverse ways, been aiding the re-emergence of theatre in the same way Nollywood is helping the resurgence of cinema in Nigeria.[13]

Professional stand-up comedy

It is impossible to trace a linear link between all the aforementioned joking forms and present-day stand-up comedy. It is essential to note that Nigerian communities have always had forms of satire whose traits have filtered into contemporary stand-up tradition. Ezechi Onyerionwu (2010) traces how some of those comedic traditions mentioned previously metamorphosed, from storytelling to the MC era. However, his work does not take cognisance of some of the precolonial satiric performances discussed previously. Of course, this is understandable because it is easier to find a link between the MC era and the emergence of stand-up art itself, but not the more traditional joke-telling forms. For one, the transition became possible through developments that took place in the 1990s. The first, and the most important, was the emergence of Nollywood, especially the enabling environment it created for experimentation in cheaper mediums of artistic expression. This development gave rise to the second, which is the entrepreneurial contributions of Opa Williams, followed very closely by Ali Baba's elevation of the status of comedians.

Nollywood filled the vacuum created by the inability of filmmakers to sustain cinema productions owing to economic constraints. Before the shift from celluloid to video, Nigerian cineastes evolved numerous cost-cutting techniques, such as shooting films on 35mm down to 16mm, using reversal stock, and eventually shooting on video and blowing it up to 16mm (Haynes and Okome 2000, 55). These substandard outputs led to a degeneration in image quality, precipitating audience protests, like the one in Osogbo where members of the audience wrecked a film house due to the poor quality of the film, *Esan* (Ekwuazi 1991, 73). Video films eventually became a better alternative, especially given that people had been watching pirated versions of eastern and Chinese films for some time. The video film alternative which later came to be known as Nollywood developed in the early 1990s 'at a time when Nigeria had more than ever before drawn back within its frontiers, cut off from the world and its attentions' (Barrot 2005, 134–135). Despite the gloomy circumstances within which it evolved, the industry has achieved tremendous accomplishments. Its successes prompted the rhetorical question: 'How was it possible for a country that had only been responsible for producing a few dozen films for cinema, then produced 9000 video films in just a few years?' (Barrot 2005, 19). Coming from almost nothing, Nollywood had become one of the fastest-growing filmmaking traditions on earth, surprising everyone with its affordability, ease of production, adaptability, and proficiency at creating believable Nigerian situations. The nature of Nollywood circumvents the financial bottlenecks associated with the hitherto prevalent cinema model. Films undergo three significant processes – production, distribution, and exhibition. In terms of production, filmmakers shoot films on celluloid, which is expensive and complicated to handle.

Due to the paucity of institutions for developing celluloid films in Nigeria, filmmakers had to take their rushes overseas to edit them. This problem, no doubt, added to the cost of production, and with the falling rate of the local currency against others, it was not feasible for filmmakers to break even. However, for Nollywood, all that the producer required, especially at inception, is a VHS video camera and a cast. Post-production entailed using cheap computer editing software and duplicating the finished work onto VHS videotapes, VCDs and DVDs, hence tremendously reducing production costs. Distribution of such films is economical because of the convenience and near-uncomplicated manner of just putting the end-product in the open market. Nollywood created a functional informal distribution channel, made possible because the industry's original financiers used to market pirated foreign films. There are no specialised agents, institutions or intermediaries needed to get the movies to consumers because they must buy these tapes from the market and watch them in the comfort of their homes. As such, the structure here was less formal than what cinema requires. For example, strict copyright laws often erected through expensive legal deals between the producers and distributors are needed for cinema before a film gets to the public. Such laws make it impossible for the films to be mass-produced, as is obtainable in Nollywood. The implication, therefore, is that fewer people have access to these films. Nollywood circumvents these procedures, making itself available to a more significant percentage of people at a cheaper rate than cinema could have done with fewer people.

Moreover, cinema requires specialised screening spaces where audiences can gather to see the films. Consequently, the filmmaker or the distributor runs the additional cost of providing and maintaining viewing facilities to screen films. It is different for Nollywood since the video technology being used is optimised for private home viewing. In conclusion, Jonathan Haynes gives a very compelling outlay of the achievements of Nollywood as follows:

> I believe Nollywood deserves credit for its roles as a chronicler of social history, as an organ of cultural and moral response to the extreme provocations and dislocations of contemporary Nigeria, and as a bearer of true nationalism. It arose in Nigeria's hour of need, when everything was crumbling, including the ideologies on which the state was based. In the midst of a general retreat into exclusionary, Manichean forms of religious and ethnic thinking and—most of all—into a sheer head-down struggle for survival, Nollywood managed to stage debates about fundamental issues and sustained an image of the nation as resilient, grounded, tolerant, plural, certainly tormented and suffering but also managing to laugh and to get on with life. The films were always good at expressing aspirations, and now that things are better—for some people, at least—Nollywood is a symbol and source of Nigerian pride, the most visible dimension of the new buoyancy, projecting Nigeria's self-image across the African continent and beyond. (Haynes 2016, xxvii–xxviii)

Thus, the emergence of Nollywood and stand-up comedy emanates from the inability to sustain further art productions in the conventional genres of theatre and cinema, respectively. Specifically, the kind of liberalisation occasioned by Nollywood engendered the flourishing of stand-up comedy. Just like cinema, theatre at that time was (and is still) going through the throes of inactivity and attrition. Akin to how Nollywood made it cheaper to produce films, stand-up comedy makes for cost-effective live performance. The two industries share many professionals like Opa Williams, Okey Bakassi, Basorge Tariah Jr., to mention but a few. Opa Williams launched the genre of professional stand-up comedy in Nigeria through his *Nite of a Thousand Laughs* in 1995. The other two made their initial entries by acting in films before finally making it onto the comedy stage.

Opa Williams started in Nollywood as a producer but veered into creating the first stand-up talent exhibition in Nigeria. There was nothing extravagant in this initial show. Nonetheless, he faced oppressive conditions in hosting this event because he had to surmount many of the challenges that had earlier led to the decline in live theatre productions and patronage in the first place. Femi Osofisan's statement captures the background against which Williams' maiden show was held, thus:

> I am talking of 'production' here in its two connotations, as the creation of scripts as well as the realisation of these scripts on stage—has dwindled dangerously among our people. The few theatres that exist have grown dilapidated out of neglect or are being converted to other uses, most often wedding ceremonies venues or centres in order to meet the costs of production. And those of our comrades who stubbornly persist and, against prevailing odds, finally succeed to get some play on stage have no assurance any more that the audience will be there.
>
> To put it more bluntly, we are in a state of crisis. (2008, xii–xiv)

None of these constraints deterred Williams from trying, featuring a posse of comedians who have become popular, like Basket Mouth, Klint da Drunk, and I Go Dye. It was not a successful outing, but Williams' persistence made sure the event was held every year afterwards and was replicated in other Nigerian cities to enthusiastic audiences. Williams' detailed account of the pathetic state of the entertainment industry when he started his first show is well documented (Akinrele 2019). One of his Nollywood industry colleagues describes Williams' venture into comedy as one driven by altruistic ends wherein he 'was to organise comedians to visit hospitals and prisons to take laughter to the people and thus lighten the yoke of pain and confinement' (Zulu-Okafor 2010).

There are disparities in mentions of the actual location and date of the first edition of *Nite of a Thousand Laughs*, adjudged to have failed woefully, prompting

Opa Williams' collaborators to withdraw from the project. First, is the mention that the event was held at the University of Lagos (Ayakoroma 2013; Owojaiye 2019), whereas in interviews Williams granted, he says that it was held at the National Theatre, Lagos (Onwuanum 2009; Iwenjora 2018). Second, most commentators mention that the event was held on 1 October 1995 (Ayakoroma 2013; Orji 2018; Owojaiye 2019), but one account puts it on the same date in 1994 (Encomium 2015). However, more consistent versions place the event at the National Theatre in 1995. The event moved to other locations in 2009 and 2010, playing at the prestigious Shell Hall, MUSON Centre, Onikan, Lagos. The 2009 event was in two parts: the 3:00 pm and the 7:00 pm shows which catered to different audiences depending on their time preferences (*Showtime People* 2009). By 2010, Opa William came up with other packages, the Regular and the Jubilee editions and the Talent Hunt show. The Regular was held in Kaduna, Ibadan, Calabar, and Jos, while the Jubilee version was held in Lagos and Abuja around Nigeria's Independence Day celebrations, 1 October, with the Talent Hunt geared towards the discovery of newer talents (*Showtime People* 2010).

The principal reason for choosing the 1 October national holiday for the Jubilee version is logical since people are most likely to seek entertainment outside their homes on such a day. Performing during the day back in 1995 was a masterstroke because, unlike the evenings – characterised as dangerous (and for which theatrical activities had lost much of its clientele) – the daytime of a national holiday became the most reasonable option for a start-up in a yet-to-be tested performance genre. Additionally, the producers did not have to bother with the additional expense of lighting the show. It was not until the mid-2000s that Williams started easing audiences into non-matinee performances. With these bold moves, Williams opened a new genre of artistic expression and production. This effort aided the transformation of MCs into full-time stand-up artists, attracting more people to the business. Even with the scaling down of *Nite of a Thousand Laughs* in the 2010s, many of its emergent replacements still retain much of Opa Williams' style: featuring many comedians, interspersing their performances with those of singers, musicians, and dancers, using the rudimentary format of theatrical staging and lighting facilities, as well as live recording for eventual distribution like Nollywood films. Performances have been moved from the National Theatre to the MUSON Centre and to halls and lounges of expensive hotels and other ritzy locations to attract better-paying clientele.

Williams undoubtedly staged the first professional stand-up event in Nigeria. However, it took several comedians themselves to earn the social and economic capital that stand-up humourists currently enjoy. Atunyota Alleluya Akporobomeriere, whose stage name is Ali Baba, in particular increased the value of stand-up performances by insisting on being paid handsomely for his work. He started in comedy in 1988 while still at university. On graduation, he joined the "Charly Boy Show", appearing in various comedy shows on radio and television. The excerpt below aptly summarises Ali Baba's beginnings in stand-up art:

> [...] comedy could fetch him serious money if well packaged. 'I did one show in the University of Benin that gave me N600. So, I figured that, if I could earn that kind of money within a month, and I do up to five events, it meant that if I could do it more professionally, I would earn more money.' He continued: 'All the schools in Edo State then, even in the University of Port Harcourt, their highest pay was N500. But Therapy students of LUTH, could pay N1000; the clubs in the University of Lagos paid N1200, and YABATECH students paid up to N1000 per show. So, I figured that Lagos possessed a lot more potentials for me,' he recalled. In coming to Lagos, the comedian made up his mind to do his business professionally, which made him invest heavily in the art. 'For something to become a profession, you have to make up your mind that you are going to do everything to enhance yourself, improve the skill and the service that you offer.' (Nwanne 2010)

When he started featuring as MC and comedian at private and corporate events, Ali Baba insisted on not providing cheap services like others before him. His big break came in 1999 when Chief Olabode George invited him to anchor a birthday party in honour of ex-president Olusegun Obasanjo. Ali Baba won the heart of Nigeria's then-president at this event. He then became the first comedian to be invited to a State function, earning him the titles "Aso Rock favourite Comedian," "The President's Jester," and "Grand Comedian of the Federal Republic (GCFR)."[14] He made sure he was well paid for every State event and, because he had numerous younger comedians under his wings, they were able to learn from him to improve on their art, being the best they could be and then making sure they were not underpaid. Furthermore, Ali Baba has always worked towards changing how Nigerians see comedians. He registered his company in 1993 and started making proposals to corporate bodies and individuals where he stated his services and charges, thus transforming comedy from being a form of side entertainment to a fully-fledged business. He also bought billboard space around Lagos Mainland, where he advertised his trade, with slogans such as: "Ali Baba – Being Funny is Serious Business" (Ayakoroma 2013). For these and many other contributions to the art of stand-up, Ali Baba is 'the major force behind taking comedy from being a sidekick to a serious business with popular comedians attaining celebrity status and commanding high appearance fees in events and shows' (Directory Nigeria 2010). He is well revered and seen as the father of professional stand-up comedy in Nigeria, especially for being a mentor to many comedians. Some of his protégés, like Ayo Makun (AY) and Bright Okpocha (Basket Mouth) have become remarkably successful. By holding out against the odds stacked against them, and deriving economic and social capital from their work, Nigerian comedians were eventually able to change the prevalent views of jokesters from 'loafers,' 'no-gooders,' and 'jobless jesters' to very respectable socialites.

Ali Baba tells his experience of being disregarded by his family because he did not study law like his father wanted, choosing to be a comedian instead. He narrates that his father was so angry that he swore never again to call him Ali Baba – the implication being that his father would never recognise his son's chosen vocation. According to Ali Baba, the story changed as soon as he bought his father a Mercedes Benz car, drove it into his father's compound, and told him, 'Daddy, this is for you.' The old man turned and called him, most lovingly, 'Ali Baba!' (Makun 2008). Though told in jest, this story symbolises the change in fortunes of Nigerian comedians since the dawn of the new century. Ali Baba remained an MC stand-up comic until industry promoters with the required capital to organise shows and pay performers started investing in comedy. Nevertheless, the business consciousness he elicited in comedians greatly affected how they viewed their work and how others started treating them. The proliferation of various kinds of gigs, mostly better-organised variants comedians arranged themselves, was occasioned by the demise of *Nite of a Thousand Laughs*. Consequently, like their peers in the film industry, Nigerian stand-up comedians are stars in their own right and are often full-time artists without other jobs, unlike their MC forebears.

Despite its humble beginnings in the mid-1990s, on the heels of the emergence of Nollywood, Nigerian stand-up has moved from being poorly organised daytime shows to expensive state-of-the-art events held in ritzy venues with the *crème de la crème* of society in attendance. From the monopoly of Opa Williams' influential *Nite of a Thousand Laughs*, solo performances, like *Basket Mouth Uncensored*, and multiple-act events like *AY Live Show* as well as numerous clubs and events have given rise to tremendous industry growth. In the three decades of stand-up comedy's existence in Nigeria, it has become the norm to have comedians at secular and sometimes religious events. There are now performers for every pocket size: from the more elitist, top-grossing comedians who anchor State and corporate events to those who perform at children's birthday parties. There are also mainstream female comedians like Helen Paul, Chigul, Princess, and others who perform in clubs and more localised venues. The proliferation of social media and internet-enabled gadgets has also aided the visibility and mainstreaming of Nigerian artists, even beyond the nation's borders. The low number of female jokesters is one major drawback of Nigerian stand-up. In the same way that Nollywood initiated video films and their spread across the continent, Nigerian-style comedy has spread to the rest of Africa, where locals are staging events and organising talent hunts to discover new humourists.

Between the second half of the 1990s and the publication of this book, there have been comedy performance exchanges between Nigeria and other English-speaking

African countries. Such cross-border interchanges facilitate mobility, international exposure, and global visibility for Nigerian humour events among diaspora communities worldwide. In this way, stand-up comedy has become quite popular and, like Nollywood, initially distributed via DVDs, then satellite television outlets, and now on social media. Upcoming humourists often have their eyes fixed on the more established stand-ups as role models and catalysts for their aspirations. Some 'already-made' comedians like AY, Ali Baba, and Julius Agwu convene talent hunts to discover and groom younger ones on their path to growth within the industry. In a bid to ensure the longevity of the genre, several practitioners are diversifying, supporting, and developing talents in other arts. For instance, AY, Basket Mouth, and Bovi have been severally involved in cinema, live theatre, music, and drama series productions. Others are involved in advertising, hospitality, and a few others have been appointed to public office at different times. These attainments have given visibility to comedians, increasing their economic and social capital in tremendous ways, thus amplifying their comedic productions all the more. This is the height that Nigerian stand-up has come to since its emergence in the mid-1990s.

Notes

1   Literally, 'my head is touching,' meaning, 'My head is exploding, not normal.' The second, literally, 'we are in crazy mode,' 'we are all crazy.'

2   Nigeria is made up of over 250 ethnic groups, each with a distinct language and culture. The Hausa/Fulani, Igbo and Yoruba are considered the major ones because they are the most widely spoken languages. It is also noteworthy that the pre-colonial humour enactments of the Niger Delta area peoples, which has produced the largest number of stand-up comedians on the contemporary Nigerian stage, are not represented by the three largest groups mentioned here. This multi-ethnic zone has one of the significant minority groups, the Ijaw, and other smaller groups like the Itsekiri, Urhobo, and Isoko. Comedy in this area has long been a necessary tool for cohabitation among the diverse tribes that use this area's waterways for trade, transport, and other activities.

3   One of the most popular depictions of a typical Igbo pre-colonial society is found in *Things Fall Apart* (Achebe 1958), where Umuofia, an independent community governed by elders and well-off citizens like Okonkwo, sits amidst other hamlets. It is at war with some of these, while peace exists with others.

4   That *ikoonu* is considered feminine is a sexist supposition that regards women as being much more talkative than men. In actual circumstances, some men engage in these forms of insult exchange. Interestingly, when this happens, it is often said that 'they are trading insults *like women!*'

5   I remember occasions in my youth when we visited my village during Christmas and other festivities, and my equally young relatives told us that *Achukwu* were about. I can now not

recall whether it was the night masquerade's sound, made up of a concatenation of eerie noises created from different instruments, or the stories that we had heard about it, that made our skin crawl. There was always that fear in my young mind that our compound would be besieged on the very nights that this happened.

6 'Traditional clowns' just like *'yan* is plural form for *dan* in Hausa.

7 'Traditional clowns' just like *'yan gambara*, rap artists that evoked burlesque enactments, are now making appearances in Hausa films known as Kannywood (Ahmad and Furniss 1994).

8 The things that happen under the sun.

9 Translated from Hausa as 'Sergeant Major, the men at work.' *Samanja* is the Hausa rendering of 'Sergeant Major.'

10 Originally, *The Masquerade*, but returned after a lay-off as *The New Masquerade*.

11 Ken Saro Wiwa was the Ogoni rights activist executed by the military in 1995.

12 These and many other reasons for the decline are elaborately discussed in Musa 2005, Okoh 2005, Ohiri 2006, Osofisan 2008, and Nwankwo 2010.

13 In the first instance, stand-up comedy revived attendance at live performances which is favourable to the few theatre events taking place around the major cities of Lagos and Abuja. Secondly, comedians like AY presently include theatrical enactments within their shows, thereby normalising stage productions for newer audiences not accustomed to such shows.

14 GCFR (Grand Commander of the Federal Republic) is the highest honorary award in Nigeria. Here 'Commander' is replaced with 'Comedian.'

2
People and personae

Categories of Nigerian stand-up artists

In his satiric song, "Shuffering and Shmiling" (1978), Fela Anikulapo-Kuti details how Nigerians have been smiling through myriad socioeconomic and political woes occasioned by the corrupt practices of successive governments. It would appear that his song is prophetic because living conditions have worsened, and people are still finding some comfort in humour. From the television, radio, and stage comedies of the 1980s discussed in the preceding chapter to the emergence of professional stand-up comedy in the mid-1990s, Nigerians have been feted with laughter in diverse genres and media as a panacea to the hardships of penury. Nevertheless, academic enquiries on stand-up art in Nigeria mostly detail developments in the west or those of African theatre and oral performances, with little or no explications on how it emerged (Fosudo 2009, 2010; Onogu 2013; Adekunle 2014; Awaritoma 2015; Okon-Ekong 2017b). Journalists and bloggers are more interested in the glamorous aspects of comedians' finances (*Showtime People* 2014; Awaritoma 2015), their alternations between being jokesters and film actors (Okon-Ekong 2017a; *This Day* 2016), and their social capital politics and society (Adebowale 2013; Akoni 2020). Despite the problems of documentation of reliable details of Nigerian stand-up, there are synoptic but useful summaries of some historical tracts by Igomu (2018) and Nwankwọ (2015).

It is important to note that there is no easy way to capture the timelines regarding the evolution of stand-up art in Nigeria. This is due to several reasons, primarily because there is gross unavailability of reliable data. Much of what is known today has been taken verbatim from the recollections of individual comedians. Some data come from inferences made from video recordings of events, especially of Opa Williams' *Nite of a Thousand Laughs*.[1] Since there is no centralised stand-up administrative unit or guild, there are no official records about the progression of individual artists, specific shows, or general development of the industry. Some of the testimonies of stand-up practitioners sometimes contradict each other, especially about commencement dates, joke ownership, gig participation, and contributions to the industry. Comics also make claims about working in comedy clubs for a long time before coming to public notice. Of course, some of the dates proffered cannot independently be confirmed because most clubs do not keep such records, some are no longer in existence or have changed ownership, while most are not disposed to opening up their transactions to the public. Further exacerbating the dearth of data on the history of stand-up is the fact that most extant videos are heavily edited, sometimes with no dates, scanty credits, and bereft of other production details. Other drawbacks are a montage of different events without clear indications of where and when some of them were staged. Moreover, 'seniority' is legal tender since it is used for several claims to privileges such as allocating performance spots and time, amounts to be paid, and invitations to specific shows. This adds to the confusion around the historical trajectory of stand-ups' careers since those comedians whose stage work started earlier than others have often exerted their 'seniority' in ways that suggest generations in the ranks of performers. However, closer investigation indicates an ongoing first generation of comedians with different dates of commencement and contributions, spanning up to three decades for different talents.

Since its emergence in the mid-1990s, up to the time of writing (2021), each decade has marked a turning point for Nigerian stand-up practice. The 1990s saw the transition from MC-ship to stage humour, principally starting with Opa Williams' 1995 *Nite of a Thousand Laughs*. The 2000s heralded economic and social capital acquisition for stand-up comedians. In the 2010s, there was an explosion in the diversity of platforms and genres, with increased diaspora and social media presence. The categorisation of talent in this book aligns with these three decades. In this manner, individual comics are differentiated by the period in which they became active on the professional stage since it is impossible to identify chronologically accurate information of performances before they started participating in mainstream events. Principally, appearances on *Nite of a Thousand Laughs* are used in this book to determine involvement in professional practice between 1995 and 2010 because it was the highest platform with which comedians and Nigerians alike measured popularity, relevance, and status. There is a long list of comedians who became relevant through Williams' *Nite of a Thousand Laughs*. They include 'Mohammed Danjuma, Okey Bakassi, the Late Sam Loco Efe, Boma Erokosima, the Late Sammy Needle, Late Junior and Pretty,' closely followed in succeeding years by 'Francis Duru, Yibo Koko, Ayodeji Makun, aka AY, Julius Agwu, Basketmouth, I Go Dye, Bovi, I Go Save, Gandoki, MC Abbey, Gordons, Michael Ogbolosingha, Klint de Drunk, Teju Baby Face, Maleke, Holly Mallam, Elenu, MC Shakara, Onyebuchi Ojieh (Buchi), Emeka Smith, Princess, and Lepacious Bose' (Owojaiye 2019). For the 1990s and the years before, three jokesters, John Chukwu (JC), Jude Edesiri Onakpoma (Away-Away) and Mohammed Danjuma, are worth mentioning due to their foundational work in the emergence of professional stand-up in Nigeria.

John Chukwu (1947–1990), popularly known as JC, has been described severally as a '[M]aster of Ceremony extraordinaire, actor, restaurateur, singer, comedian (name it, he's it)' (Odegbami 2014, 30).² His major contribution to comedy development was that he dedicated Friday nights at his Klass Nite Club to stand-up in the late 1980s (Sokunbi and Nwanze 1990; *Proudly Nigerian* 2016). As a comedian, JC was adept at accents and impressions of different ethnic stereotypes and is known to have been able to speak several Nigerian languages, English, and Italian (Obiozo 2019). Specifically, Wilson Orhiunu (2007) recalls watching him do 'perfect impressions of the Calabar accent in the late 70s.' JC was 'a spontaneous comedian' with a knack for 'spur of the moment' jokes which he used, to speak about societal ills and stir up laughter (Hamzia 2015). Sonny Oti gives an exciting account of his encounter with JC and Fela Kuti in June 1980, showing how deeply involved JC was in that era's entertainment sphere (2009, 29–31). Despite his unexpected death in 1990 at 43, many comedians of the 1990s defer to JC for the numerous ways his jokes, multitalented stage enactments, and exploits on radio and television programmes affected their acts. Though he did not live long enough to see the fruition of Williams' *Nite of a Thousand Laughs* five years after his demise, JC's nightclub was part of the earliest stages comedians within Lagos used to hone their trade. It is noteworthy that this platform made it possible for comedians to tell standalone jokes, not as compères at a social event, but as humourists with the primary aim of eliciting laughter.

One of JC's comedy platform beneficiaries was Jude Onakpoma, popularly known as Away-Away, who, as a fresh graduate in the late 1980s, came to Lagos to replicate the successes he was known for while he was a student at the University of Benin. Away-Away, eventually became a famous brand for the elite, especially the military ruling class, given the way he received invitations for events as MC. In 1989, he received the Best Comedian of the Year Award for his sterling performance at the Nigeria Music Awards. By wearing corporate clothes to events, Away-Away took stand-up art away from clowning. However, his industry growth ended when he moved to the US for further studies, right as his comedy career was about to take off. He did make overtures towards a comeback in the early 2010s, but that did not work out well, primarily because Nigerian stand-up had moved way beyond where he had left it. It had become more professional, creating its varying peculiarities in joke tastes, audiences, and sundry preferences. He acknowledges these in the following statements:

> I left Nigeria at the peak of my career. I had a scholarship to go and further my education in United States. […] I always wondered what would happen when I stopped making people laugh, what if I became irrelevant in few years? These were the questions that encouraged me to seek answers by accepting the scholarship to pursue education in the United States. I had a scholarship to further my education through a doctorate degree programme. However, I

will not advise anybody with opportunities in his or her country to abandon it for overseas. They should always challenge their talents and not remain in a comfort zone. (Jebose 2014)

Though Away Away left, others like Mohammed Danjuma and Atunyota Akpobomeriere persisted, eventually witnessing the transition from MC to professional stand-up.

Mohammed Danjuma (1965–2005) was part of Opa Williams' *Nite of a Thousand Laughs* for a couple of years, serving as the host in some events before his demise. Not much is known about his performances and specific contributions except through credits from other performers such as Omo Baba (PM Entertainment 2012), Tee A (Encomium 2015; Okon-Ekong 2016), and MC Basketmouth (Itewo 2010). Danjuma played 'Tanko' in a popular 1980s Nigerian Television Authority (NTA) sitcom, "Second Chance." He once told a joke of 'how he was once mid-air inside a plane only to see one man in parachute knocking on his window and telling him: "I don go-o! Na me be pilot of this plane-o. If you like-o, continue to stay there-o, but me I don go-o"' (Uzoatu 2019).[3] Several comedians and cartoonists repeated this gag to depict the nation's sorry state as one rudderless ship waiting to crash. Ali Baba also mentions him frequently, reminiscing on memorable experiences and once writing about him thus: 'I miss that fool,' before telling hilarious tales of some of the comedic pranks they played on each other (*Gbedu Magazine* 2016), stating elsewhere that Danjuma played a significant role in creating the background for the emergence of professional stand-up practice in Nigeria (Erhariefe and Chukwuma 2016). With Danjuma's untimely departure, Ali Baba became the foremost progenitor, taking up several central roles at the nadir of Nigerian stand-up comedy. By his testimony, one way Ali Baba differed from Danjuma is in their conceptions of the professionalism of stand-up art in Nigeria as their acts were becoming more recognised. Ali Baba narrates:

> I remember late Mohammed Danjuma told me comedy would never work. He would rather stick to his job as an MC. However, as time rolled by, corporate bodies would invite us for events. Danjuma would be the MC and pocket N50,000 while I would go home with N200,000 as stand-up comedian. Within a short while, he realised that comedy was the way forward and before I could say Jackie Robinson, he was doing comedy as well. (Abusidiq 2012)

This statement reveals that it was not for lack of capacity that earlier precursors were held in check, from realising their full potential at gaining economic and social capital through stand-up art. JC, for instance, never left his regular job. Jude Away-Away could not resist the lure of moving away to greener pastures. Danjuma expressed reservations about being much more than an MC. Stand-up was a hobby, a pastime engagement, and not a full profession for each of them. Others, who came later, like Lepacious Bose, initially preferred to maintain their regular jobs until they became more assured of their sustenance solely through stand-up enactments. JC died in 1990, and Jude Away-Away left for the US. Danjuma was part of professional stand-up practice for close to ten years but died right before big money started flowing in. This left just Ali Baba as the central figure, who, together with a few others now had the task of mentoring younger jokesters.

Furthermore, Opa Williams recalls that before his maiden *Nite of a Thousand Laughs* show, several comedians were practising in different media, such as 'Mohammed Danjuma, Leo Owode, Smart Orhutemu, Ehiz, Julius Agwu, Okey Bakassi, Sam Loco Efe, Baba Suwe, Papiluwe [Papa Luwe], Alarm Blow [sic],' adding that 'Alam Bloo was just a Master Compere, Leo Owode was just good on radio, Baba Suwe and Papiluwe [sic] were acting in Yoruba films' (Ohai 2015). According to Ali Baba, others who featured prominently at the time include 'Yibo Koko, Centi Jack, Basorge Tariah Jnr, Okey Bakassi, Agoma Awaritoma, Alam Bloo, Tee A …' (Adebayo 2012). Yibo Koko, a graduate of Theatre Arts at the University of Port Harcourt, gained a reputation as a comedian before turning to filmmaking and stage productions in 2008 (Okon-Ekong and Obioha 2016). His *Seki*, a Niger Delta dance drama, was quite renowned when it was produced (Seki 2018). Basorge Tariah Jnr, also a Theatre Arts graduate of the University of Port Harcourt, started with stage comedy before moving into acting and filmmaking. His *My Guy* (1999) has been described as 'the first real attempt at a fully language-based comedy in Nollywood' (Aigbokhaevbolo 2018), and he played Do Good in DStv's drama series *Do Good* alongside Kate Henshaw. Alam Bloo, for his part, started comedy while still at secondary school but paid more attention to music because stand-up had not taken off in Nigeria. According to his testimony, he turned out as one of the first to do in-flight comedy on some local flights (Babalola 2009). His comedy, which also aired on television, "Lafta Line Special" on NTA Network and later "The Charly Boy Show," subsequently influenced many younger comedians. Tee-A (Tunde Adewale) also started doing comedy acts while at secondary school and then during his days at the University of Lagos before he ran into Ali Baba, with whom he worked for some time. He and Ali Baba collaborated in developing some of the attributes that eventually made stand-up practice successful. For instance, they rented office space, wrote proposals, made billboards advertising their trade, and developed business relationships with clients, thus elevating the status of their work from 'mere' joking. In one of his many interviews, Tee-A details how things used to be in the industry, saying that all he wanted was for people to see how good he was at his art (Ogunjimi 2012).

Others, like the late Sam Loco Efe, Gbenga Adeyinka, Okey Bakassi, and Gandoki (Tony Mofe Ereku) were part of this early crop of comedians. Sam Loco

Efe and Okey Bakassi (Okechukwu Onyegbula) starred in Nollywood films, with Efe continuing in that direction until his death in 2011. Okey has recently been more involved in stage comedy and hosting a satiric news-style television show, *The Other News*. Opa Williams avers that Okey Bakassi was present at the film shoot at the National Orthopaedic Hospital, Igbobi, Lagos, where the idea of a stand-up show was conceived, saying:

> we had some hiccups [with the film shoot], so we didn't know what else to do and we started cracking jokes. Okey Bakassi and Regina Ebere were the ones cracking those hot jokes, everyone laughed so much that we all forgot our sorrows. [He continues that it was at that point that it hit him that] if the patients in their sickbed and the doctors were laughing that much, this is something that cut across people's race, faith and creed. This is something I should do. (Akinrele 2019; Ohai 2015).

True to this assertion, Williams started what turned out to be the first professional stand-up event in Nigeria. Julius Agwu, for his part, participated in the 1996 edition of *Nite of a Thousand Laughs* in Lagos while he was still studying at the University of Port Harcourt. Today, he is one of Nigeria's top comedians, reputed for his *Crack ya Ribs*. His autobiographical book *Jokes Apart* (Agwu 2013) details his early life (what he refers to as his 'pikinhood'), foray into theatre and entertainment, as well as becoming a stand-up comedian.[4] Gbenga Adeyinka, on the other hand, has worked as a comedian, MC, and anchor to some TV game shows for Nigerian Breweries. He has performed very much less on stage in recent times than he did in the late 1990s. Gandoki holds the Guinness World Record for the most extended joke rendition on stage, having told jokes for 42 hours continuously without repeating any (Augoye 2016; Ohai 2016; Chima 2016). Opa Williams calls him the 'funniest' comedian, adding that,

> [i]f you go round and ask other comedians, they will tell you the same thing. With an ordinary story like I am going to the airport, Gandoki will make you laugh and laugh till you can laugh no more. For me, the right word to describe Gandoki is spontaneous and not funny. (Anokam 2011)

Then, Awaritoma Agoma featured in the early shows before moving into other pursuits, eventually becoming a lecturer at the University of Abuja. His book, which details his contributions and other early-stage aspects of Nigerian stand-up comedy, was published in 2009. Among all these earlier stand-up artists, Julius Agwu and Ali Baba emerged as events managers with different shows under their belt, while Okey Bakassi remains a force to be reckoned with in the industry, and Gandoki still gets featured in a handful of enactments.

Female humourists in Nigerian stand-up

Female participation in Nigerian stand-up since inception has been both marginal and minimal. This has its roots in the dearth of female comics in television and radio comedies in Nigeria well into the 1980s. Those who featured in some of the dramas of the 1980s era appeared as wives, mistresses, and even selfish spinsters like Madam de Madam in Ken Saro Wiwa's *Basi and Company*. If comedy is an often-understudied performance genre, this is doubly so for women because even where they exist, the comedic feminine body is often masked by contrived invisibility. In addition, with the dominance of men in the nascent industry, women's gaze and voice became utterly subdued and underrepresented, leading to the emergence of jokes fraught with politically incorrect references to women. The overall upshot has been that the handful of professional Nigerian stand-up female performers who appeared on the national stage in the 1990s and early 2000s have disappeared.[5]

Mandy Uzonicha refers to herself as Nigeria's first female stand-up artist, positing that her foray into comedy began with her anchoring of the "Candid Camera" segment of "The Charly Boy Show" on NTA 2 Channel 5 Lagos in 1992 (Girls Killing It 2016; Lawal 2011). Her work as a stand-up artist started a couple of years later as the industry started taking a foothold in Nigeria. From the onset, Mandy, as she is called on stage, had her reservations about living solely on joke-telling. She tells of laughter being commonplace at home while growing up due to the excellent sense of humour that her mother and grandmother exhibited and imparted to their children. She surmises that she 'never knew such would one day put food on my table and help take care of my daughter' (*Commics News* 2009b). Despite being there at the beginning and laying an exemplary foundation for other women, Mandy did not continue making waves like her male counterparts. She slowly dropped out of the scene by the turn of 2010 after successively performing in fewer shows in the preceding couple of years. Even though she is regarded as the female version of Ali Baba, for leading the coterie of female humourists in professional stand-up, the way she disappeared from the scene continues to be the norm rather than the exception for other female jokesters, except for a few that have become quite dominant in the last decade.

Speaking about the gendered constraints of becoming a successful female comedian in Nigeria, like their male counterparts, Mandy says,

> [o]ne challenge in Nigeria is that women don't get the better paying gigs and when you don't get good gigs, people don't see you. Corporates in Nigeria don't think of female comedians when it comes to endorsement, it basically boils down to the fact that most decision makers in the corporate world are men and men in my country generally seem to feel that the right to humour belongs to their gender forgetting that the 1st female comedian they ever came across was

their mothers. As kids our [mothers] would make funny faces and we smile she would say some certain things and we roll with laughter. Most of us are lucky to get some jobs tailored to suit our gender. (Girls Killing It 2016)

This narrative of Mandy's underscores the commonality of comedy and humour and the female capacity to evoke laughter in many homes, something that has sadly not been replicated in public spaces. For this reason, performers like Mandy blazed newer terrains for future female comedians through their daringness to become stand-up artists in a society where women's ability to engender laughter is often constrained to remain within closed environments. However, she acknowledges the support that she and her colleagues have received, specifically mentioning Opa Williams for picking her to perform at his event in and outside Nigeria (Eseoghene 2017). Nonetheless, even with the emergence of newer shows from the 2010s to the time of writing (2021), female stage presence remains relatively marginal. It can only be surmised that support for female humourists, such as that provided by Opa Williams, has either been insufficient or countered by other exacerbating factors that suppress female participation in Nigerian stand-up. Hence, Mandy mulls the absence of femininity in the industry, averring that 'one of the reasons can never be that we are not good. We are good' (Pius 2008). She notes Nollywood films as an example of one sphere where women show immense talent and skills in Nigeria's performance industry.

True to Mandy's words, Najite Dede was one of the earlier female comedians who eventually moved to live theatre acting and directing before eventually turning to Nollywood, where she has successfully participated in and directed some movies. Concerning her foray into stand-up comedy in the late 1990s, at about the same times as Mandy, Dede says, 'I had a generous mentor in Patrick Doyle. The first day I got on stage, I didn't know I was going; he literally pushed me on. It worked. I suppose that's what they say about opportunity meeting preparedness' (In Allure 2010). Through Doyle's film, *All About Ere* (1998), Dede made her eventual exit from comedy into the Nollywood world (Amatus 2005, 2020). Records of her stand-up acts are not readily available since much of it happened well before 2000. On the place of women in the Nigerian stand-up sphere and her reason for going into other endeavours, Dede avers that,

[m]ost minorities are always talking about being marginalised; 'we're not being carried along.' All those phrases that frankly get on my nerves. Women in this country are contributors in all aspects. If you want to be part of the comedy business you have to step up to the market like Mandy, Helen and Princess. I stopped doing Standup because it's not my calling. Yes I'm funny but I want to put my comedy into my theatre work. It was pure bread and butter. (In Allure 2010)

Dede thus re-echoes Mandy's inference that what is needed is talent and persistence for women to grow alongside their male counterparts on the stand-up stage.

By the 2000s, the Nigerian stand-up industry moved from being a hobby to becoming a career, thereby bringing an influx of newer talents, mainly enabled by auditions for *Nite of a Thousand Laughs*. Damilola Adekoya (Princess) was one of the female jokesters who made it to the *Nite of a Thousand Laughs* stage in 2005. Before this appearance, she acted in Wale Adenuga's *Papa Ajasco* television comedy series for a couple of years (NFC n.d.) and participated in Tee-A's television shows around 2004 (*Commics News* 2009a). Bose Olufunke Oseyemi Ogunboye, popularly known as Lepacious Bose, was another female comedian to emerge alongside Princess. Both worked tirelessly and successfully, speaking about and for women, telling jokes that mattered. Ogunboye studied Theatre Arts and later went back to get a Law degree at the University of Ibadan. She started comedy professionally in December 2006 after trying quite unsuccessfully to get an acting role in Nollywood. She often talks about the dashed dreams of making it to the screen, positing that the stand-up industry was easier for talented artists, confirming Mandy and Dede's views above. She draws a comparison between stand-up and the film industries in Nigeria thus:

> In the comedy industry, somebody would always give you a chance to climb the stage. But what you do with that chance is your business. If you perform well, good. If you don't, nobody remembers you the next day. But in the movie industry, you have to know somebody, who will know somebody, who will know somebody and on and on. There is so much pretence and hypocrisy (sic), which were enough to put me off. I couldn't just handle it. (David-Adegboye 2010)

In these words, Lepacious Bose affirms her reasons for her preference for stand-up comedy.

Coming to their stage artistry, Princess and Lepacious Bose possess forceful stage voices and assertiveness from how they deploy their bodies as part of their acts. Princess tends to be more abrasive, eliciting a right-in-your-face kind of comedy, than Lepacious Bose, who mostly builds hers around body sizes. Princess became immensely popular for her adornment of a semi-literate lady who speaks with a British accent and uses horrible English language syntax. She thus switches between this persona, her true narrative voice, and other forms of embodied evocations of the various characters of her joke narratives. She deploys observational comedy, facial expressions, body movements, and interactions with the audience, especially through adjacency pairs. Princess too made references to her body size at the peak of her career. She concerned herself with verbally eliciting imageries of possible awkward positions that arise when a heavily-bodied woman is in bed with a skinny man. For her part, Lepacious Bose built much of her stage joking around body sizes and how various people react to them. Her stage name, 'lepacious', is an Anglicisation of the Yoruba term for a very slim person, 'lepa.' As such, calling herself 'lepacious' contrasts with her actual looks. On how she got the name, she says that people used to call her 'orobo' (Yoruba word for large-bodied persons) and that she always replied, 'Na me bi Lepa now, na una bi Orobo' [I am the skinny one, you are the 'fat' ones], and it was from one of such exchanges that she decided on appending 'lepacious' to her name (*Comics News* n.d.). Both Princess and Lepacious Bose ostensibly sought to override the received western notion of female beauty, mostly embedded in having a very lean figure, arguing that it is the opposite in most traditional African societies. As such, instead of using 'their body features in a self-denigrating manner, they [Princess and Lepacious Bose] emphasise positive perspectives about themselves, unlike female comedians in America, like Joan Rivers, who denigrate their appearances and features for comedic intentions' (Sunday and Filani 2019, 98–99). Despite this claim, there are instances where both performers turn on themselves for laughs, especially when they make references to some of the things that they cannot do owing to their weight.

Nevertheless, both female comedians maintained a strong stage presence until the mid-2010s when Lepacious Bose engaged in weight-loss programmes, which eventually led to her losing so much weight that her clothing size dropped from 32 to 18 (Ajumobi 2016; Njoku 2017; Allure 2019; Allure1 2019). She then moved on to other endeavours, especially promoting body slimming products. She recently spoke about her stand-up days, saying:

> I hated myself and was constantly suicidal yet I made people laugh (what an irony). I cracked jokes about my weight because it was the only way I knew to look like I didn't care. Yet I cared!!! Countless times, I would have a great performance but drive home in tears, it was a crazy, roller coaster feeling. It was not just the weight it was much more but I could not explain it. (Njoku 2017)

For her part, Princess went through a short-lived marriage that brought her some bad press (TNC Reporter 2016) and then began to appear less frequently in stand-up circles. Though they are no longer frequent features on the Nigerian stand-up stage today, the legacies of Mandy, Princess, and Lepacious Bose as pacesetters in both their comedy style and gender remain reference points for those who came afterwards.

Four other female artists who have made their mark on Nigerian stand-up comedy are Omotunde Adebowale David (Lolo 1), Helen Paul (Tatafo), Chioma Omerua (Chigul), and Anita Alaire Afoke Asuoha (Real Warri Pikin). Lolo 1 wears many hats – as a television drama actress, radio on-air-personality and stand-up comedian. She trained as a lawyer, a profession she practised for just three years before finding herself in the world of entertainment. She is best known for her Nigerian Pidgin

English radio programme, *Oga Madam Office*, which she has also taken to the stand-up stage annually since 2012 as *Oga Madam Live on Stage*. Though this event is one of the few organised by female performers in Nigeria, it still features more than ninety per cent males. Each of its editions features various renditions from songs by famous musicians to drama and then stand-up comedy. Lolo 1 engages in the same topical issues of the day in her stage performances that she is known for on her radio programmes. She uses a blend of alterations in accent and insightful analyses given in Nigerian Pidgin English with jocular twists and hues. It is pertinent to add that Lolo 1 is making raves in radio, especially around Lagos, with her interviews, news analyses, and other renditions usually done in Nigerian Pidgin English. She is better known around the country for her role as Adaku in the popular television comedy series, *Jenifa's Diary*. In 2019, *Oga Madam Live on Stage* became the stage musical, *Alero The Musical With LoLo1*, losing its earlier stand-up joke rendition format.

Unlike Lolo 1, Helen Paul has had a more sustained presence on the mainstream stand-up stage in the country since her emergence on the Nigerian entertainment scene. Her main popularity came from her satellite television role as co-presenter of *Jara*, an Africa Magic programme that features news and events about Nigeria's entertainment scene, especially Nollywood. On set, she deploys the same comedic narrative skills for which she has become well-known, such as rendering jokes or passing social commentaries through a child's voice and perspective. Her mimicry of a child's manner of speaking is often very apt and convincing. She also has a knack for talking about 'packaging', which is slang for putting up false appearances, and she mostly ends such enactments by removing her wig to reveal her real hair. Unlike other female humourists on Nigeria's stand-up stage, Helen Paul has a diminutive stature. As such, when she gets into self-denigratory jokes, it is the opposite of what Princess and Lepacious Bose would say about their bodies. Also, some of her jokes include speaking bad English with a fake American accent, song parodies, and hurling jocular insults at specific individuals both in the audience and elsewhere. She brings sharp wit, spontaneity, and versatility to all her renditions. Helen Paul has also had some stints in film, radio, television, and stage drama during and after her Theatre Arts study at the University of Lagos, where she recently received a PhD. Thus, at the time of writing, Helen Paul is the only comedian with a doctorate still performing. Her first professional comedy feature was on the *Nite of a Thousand Laughs* stage in 2009, performing in Lagos and Calabar and successfully in other editions and platforms across Nigeria. She is one of the two female comedians who have become regular features in Ayo Makun's *AY Show Live* across the nation's main cities and overseas (Nigeria Galleria 2017b). Helen Paul has held a steady place in the comedy industry through her hilarious social media skits where she plays the role of Alhaja, a semi-literate Yoruba market woman, and her daily dealings with customers, friends, and family. Specifics of her stand-up renditions are discussed in subsequent chapters, where the enormity and importance of her contributions to the heterogeneity of the Nigerian stand-up environment are made apparent.

Chigul is another towering female figure in Nigerian stand-up. Her journey to comedy stardom started with a BlackBerry Messenger (BBM) recording of herself singing, which went viral and unlocked many opportunities. She started making such videos and sharing them with friends until one of them was shared with others outside their circle, and from there, it rapidly circulated reaching even the Nigerian diaspora overseas (Muomah 2014). One peculiar aspect of Chigul's set is her ability to mimic a diverse range of accents. With these voice impressions and multiple embodied representations, she peoples her enactments with different stock characters made up of her particularly Igbo accented narrative voice, two other recognisable roles of Modinat (an urbane Yoruba girl) and Bintu (a Hausa girl). Her ability to speak many languages – Igbo, Hausa, English, Spanish, French, and Italian – aids her in creating up to a dozen other different stage personas. She has spoken about her challenges with depression (Okanlawon 2020), her short-lived marriage (Awojulughe 2017), and flaunted her weight loss success on social media (Oke-Hortons 2020). Being multi-talented, Chigul expresses her comedy in various forms, through joke-telling, song parodies, character imitation, and being compère at official events. She distinguishes the comedian's work from that of an MC, among other things, by saying,

> [i]f you want to become an emcee, you have to learn to be bold and navigate the crowd because an emcee and a comedian are two different people, even though there is a thin line between both of them. There are very few of us that do these two jobs effectively together. People feel that once they can do the work of an emcee, they are definitely comedians as well and that is not true. You must also decide on what genre of comedy you want to do- are you going into singing, voice-over or telling jokes? In doing that, you must be aware of your audience. Not everybody wants to be talked to and made fun of so you need to be aware of your surroundings. (Ojoye 2017)

Undoubtedly, Chigul has become an influential female comedian in Nigeria. Aspects of her stage performances are discussed in the succeeding chapters.

Another important female comedian to have emerged in recent times is Real Warri Pikin. She started first as a dancer, participating in national competitions between 2008 and 2012, before gravitating towards compèring shows and stand-up comedy (Okunola 2020). She insists that she was 'pushed' into comedy by depression (Akinkahunsi 2018; Ojoye 2019). She is the one female comedian that participates in AY's stage events, other than Helen Paul. Her stage personality and jokes often centre around her body and her Warri heritage.

Apart from Real Warri Pikin and those already mentioned, many others have made appearances on the stand-up stage for various lengths of time.[6] In recent times, female comedians have become more popular on social media than on stage. According to Lepacious Bose, there are two major sociological factors that limit female participation in Nigerian stand-up comedy. The first stems from the constraints of tradition, determining what each gender is allowed or barred from doing or saying on stage. She describes it thus:

> Comedy was dominantly a male-led industry and a lot of the challenges [were] in our heads anyways. In my own head for example, being an African and a Yoruba with my background with teachers as parents. There were things I wanted to say. I knew they would be funny but my parents would kill me if they heard that I said it. Sometimes, you'd want to poke fun at a married man in the crowd and his wife is by his side and you don't have the liberty to do that because no woman will sit around and allow you make fun of her husband. But a male comedian will do that and everyone will laugh and find it funny but a woman won't let another woman do that. (Mike 2020)

The second derives from environmental conditions, which confer varying senses of insecurity and danger for individuals based on their gender. Lepacious Bose describes this situation thus:

> You know you are single girl, you go for an event, you don't have a car and you're returning home at 12 a.m., it's not easy for a lot of women. Sometimes you are not called on stage until around 10 p.m. The guys can decide to leave an event at 1 a.m. and take a bike from MUSON to Ajegunle, it's not easy for a lady. And a whole lot of other things. A guy can perform badly, people boo him and he takes it in its stride, and goes home and sleep. For a lady, it's not easy on our emotions. Most women are not able to manage that. It's more of a confidence thing for the woman and the fear of failure. Not necessarily because they do not call us for events. (David-Adegboye 2010)

Men typically dominate the stand-up stage in several parts of the world, mostly because women everywhere are erroneously considered less funny. This underrepresentation of women has negatively impacted female participation in comedy production so much so that in 2016, just 14% of Netflix comedy specials uploads were for female comics (Stuart 2018). The unfavourable conditions female stand-up artists contend with are so bad that when 'men fail at comedy, failure is not seen as a product of their maleness or endemic to men as a whole; however, when women bomb, the default explanation is her being a woman' (Krefting 2014, 113). Suffice it to say that being a stand-up comedian is tough, but being a female comic is over four times more rigorous due to the reasons adduced above and the supposition that women are recipients, not producers of humour.

Comedians of Nigerian stand-up

For male humourists, the challenge continues to hover around gaining and retaining relevance amidst the ever-growing crowd of performers in the country. The talent hunt shows of the 2000s and the burgeoning social status of comedians have lured more and more youths into the joke-telling business. The late 1990s to the mid-2000s saw the introduction of comedians like Bright Okpocha (Basket Mouth), Francis Agodan (I Go Dye), Godwin Komone (Gordons), Koffi Ayinde Idowu Nuel (Koffi), Ayo Makun (AY), Onyebuchi Ojieh (Buchi), Ahamefula Igwemba (Klint da Drunk), Bovi Ugboma (Bovi), Owen Gee, Teju Babyface, Maleke, I Go Save, Michael Ogbolosingha, Holy Mallam, Emeka Smith, Omo Baba, and a host of others.

Bright Okpocha (Basket Mouth) started as a rapper before going into stand-up. Around 1996/97, a specific audience booed his band while they were performing. In order to placate them, the band stopped playing, and he had to pick up the microphone again, this time as a comedian. His joke-telling at that event thrilled the spectators more than the rap music he and his band had prepared to present (Nigeria Galleria 2017a). He is one of those who have successfully pulled off many shows of their own, especially internationally. I consider him to be Nigeria's most travelled comedian because he has featured in events in more countries on the continent than other stand-ups. Since 2019, some of his engagements include making movies alongside his long-running television series, *Flatmates*, and music production, resulting in an album titled *Yabasi*. Ahamefula Clint Igwemba (Klint da Drunk) is another comedian who has also dabbled in music and film. He is one of the few Nigerian comedians with a stock personality, using dance routines and song parodies alongside persistently acting like a drunk. Like Basket Mouth, he started as a musician, later becoming a comedian. He says his stage art was inspired by Scatter Mojo, a drunkard from his village, whom he had imitated since childhood (Alhassan 2012; Odeyemi 2012). Two other comedians, Adebayo Ajiboye (Holy Mallam) and Olufemi Michael (Aboki 4 Christ), also played stock characters in the 2000s with their stereotypical enactments of Hausa men, complete with the accent, mannerisms, and outlook. The fact that these two are Yoruba men performing with Hausa accent and traits is remarkable because it bears witness to the trans-ethnic aspect of joke-telling in Nigerian stand-up.

Francis Agodan (I Go Dye) is another important jokester of the late 1990s and the 2000s. He started doing comedy on Delta Broadcasting Service and later performed in a Benin hotel in 1994 before appearing on the *Nite of a Thousand Laughs* stage in 2000. He is one of the many Nigerian comedians who popularised the Niger Delta city of Warri, presenting it as a unique comedy brand by glamourising *Waffi* slang, character traits, and worldview.[7] He achieved this feat by characteristically punctuating his narratives with Warri registers. Ayo Makun (AY), a direct protégé of Ali Baba, also grew up in Warri, and plays the *Waffi* when it is necessary. He has become quite popular, not ineludibly because of his jokes, but for his prestigious *AY Live Shows* which have been running for over a decade now. AY started in comedy with memorable imitations of famous Nigerian pastors, especially Chris Oyakhilome and Chris Okotie, his own pastor. He has since rested imitations of these for others and the use of short dramatic skits in his events.

Some significant comedians to have emerged in the late 2000s include the trio of Lawrence Oluwaseyitan Aletile (Seyi Law), Akinlami Babatunde Julius (Elenu), and Jephthah Bowoto (Akpororo), who came into the national limelight following successes at talent-hunt competitions organised by AY and Opa Williams. Akpororo infuses dance and music in his performances, Seyi Law imitates and replicates Yoruba stereotypes, while Elenu does standalone and double acts with AY. AY plays the main speaker, and Elenu interprets for him in Yoruba, enacting humour through nonsensical (mis-)representations. Double act comedy has a recent development in Nigeria's stand-up because most comedians perform as individuals. It is better known globally with the Japanese *Manzai*, involving two performers known as *boke* and *tsukkomi*. Two pairs of double-act comedians have emerged in Nigeria recently: Still Ringing and Sam and Song. Their acts, just like AY and Elenu's, are modelled on the format of a Christian preacher and his interpreter. Laughter is generated from the second speaker's deviations (often riddled with misinterpretations and nonsensical allusions to unrelated happenings, personalities, and places the audience is familiar with) from the main speaker's statements. There is also a whole genre of jokes revolving around false interpretations usually set in the colonial past throughout Nigeria. Furthermore, the 2010s saw the emergence of myriad comics like Stanley Chibunna (Funny Bone), Ogechi Nwanevu Cyril (Pencil), Daniel Chibuzor Nnwoka (Dan d'Humorous), Oghenekowhoyan Onaibe Desmond (Destalker), Bennet Chinedu Daniel (MC Acapella), Diribe Chidi Richard (MC Pashun), and Obinna Simon (MC Tagwaye).[8] MC Tagwaye performs with a Hausa accent, mostly enacting impressions of Nigeria's president, Muhammadu Buhari (at the time of writing), with whom he shares some resemblance. The list of Nigerian humourists goes beyond this because there are more active comedians than can be exhaustively covered in this book.

It is noteworthy that while most mainstream performances are held in the major Nigerian cities of Lagos, Abuja and Port Harcourt, stand-up events also occur elsewhere and in less formal locations. It is further pertinent to note that Warri and its environs have produced more comedians in mainstream practice than any other part of the country, ranging from pioneers such as Ali Baba and I Go Dye, and more recent joke-tellers like Real Warri Pikin and Destalker, to those with Yoruba parentage born and raised in Warri, like AY and Akpororo. Despite the sheer number of people from the Niger Delta region in Nigerian stand-up, there are people from other ethnicities who have become equally successful and popular. With the large number of performers and increasing competition for joke materials, comedians try as much as they can to diversify their themes and techniques as we shall see in the next two chapters.

Notes

1 Some of these individual accounts can be found in the following, mostly journalistic essays: Ijalana 2010; Nwanne 2010; Olukole 2010; Odeh 2011; Tolu 2013; Umukoro 2013; Okon-Ekong 2016; Awosiyan n.d. Apart from *Nite of a Thousand Laughs*, many events took place simultaneously but were mostly unrecorded. Information about them is only available through word of mouth, which is sometimes contradictory and imprecise in terms of the exact time each person became a professional comedian on the Nigerian stage.

2 Also known as John 'God' (English version of his Igbo surname) or JC.

3 'I am gone already. I am this plane's pilot. You may continue to stay on if you want, but I am gone.'

4 Julius Agwu often tells the tale of how children born in the village should be called 'pikin', which is a Pidgin English word for 'child.'

5 Examining the reasons for the near absence of femininity on the stand-up stage in Nigeria is beyond the scope of this book.

6 Other female comedians include Ebinyo Michael, Dud Evans, Deola Chatterbucks, Chinyere, and Emmanuella. These have performed at many social functions, and some of them on mainstream stand-up shows. However, except for Emmanuella, they have not reached the same national recognition as those mentioned. I consider Emmanuella more as a social media comedy personality even though she has been featured on one of AY's stage events. She was born in 2010 and has a large following on YouTube, where her account, MarkAngelComedy, managed by her uncle, has close to 7 million subscribers.

7 *Waffi*, a reference to the inhabitants of the city of Warri, is discussed in the next chapter.

8 'Tagwaye' means 'twins' in Hausa, and this performer has a twin brother.

3
Techniques and devices

The art of yabbing and wording

A popular saying attributed to E. B. White posits that '(e)xplaining a joke is like dissecting a frog. You understand it better, but the frog dies in the process' (Hirsch 2020, xxv). In the light of this statement, we delineate two aspects of joke criticism, separated into interpretation or dissection, and examination or interrogation. Interpretation/dissection seeks to replicate forms of analyses suitable for other genres of arts like literature and theatre, where post-mortem critiques are needful and instrumental to a fuller understanding of the work. The second (examination/ interrogation) denotes the kind of work this book is doing, which is examining the processes of joke-telling. Specifically, where the former may be applied to individual art pieces, jokes or artists to (in)validate their worth or laughter evoked, the latter is more concerned with the procedures and mechanics of joke production and reception. Additionally, as dissection and/or interpretation kill(s) jokes or the frog as contained in White's observation above, the second type of joke criticism readily adheres to the notion that 'how a joke works does not necessarily sabotage it … [because] theory and practice occupy different spheres' (Eagleton 2019, ix–x).

As part of understanding the inner workings of joke-telling within stand-up renditions, Ajaye (2002) identifies elements such as point of view, honesty, delivery, timing, visuals, and smooth transitions. For Ajaye, the first element of stand-up art, 'point of view/true thoughts', is the point where joke-telling starts. Here, comedians tell tales predicated on real-life situations, expressing their true feelings about the subject. The second is 'honesty,' wherein the jokesters funnily

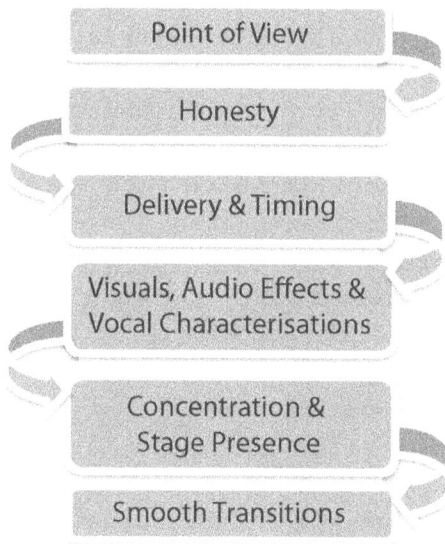

Figure 3.1 Franklyn Ajaye's elements of stand-up comedy

give opinions and not just 'try[ing] to give a funny opinion' (Ajaye 2002, 12). Honesty supposes that narratives are conveyed in as much a convincing manner as possible to compel believability and not that stories are not made-up stories. Other elements such as delivery, timing, visuals, and smooth transitions (Ajaye 2002, 10–19) designate ways in which comedians regulate and manipulate the rate, exact moment, accompanying imageries, and mode of succession of their joke renditions to extract maximum laughter from the audience. It is noteworthy that these elements work simultaneously and not independently in aiding the jokester elicit laughter. For this study, the elements are merged, as seen in Figure 3.2, to show how they work together.

Stage Presence is the first element of stand-up comedy because it is through it that the comedian can grasp and hold the audience's attention. It includes the manner of entrance, appearance and other performance mechanics the artist adopts in directing the audience's interest. Furthermore, stand-up comedy requires direct performer-audience interaction and good stage presence to enhance such relationships. Considering Stage Presence before every other element is borne out of the conviction that performers need to hold the stage before any other element can successfully come into play. This is because comedians who cannot control the audience's attention while on stage will not carry through with Honesty. They may eventually fumble in the area of Delivery and Timing too. Stage Presence is mostly achieved through being emotionally and psychologically present, using appropriate body language to woo the spectators, establishing an enjoyable rapport with them, capitalising on this connection, and ultimately managing it in ways that create unforgettable moments in the show.

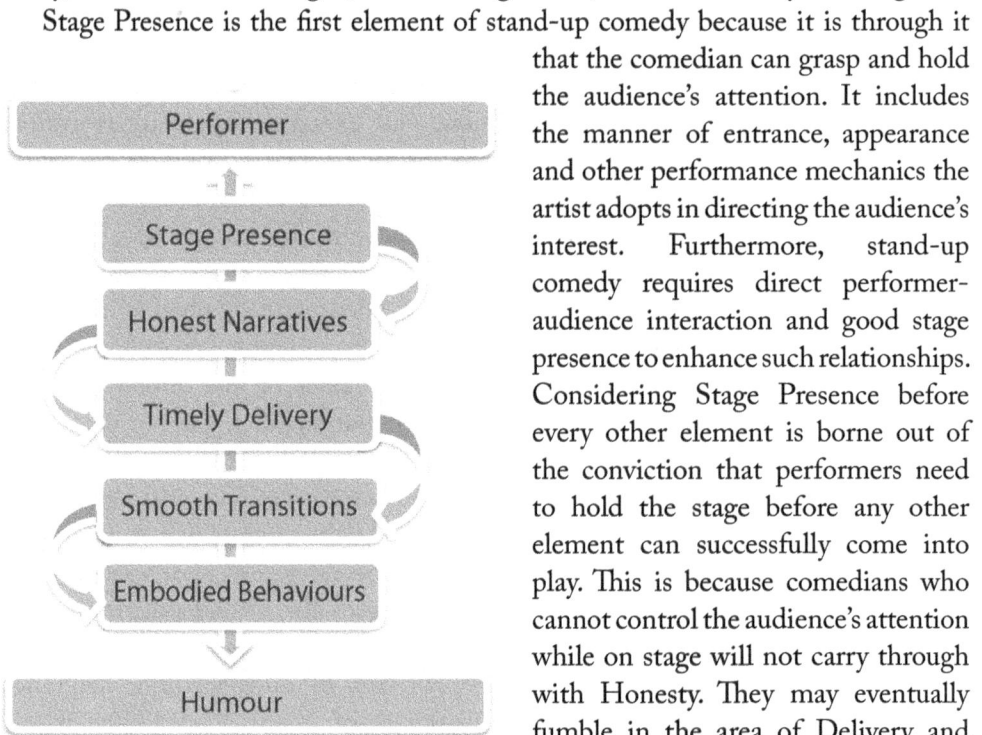

Figure 3.2   Elements of stand-up comedy

Honest Narratives is a fusion of Ajaye's Point of View and Honesty. This merger captures the essences of having personal perspectives and bringing them out in very believable ways. Every comedian possesses specific ways in which they convey their jokes. They also strive to present them to attain the highest level of mirth. By the nature of jokes, familiarity with the object being discussed is essential for the joke-teller and the receiver(s). This is because since jokes work mostly with incongruities or a distortion of the usual, there is a need for the spectators to be aware of the issue being raised. In situations where the audience does not share common socio-cultural circumstances, worldview, and knowledge with the comedian, it is often very difficult to make them laugh unless the artist can discover common issues from which to create jokes. It is familiarity with the topic that enhances plausibility even though performers often proceed from the known into incredible tales. Honesty entails delivering the thoughts in a manner that suggests that they are true and actually took place. Even though the audience knows that comedians make up their stories, they still believe them based on the fervency and conviction with which the jokes are told.

Timely Delivery works with Honest Narratives because apart from telling believable tales, comedians also perform with an eye on audience response. From their reading of such responses, they determine when best to drop, alter, or draw out specific lines of their joke narratives. In stand-up comedy, Timing and Delivery are indistinguishable since when talking about one, it is very likely that the other will be mentioned. Delivery is the appropriate use of cadence, pause, and a good understanding and utilisation of audience response in the presentation of every segment of each joke. Timeliness is essential to stand-up performances because a good line delivered poorly will not produce its fullest potential of mirth. A bad line delivered appropriately could do better than a good one presented badly. Timely delivery is thus central to the risibility of the joke; when coupled with Smooth Transitions, the entire performance becomes a complete whole with a beginning, middle, and end, even with the absence of a unified storyline. Comedians adept at creating connections where there are none, are more likely to make their audiences laugh increasingly up to a crescendo, eliciting an applause break. Because they work with materials that are often unrelated thematically and structurally, good comedians frequently invent multiple mechanics of transition to unify their presentations. Some of them use tag words that are common to both the preceding and succeeding tales. In this instance, they first highlight the word in the former tale and then use it to proceed to the next one. This way, they can create a transition loosely but smoothly, and because the appreciation of stand-up comedy is immediate, the audience sees the entire performance as coherent, even though a post-mortem appraisal will expose the loose connections the comedian has used.

Embodied Behaviours in stand-up comedy include speech, movement, gestures, and facial expressions used to accompany the jokes. Speech here does not solely refer to everyday spoken words but also to imageries and suggestions which comedians elicit. It also includes all manner of narrative twists which comedians deploy to make meaning. In addition, embodied actions are part of what performers use to enhance stage presence. They are important in adequately portraying the kind of picture that comedians want the audience to see. Bodily movements can also be used to counter speech when comedians choose to play multiple roles with embodied actions. Here, the audience sees that what the performer is saying runs counter to what he or she is doing in gestures, facial expressions or even movements. Suffice it to say here, that Embodied Behaviour is a substantial part of what makes stand-up comedy a theatrical art.

Comedians 'develop' these and many other 'techniques to compensate for those times when [their] talent or creative spark isn't there' (Ajaye 2002, 10). Stand-up art is quite tasking because the path to amusement is potentially fraught with offence, thereby making comedians exert their initial efforts towards successfully navigating their materials away from eliciting repulsion. Particularly, it is dependent on timing, entails on-the-spot criticism, instigates ambivalence through its abuse/amusement nature, elicits laughter from audiences it ridicules, privileges direct speech, and almost always requires new materials at every performance since repeated jokes receive fewer laughs.[1] Thus, stage humourists perpetually tread a thin line between amusement and abuse, rely heavily on their reading of audience reaction for timely delivery, and produce new jokes or at least tell older ones in newer ways to sustain the element of surprise without which laughter may not be effectively evoked. No other artist is confronted with such demands, especially in the way comedians craft and devise unique signature mechanics for surmounting each challenge.[2] Such mechanics are mostly subterranean since the audience is not required to know them to laugh. They are applied variously to the five parts of most jokes as shown in Figure 3.3: setup, punchline, pause, tagline and follow-through.

Setup ⟶ Punchline ⟶ Pause ⟶ Tagline ⟶ Follow through

Figure 3.3   Parts of a joke

The setup designates points where the comedian 'establishes the context of the joke and introduces any necessary background information to prepare the listener for the punchline,' and the punchline means a 'twist on the information provided in the setup,' from which laughter is created (Miller 2010). Whereas the setup creates a familiar situation or condition, the punchline is precisely an unexpected alteration in the familiar story. It is therefore a mixture of the curiosity created by the setup and the accompanying unexpected ludicrous turn of events engendered by the punchline that creates the humour. The pause is a deliberate break in the performance within which the comedian does a range of activities – heightening suspense, allowing the audience to laugh, clap, and savour the joke, making them fill in spaces after a suggestive statement, and transiting to an adjoining joke introduced by a tagline. Functional pauses come from adeptness at reading audience response accurately and determining when best to deliver every component of the joke narrative. Taglines are additional punchlines often given without a new setup to elicit further mirth. Follow-throughs are transitional statements with which unrelated jokes are connected with new setups, which lead to newer punchlines. When the pause, tagline, and follow-through are used appropriately, the performance appears to be one linear narrative, whereas it is in fact just a series of episodic stories strung together by wit.

Nigerian comedians deploy the same comedic devices – parody, narrative dexterity, direct insult, lampoon, satire, imitation, and the like – used by humourists everywhere. There is no homogeneity in style or uniformity except in joke content mainly drawn from the same depository of knowledge shared by audiences and performers alike. From this familiar base, the setup of most jokes comes, which is then immediately followed by the punchline that emanates from an alteration or deviation from the norm in irregular, grotesque, or uncommon ways. Put differently, jokes:

> rely on audiences' metafolkloric expectations for their composition and delivery [and the joke-tellers need to] embrace a multifaceted gambit in navigating through the intricacies of style, form, content, and audience expectations. (Blank 2016, 191)

In addition to pilfering materials from shared cultural knowledge, comedians also explore and exploit pre-existing jokes and joke forms in their society (Tolbert 2016, 176–177). For instance, Nigerian comedians deploy forms of *yabbing* and *wording* in their acts: two terms often used interchangeably to refer to pre-colonial forms of joke play and insults between individuals and groups.

The Nigerian Pidgin English verb, *yab*, means to insult, abuse or offend, whereas *wording* comes from the English term, *word*, which is used to designate a playful exchange of insults, a test of wits between individuals or groups. *Yabbing* is described as

> … an oral repertoire during which friends hurl serious jokes at each other or lampoon each other; not as an act of enmity but as a mark of friendship. *Yabbing* is the peak of interaction in a social gathering of Nigerian men. (Onyeche 2004, 54)

Although its specific origin is unsure, *yab* is sometimes said to have emerged from the English 'jab.' Its origin notwithstanding, the term became popular with its repeated use by the Afrobeat music maestro, Fela Anikulapo-Kuti, who designated his satiric songs and exposé against the government of the day as *yabbis*. Sola Olorunyomi calls it a declamation, the sort of 'verbal rebuttal that could move from light-hearted banter to a crude ribaldry;' positing further that *yabbis* has 'its own limit and its license goes only as far as there is no physical assault, following the Kalakuta dictum: "Yabbis no case, first touch na offence"' (2003, xix).[3] Furthermore, within the context of Fela music concerts, Tejumola Olaniyan further explicates Fela's use of *yabbis* before the emergence of professional stand-up practice in Nigeria:

> While the precise meaning of 'yab' in urban southwest Nigerian pidgin English is to roast, criticize, or abuse, its connotations are much wider—to expose one's wrongdoing in public, to discomfit, humiliate, deconstruct. Indeed, one of the most beloved features of a Fela concert was '*yabis* time' during which, to intermittent interventions from the audience, he would range widely round the world critically picking apart and ironizing news items and events … *Yabis* time was a consummate scene of educational instruction in which, led by Fela, the audience came to know a lot about itself and its place in the contexts of the nation, the continent, and the world and the dominant relations, historical and contemporary, among those entities. (2004, 145)

For Fela, therefore, *yabbing* is a mode of subversion using abrasive verbal attacks on power. Thus, *yabbis* is his way of getting even with power and its wielders. Professional comedians like Basket Mouth deploy *yabbis* (Al Jazeera English 2015) as a joking pattern within their stand-up renditions. Unlike Fela's, accompanied by music, *yabbis* time is not delineated but is integrated into joke performances. Within stand-up art, *yabbing* is expressed through satire, lampoon, parody, and sundry forms of ridicule comedians elicit in deploring the powerful and their insensitivity to the plights of ordinary people.

Wording is more playful and less provocative since it is usually a game between peers, dwelling mainly on domestic and personal matters. Though the nomenclature has a recent origin in Nigerian Pidgin English, it is a joking relationship that existed in various pre-colonial localities in Africa, with slight differences based on the specificities of location, people, culture, and observances. The principal idea among all localised variants remains the playful exchange of jokes between people who belonged to different social categories given that joking relationships are inter-generational and inter-ethnic, imbued with the capacity to bridge differences and forestall conflicts. The *dozens*, a game of throwing insults at opponents, practised among African-Americans is similar to *wording*. It came to the US through African slaves (Baraka 1968; Dollard 1973), with origins traced directly to the Igbo *ịkọcha nkọcha* (verbal abuse), which is a generic name for *ịkọọnụ* and *njakịrị* (Chimezie 1976). It is noteworthy that the Igbo do not have a monopoly of this genre of joking since there are reports of similar practices all over Africa (Radcliffe-Brown 1940; Moreau 1944; Wegru 2000; Diallo 2006). Specifically, there were artistic expressions of satire and insults in folksongs and masking traditions in Mali, Ghana, Zambia, and Ethiopia (Finnegan 1970/2012, 269; Okpewho 1992, 276) as well as in Somalia, Tanzania, and South Africa (Ebewo 2001, 49–50). For present-day *wording*, therefore, its valorisation within contemporary stand-up art in Nigeria is in two forms. Firstly, comedians often deploy joking devices associated with *wording*, such as mild personal attacks, ridicule of someone's appearance or social status, farcical imitations of the opponent's mannerisms and peculiarities, as well as general ridicule of one's relations and circumstances. These representations range from serious and factual happenstances to silly, contrived inventions and claims, some of which can be politically incorrect. Comedians use this form of *wording* in the description of situations and individuals within joke narratives. The second aspect of *wording* in Nigerian stand-up is the deployment of the devices mentioned above to respond to and handle heckling within a comedian's set. Being interrupted while performing is a form of challenge that comedians deal with in several ways. *Wording* devices can be quite helpful in this regard, especially by aiding the comedian to maintain playfulness while quashing heckling and other confrontations from the audience. The difference between these uses of *wording* are not so far apart, but there is always the understanding between audiences and comedians in live situations that the two parties are involved in a joke situation. This background imbues the environment with playfulness thereby framing the taking up of offence by anyone in the audience as an aberration. In this wise, *wording* is an enabling strategy for the suspension of offence-taking within the Nigerian stand-up environment because the consciousness of its peculiarities in real-life situations (especially given that most people were conversant with it while growing up) conditions people to be more receptive to being ridiculed in a clearly defined stand-up environment.

The stage battle between Helen Paul and Gordons at *AY Live Show* in Lagos is an excellent example of how comedians deploy *wording* devices. Helen Paul *yabs* comedians from AY to Ali Baba during her set, saying that AY wears the same jeans and 'white canvas,' Ali Baba's jokes are for old people like Obasanjo, and ultimately that Gordons 'looks like a herbalist.' When it is his turn to perform, Gordons decides to retaliate with more hurtful verbal abuse. Helen Paul joins him on stage with a microphone, responding to his 'insults.' As the exchange of very personal attacks becomes more intense, AY comes on stage and carries Helen Paul off (Kilarigbo Live 2015; AY Comedian 2016b). In this example, Helen Paul turns other comedians in the audience into targets for her sarcasm, and no one attempts to stop her as she performs. Afterwards, I Go Dye decides not to respond to her comments when it is his time to perform. However, Gordons says that he is a Warri boy and 'Warri people no de quick forgive!'[4] He *yabs* her directly, using insulting language and expressions, which prompts Helen Paul to return to the stage. With Paul's entry, there ensues a shouting match, a heated *wording* between the two. The audience laughs profusely, following the examples of the comedians who were equally laughing as they insulted each other, indicating that it was all in jest. If there is any other extenuating or underlying issue between the two, it does not matter to the listeners because everything on that stage has become part of the performance.

Each jokester possesses recognisable styles of joke presentation built around stage presence, use of space, and peculiar delivery pattern, which, at once, distinguishes and hemlines their art. Appropriate use of space is vital to stand-up situations due to its direct relations with movement and embodied expressions as complements to spoken words. Each of these performance devices is combined variously for maximum impact as instruments of joke performance. To better understand the mechanics of joke routines, they are examined below under two broad categories: embodied and structural forms.

Embodied devices

Embodied expressions are relevant to cognition and expression in human existence. This is so because '(w)ithout the bodily, we would not be able to organize ourselves in our environment: we will not know where/what we are, what/how we are learning or how we can communicate about our feelings, experiences and modes of being' (Coetzee 2018, 1). As such, speech and movement (of the body and in space), which are essential bodily actions within performance, are not performed in isolation from other body actions in real-life situations or within stand-up renditions. Being one of the two most evident bodily actions of stand-up artists, speech designates verbalisations incorporating devices such as a deliberate slip of the tongue, hanging and incomplete statements, stuttering/stammering, voice alterations and modulations, and the use of accents. Movement, which is the second most significant embodied action of stand-up enactment, has two parts: spatial and bodily motion ranging from gestures, facial expressions, sitting, standing or squatting, and other non-verbal use of the body, to relocate from one part of the stage to another as accompaniments to speech and accentuation of stage personalities. The importance of these non-verbal bodily strategies serves to emphasise, negate or uphold utterances. They can sometimes be standalone expressions devoid of words and other verbalised actions, indicating that humour can also be evoked through pantomimic, farcical, embodied actions.

Peculiar speech devices found in Nigerian stand-up include the deployment of *ghetto credibility*, *nto*, and accents. *Ghetto credibility* refers to the exhibition of localised identification markers – registers and slang, speech mannerism, and general character disposition of ghettoised spaces such as Ajegunle or Mushin in Lagos, Warri other not-well-to-do settlements adjoining different cities. The use of *ghetto credibility* is widespread as comedians consciously enact experiences and/or affinities with certain areas and conditions even when it is evident that they had a more privileged upbringing. The most identifiable *ghetto credibility* is that of Warri, better known as *Waffi* credibility. Described as a city in which the inhabitants 'have always drawn inspiration and determination from the power of their wits' (Tidi 2018), Warri has become the comedy capital of sorts in Nigeria. It is also an area that has produced the highest number of comedians in Nigeria, sharing commonalities [in the use of] language, gestures, response to reality [… and] in the manner they utilise Warri's history as a city of sailors, *boma* boys, multiplicity of ethnic groups, and a certain proclivity for flamboyance and grand gestures despite often harrowing times.[5] (Ojaide and Ojaruega 2020, 90)

Comedians like Ali Baba, I Go Dye, Gandoki, AY, Gordons, Akpororo, Real Warri Pikin, and Destalker have affiliations with this city. Hosting three major ethnic groups and a few others, Warri is a melting pot of cultures. There is an ascription of the city's dominance in comedy to its minority status within the larger Nigerian society and the desire to hit back at 'the oppressor nations of Igbo, Yoruba and Hausa' ethnicities, the 'big tribes,' for their unnamed 'faults and foibles' (Ego-Alowes 2017, 46). Contrary to this claim, three significant reasons for the supremacy of humour in this region can be identified:

1. the area's volatile nature due to a history of violence conditions people to adopt playfulness and humour to avert conflicts,
2. the proliferation of pidgin English to break linguistic barriers among the three major tribes – the Ijaw, the Itsekiri, and the Urhobo, enabled the evolution of peculiar registers through the influence of local languages, localised speech patterns, and a unique pidgin English variant, and
3. the successes of the precursors of stand-up art like Ali Baba, I Go Dye, AY, and their direct support from performers from the region aided the entry of many Warri youths into the profession.

Ego-Alowe's claim fails to recognise the presence of people of other ethnicities, AY and Akpororo, for instance, as comedians making waves under *Waffi credibility*.

Warri shares some characteristics with other ghettoised spaces like Ajegunle, a suburb of Lagos, where other non-Warri comedians claim to have been raised. Warri and Ajegunle share the trait of being locations where the general populace lives in penury amidst the offensive opulence of the super-rich. For Warri, the popular archetypal *Waffi* character, Akpos (featured in common everyday stories and comedy skits on stage and television), has been created with identifiable affinities with the trickster character of oral literature. Akpos reportedly 'operates outside of normative constraints and socio-cultural orthodoxy' (Yékú 2016, 252), not in politically incendiary and subversive modes, but as a comic persona imbued with *Waffi credibility*. Two prominent catchphrases that have made it from the streets of Warri to the stand-up stage, 'Warri no de carry last,' and hailing people as 'Area,' evoke the form of indefatigability for which people from Warri are known. I Go Dye uses them extensively, for instance, and Real Warri Pikin adds, 'Wetin de play?' [What is playing/going on?]. The primary designation of *Waffi credibility* is the portraiture of a relentless and survivalist nature, as seen in I Go Dye's jokes and tales of underaged Warri boys claiming to have got

HIV/AIDS through sex so they can claim palliatives (NTL5 n.d.; NTL14 2008), being knowledgeable about foreign currencies and exchange rate (NTL15 2008) and being so fearless that they tread where armed soldiers fear to go (Juvenis TV 2020). Also, with his thick, intimidating voice, build and bald head, Gordons uses *Waffi* credibility just as in his exchange with Helen Paul. Destalker approaches his *Waffi*-ness by speaking in a calmer, reassuring but very emphatic manner, riddling his speech with proverbs and epigrams gleaned from oral tradition. Real Warri Pikin compares with Gordons in abrasiveness, the talk, walk, and the confrontational, in-your-face interaction with the audience. Despite negative stereotypes adduced to *Waffi* credibility, it confers Nigerian comedy the capacity for self-ridicule and absorption of verbal insults by comedians and audiences.

The second distinctively Nigerian narrative style known in Igbo as *nto* refers to exaggerated bombastic, highfalutin tales of exploits told to see how many lies one can get away with. It often starts simply, before delving into the realm of the implausible. Sometimes it also ends in pure bathos as exemplified by Basket Mouth in his tale about being invited for a big comedy show by HBO in the US with America's best, which he tells with relish and heightening suspense until the end where he says that he woke up and all was a dream[6] (Globacomlimited 2010). Comedians make up narratives, but the difference is that *nto* is always high sounding, unwinding, and often ends disappointingly. In I Go Dye's oeuvre, there is this exciting tale with an anti-climactic ending:

> Basket (Mouth) just vex. Before 'im vex na P-Square, D'Banj vex go buy BMW Z5. Radio, fridge dey inside. ATM machine dey inside [prolonged laughter]. Basket Mouth just vex, una de see Basket Mouth de carry dreads, de do advert for Malta Guinness. If you know how much 'im hol'. When Basket do 'im own, all of us jus' quiet. He jus' buy, de same day, four different jeeps. No name. I just see 'B' [pause]. Customised. Na later I come see 'Mouth.' If you see car, 'e just wowo, 'e be like wetin wan catch person [he demonstrates]. Ol' boy, na 'im I say me wey be Warri boy, they can't fall my hand. [with greater emphasis] Me, Warri boy! Wetin de worry them! Na 'im I vex, I say I wan find my own choice. Na 'im I vex waka go find one wicked Infinity Jeep, 2008 model. Black! As I de waka again na 'im I see another wicked Infinity Jeep, 2010 model. De oyibo man say dis thing is cost. Na 'im I say na dis one I want. Na 'im I vex, with my church mind, na 'im I find de Infinity jeep side mirror![7] (NTL16 n.d.)

In this narrative, there is a progression that climbs increasingly into exaggeration, but the conclusion that he ended up buying the side mirror of the vehicle he has so gloriously described is significantly bathotic. This descent is unexpected and downright ridiculous. One would wonder how his ownership of a side mirror of the 2010 model of this monstrous 'Infinity Jeep' would elevate him to compete with those who own the real thing.

Furthermore, Emeka Smith's set at an *AY Live Show* in London is erected on the hassles of travelling abroad on a Nigerian passport. He tells of an experience at Atlanta airport in the US where he claimed that he was Tanzanian to avoid being treated as poorly as other Nigerians ahead of him in the long queue of black people. According to him, the immigration officer asked him to sing the Tanzanian national anthem as proof of his nationality, and in response, he bursts into a popular Ijaw gospel song, the audience helps him sing it, and he exits to resounding applause at the end of that song (AY Comedian 2017). It was a sterling performance by Emeka Smith until Klint da Drunk comes on later at the same event and decides to start his performance by exposing the falsity of Emeka Smith's claims. He rhetorically asks why the immigration officer believed Emeka Smith is Tanzanian when he must have had a Nigerian passport or 'Did your passport change colour?' he asks in revelatory finality to bouts of laughter from the same audience that enjoyed the joke earlier (AY Comedian 2018b). Here, Klint exposes the implausibility of Emeka's tale and the audience's gullibility in believing it. Thus, *nto* does not yield its ludicrousness until either the teller admits or exposes the inherent lies as Basket Mouth and Klint did in the examples above. There is yet a third variant like Okey Bakassi's at an event in Asaba where he tells many bombastic tales but without making any revelations as to their incredulity (AY Comedian 2014). Seyi Law's set at *AY Live* in Abuja, where he claims that he is so dark-skinned that people fail to see him sitting inside a car at night, is yet another good example of this third variant. He claims that he was once shot at by armed robbers, but the bullet could not locate him in the darkness, so it had to go back to the robbers to report that it could not find him (De-9ja Music Ent. 2017b). These glaringly false narratives aim to get the audience to laugh at the verbiage, the manner of exaggeration deployed by the storyteller, and do not necessarily evoke laughter because audiences believe them.

The third peculiar aspect of speech in Nigerian stand-up is the use of character designations and variations employing accents, code-mixing and other specialised rendering of Nigerian Pidgin English. Many comedians align their art to designate specific regions and tribes while others remain neutral, adorning personalities and representations depending on specific demands of jokes. Some of the jokesters with *Waffi* creditability mentioned above belong to this group. Others elicit Igbo, Yoruba, Hausa, and other ethnic stereotypes.[8] Accents are discussed further in Chapter 5, but there are other specialised forms of speech patterns. These include feigned difficulties in vocalisation and inventive voice impressions implicated in comedians' deployment of slips of the tongue, deliberate mispronunciations, stuttering, and sundry forms of narrative variations in delivering jokes. Klint da Drunk, for instance, plays a sustained stock character role of a drunk person, which requires enacting amnesia and multiple types of speech difficulties to complement his unsteady gait and posture. Thus, as part of his stage acts, Klint stumbles on words complete with manifest exertions to make himself understood through his feigned intoxication. For example, he gets stuck in alternations and nonsensical misplacements of the syllables and stress patterns of people's and places' names such as rendering of Uche Ogbuagu as 'Ugbo Ochiagu' (NML n.d.), D'Banj as J'Ban, D'Chan, among others (NTL11 2007), and Mozambique as 'Bozambique,' or 'Mobamzique' (Kilarigbo Live 2018).[9] Klint does not necessarily tell jokes with these devices because his imitative acts turn out to be innately comical.

Speech devices also include replications of how specific individuals speak, voice imitations and variations, capturing stereotypical speaking patterns, and, of course, singing both seriously and comically. Basket Mouth has a range of voice impressions: thickening his voice tone to characterise a jealous boyfriend to fend off competition from a more privileged suitor (NTL12 n.d.) and in mimicking a gluttonous person ordering food at an eatery when someone else is paying (NTL20 n.d.). I Go Dye deploys voice imitation severally to depict children (NTL5 n.d.) and adults in various circumstances (NTL12 n.d.). AY uses voice modulations in his depictions of the clergy and Nigerian celebrities, while Helen Paul presents a very convincing replication of a little girl using just her voice. Others like Koffi, Chigul, and MC Tagwaye use accents to characterise different nationalities and individuals in their stage jokes. It is noteworthy that appropriate and adequate voice use is central to successful stand-up renditions. The aim is not to have a good voice since it is not a singing contest but that one can deploy a limitless range of vocal tonal effects.

Body and spatial movements such as facial expression, gestures, body postures, and other acting strategies complement speech in performance. Movement distinguishes performed jokes from written ones, adding depth and layered meaning to separate stand-up comedy from mere joke-telling. Though comedians dramatise some of their materials as AY often does, movement is not always employed in imitation of others, but also to emphasise statements, create antithesis to spoken texts, and make visual aids for the audience.[10] I Go Dye crawls on all fours in imitation of dogs (NTL12 n.d.), demonstrates how women apply make-up to their faces (NTL16 n.d.), comically collapses to represent how older men faint from exhaustion while trying to satisfy younger women sexually (NTL19 n.d.), and drags a plastic chair across the stage in imitation of people hauling their luggage through airports (NTL20 n.d.). Ali Baba surprisingly uses the entire expanse of a church stage to show how the tennis skills of Serena Williams is akin to how African mothers beat their many children at once as they run around the house (De-9ja Music Ent. 2017a). AY has a characteristic body movement with which he plays female roles: placing his palms under his chest with index fingers pointed forward to indicate provocatively pointy breasts, accompanied by a near-squat position enhancing protruding buttocks, then bulging eyes, and his tongue hanging out.

Basket Mouth uses facial expressions, calling attention to them by, for instance, asking for a close-up shot of his face to be projected on the screen in a live event (BMU3 2009). He generally deploys embodied representations like replicating the action of a physically challenged lady wheeling away on a wheelchair from a man trying to woo her (NTL19 n.d.), the mannerisms of *ajebutter* (privileged) and *pako* (less-privileged) children (NTL3 2004), and those of people who are drunk or high on weed (Hiphopdivas100 2012). He has an outstanding ability to elicit appropriate imageries to accompany his narratives. The most common way Basket Mouth does this is by initiating familiar situations before progressing to the realm of outlandish claims. Before telling the joke about Adam's nakedness, for example, he says,

> I don de imagine […] sometimes I de imagine some things wey 'e be say dem de surprise me. Imagine say […].[11] (NTL15 2008)

Basket Mouth characteristically uses variations of this statement to seemingly lead audiences into taking a stroll with him on tracks of wild imaginations. He does not belabour the validity of his claims but instead encourages the audience to see the journey as an excursion in the realm of the unreal. For instance, in the case of Adam and Eve, he takes the audience into an exploration of a world in which men and women go about their daily work naked – the police, comedians, the president, just about everyone. The picture is difficult to shake off, especially as he mentions specific individuals who are well known to the audience. There are also examples of the voice-overs on Nollywood and Hollywood film trailers and his idea about comedians like him becoming president. He says that he will not be a 'chop alone' (selfish) leader but will apply the 50:50 pattern so that when the government does not provide any social amenity, individuals can use their 50% to do the work (NTL15 2008). The 'chop I chop' (eat and allow others to eat) policy of a Basket Mouth presidency is also an opportunity to delve into the realm of imaginations. For an audience used to failed government promises, the possibility of receiving direct payments to fend for themselves is laughable but worth momentarily mulling over. In each of these examples, audiences are guided towards imagining how life would have been if Eve had not taken the apple and how everyone would still be going about their daily chores, oblivious to their nakedness. People know the Bible story on which this imaginative conjecture is built. Thus, humour is evoked from the deviation from the story, the daring imagination of what would have been. Each of these narratives is accompanied by commensurate movement and gestures aimed at increasing the visuals of their joke-telling, thus enhancing meaning and audiences' appreciation of what is being discussed.

Structural devices

Narrative arrangement, joke forms, and language comprise part of the structural devices of joke-telling. Narrative arrangement encompasses the totality of ways comedians determine the best moment and ways to set up their stories and drop punchlines, more specifically, delivery patterns and timing. Stand-up comedy requires no 'plot, closure, or point ... [the] comedian is free ... to thematize or editorialize or beautify' as s/he deems fit (Limon 2000, 12). For this purpose, comedians create laughter from rightly gauging delivery, maintaining a compelling stage presence, and proportionally deploying accompanying spatial and body movements to their performance but also by their selection of appropriate structural and physical devices. Joke forms refer to patterns of ridicule and modes of laughter elicitation. Disparate jokes are tactfully strung together, thereby creating a link that can be considered a form of order, or even plot. As such, Limon's idea of 'no plot' becomes problematic because when comedians tell jokes in no particular order, they risk losing their audience, and that means they will certainly bomb. As mentioned earlier, one way to join different jokes is through the imposition of thematic links that allow comedians to move seamlessly from one narrative to another. Nigerian comedians have been extolled for using this device appropriately, because as custodians

> of the idea of total art [they understand] the simple logic that effective art subscribes to an orderly, acceptable and functional arrangement, which not only speaks volumes of the artist's sense of organization and structure, but also penchant for meaning. Thus hardly is any other artist more besaddled with the heavy onus of total art than the stand-up comedian. [They also ...] know cultures, psychologies, societies, religions, histories, etc, (sic) but [they subject themselves] to the tedious chore of fitting into all these and fashioning out an appropriate module of presentation. (Onyerionwu 2010)

Akuidolo Orevaoghene (Forever) enacts this total art form in the extract in Figure 3.5 by appropriately applying the joke narrative progression.

The set opens with 'Happy New Year,' a subject that is not explored further until later, as shown by the black dots. Next comes the initial two setups (ST), which Forever builds around 'his marriage' and the first two punchlines (PL1 and PL2). Then comes the tagline (TG) about the shift from being an Arsenal fan to 'supporting' Nickelodeon, which ushers in the follow-through (FT) about the further transition from watching football to the Indian soap opera channel Zee World. Here, I left out a few lines about how the language of expression in his house has suddenly become 'Indian', from which Forever erects a new setup using his wife and their marriage. This time, he shifts into another discourse using Benin city's typical stereotype as the capital of witchcraft in Africa. Here he avers that 'Bini' people, including his wife, do

- Happy New Year. Please clap for me, am a married man (audience obliges, laughs). It's
not easy to marry in this country, to marry successfully. I've been married for a very long   ST
time…(pause) for like two years now. (audience laughter). Before I got married one,
man lied to me… I'm looking for that man because I want to arrest him. He said, Forever,   ST
when you marry, as the head of the family, don't let your wife control you. Be in charge!
(pause) Lagos! (pause) For two years now, I'm not in charge. Before I got married, I was
an Arsenal fan. As I speak to you, I support Nickelodeon. (audience laughter) I can't   TG
even touch remote control, talk more of changing channel. How I started watching Zee   FT
World, I don't know (audience laughter) […] Am already speaking Indian in my house
(pause. Audience laughter) I got married from Edo State. Anybody from Edo State here?
(raises his hand to prompt his audience to do same) wonderful people! Benin City is the   ST
only city that has airport, no plane. (audience laughter) Because they don't need it.
Everybody flies. As am talking to you now, I no know where my wife dey. But I know   TG
- she's going somewhere […] You know 2019 is a great year. That's what they will tell
us. Motivational speakers will now give you hope. They will give you quotes that don't
work for them. They will tell you. "My brother, in 2019. you need SCOPE to COPE.
(pause) Without SCARS, you can't have CARS." I say, "My brother, give me motor."   ST
(Empire Entertainment Smile 2019)

PL1
PL2
PL3
PL4
PL5

Figure 3.4 Excerpt from Forever's performance

not need planes and airports because they all fly. I left out a couple of sentences about
how they save more by flying 'at night' rather than by day. The punchline evolves from
this unverbalised admission of involvement in witchcraft and the bombastic claim
that they fly about without planes. Therefore, the suggestion is that he has given up
his television programme preferences and joined his wife in flying at night. He then
goes back to his opening greeting, where he said 'Happy New Year' to the audience.
Using the background of the concert being held on 1 January, at the peak of new year
resolutions and setting targets for the year, Forever erects a gag that satirises people
who make unfeasible plans at the behest of dubious motivational speakers.

Not all sets follow this arrangement pattern because more spontaneous comedians
build their acts around audience interaction and responses. Those who use well-made
patterns still find their ways back to their main themes after unexpected disruptions.
For instance, in a set about Nigeria's forty-second independence anniversary, Basket
Mouth makes scathing remarks about the nation's inability to become prosperous
despite its potential for economic growth, pauses, and then calls the country *agbaya*
(Yoruba term for an adult behaving like a child). He mentions corruption as the

root cause of the country's problems and ties that to someone, especially the then-president being ugly, thereby conflating both terms as one before giving a one-liner, 'Anybody wey wowo fit become tief [pause] … like our president now!'[12] (NTL3 2004). One cannot say for sure where his script starts and where it ends. Basket Mouth has a knack for dropping punchlines and taglines as if they are spontaneous or slips of the tongue when, in actuality, they are all part of his script. Throughout his enactment here and in his entire stand-up oeuvre, Basket Mouth uses self-censorship devices to keep his utterances in check. His rapid transitions from one jocular tale to another is a peculiar narrative style, a form of creative verbosity with which he allows his audience no room to heckle him. He uses functional pauses to enhance his jokes' risibility because only they allow the full import of his statements to sink in. His delivery pattern is so prompt that his pauses are neither so long that laughter dies out entirely nor so short that he cuts off audience laughter and applause.

Other successful comedians use these mechanics in their stage work. I Go Dye shows immense flexibility in the cadences of his joke delivery while transiting between its disparate parts. In one event, he starts by avowing his Nigerian*ness*, berating people who deny their nationality due to hard times. He then adds,

> Believe it or not, *ogoro* must jump. Devil na area boy, God na godfather. Warri boy no de carry last.[13] (NTL19 n.d.)

With the last statement, he delves into how Warri people make comedians explain their jokes, then to performers who throw their 'boxers and singlets' into audiences that serve as the setup for talking about Tuface and musicians who do drugs. He narrates how someone advised him to take weed, which eventually got him into trouble. I Go Dye confesses that he does not need people to tell him what to do anymore because someone asked him to put on more weight to look better. He wonders why this person is so concerned that he or she asks him to 'get fat' when his girlfriend is not complaining. According to the narrative, his main grouse is that it was in the same way that girls force older men to go harder in bed and in the same manner lose their lives in a bid to please younger, more energetic girls (NTL19 n.d.). To move to another tale not related to the preceding, I Go Dye says, 'Warri no de carry last' with which he delves into talking about Warri people and their indefatigable nature. Next, he shifts to advice mode with which he links three tales about smoking weed, gaining weight, and young girls tiring out older men during sex. As he progresses, his voice and emotion increase, making him more spirited and demonstrative, heightening tension and increasing audience laughter. From his head movement (since his eyes are usually hidden behind glasses), I Go Dye studies the audience during pauses. He hardly gets carried away by the responses he receives during performances. He typically stands aloof of audiences' uncontrolled laughter, waiting for a lull in the hullabaloo when he tells another joke to take the resultant hilarious uproar a notch higher. His narrations appear long, windy, and sometimes disjointed on the surface, but that is precisely his joke arrangement pattern. He uses similarity in themes and statements to link each disparate part.

Comedians make good use of the different parts of joke narration, interspersing their renditions with spontaneous interjections in response to on-the-spot audience responses. Basket Mouth and MC Acapella have also brought scripts on stage, making a show of ticking off their list after every joke and noting the response to each statement. This is antithetical to the usual attempt by most jokesters to make their performances appear unscripted even when lots of preparations has gone into preparing the routines. Aside from these narrative patterns, there are other forms of joking and laughter elicitation used by Nigerian jokesters, such as observational comedy, adjacency pairs, song parodies, self-denigration, imitation, and caricature, as well as sexual jokes and farce. Observational comedy is widespread, with setups derived from commonplace happenings and discourses of everyday life. They are the most common forms of mirth-making, catalysed most frequently through advice to audiences about how best to handle life situations.

Adjacency pairs in performer-audience interactions are peculiar forms of call-and-response exchange between comedians and audiences. They are described as 'a sequence of two utterances [...] produced by different speakers, ordered as a first part and second part [...], so that a first part requires a particular second part or range of second parts' (Schegloff and Sacks 1973, 295). One recurrent example is the *Waffi* (Warri) register, 'Area!' which characteristically elicits a response. Adjacency pairs also occur in question-and-answer sessions between comedians and audiences, as in Forever's set above, where he asks if anyone in the auditorium is from Benin. The third type of adjacency pairs available in Nigerian stand-up is heckling. Performers like Klint da Drunk build their acts almost entirely around this device, mostly using his feigned inebriety to elicit comments and queries from the audience even before he starts speaking. He also picks on individuals, as seen in instances where he makes fun of the phone of someone trying to take a picture of him (NTL11 2007), or another that he says has 'mouth odour' because the individual heckled him (NTL5 n.d.), or where he tells someone that the suit he is wearing looks like a 'monkey jacket' (NTL2 2003). There are also situations where Klint asks for permission to borrow someone's boyfriend, an exchange which devolves into a short discourse on whether the man is the lady's husband or boyfriend (NTL3 2004), where he asks a man to remove his cap and as he obeys Klint exaggeratedly screams that the man's bald head is scary, and to another person, in the same event, he says, 'Look at your shirt, I am very sure that a tablecloth is missing in your house' (NTL4 2004). Elsewhere, he tells another audience member that he has been wearing the same shirt to over forty of his shows (CYR4 2008). All these underscore Klint's adeptness at building his acts around real-time performer-audience interactions and innovative putdowns for heckling using devices of *wording*. Many of his responses are, in hindsight, offensive.

Double-act comedy manifested by the duos Still Ringing and Sam and Song, whose laughter elicitation patterns are discussed in Chapter 5, is also considered a form of adjacency pairs. In this case, the exchange is between two jokesters on stage and not between a comedian and the audience. Elenu and AY's pairing has been mentioned previously. There are other examples, such as Klint's, where he plays the role of a policeman, wearing the right uniform and holding a torchlight. He receives a phone call from a witness to an ongoing robbery whose voice plays over the speakers. The role is played by I Go Save, who complements Klint's comedic utterances through his responses. There are two levels of satire in this exchange: the condemnation of corruption within the Nigerian police and the hilarious miscommunication between the two. These two are fused because the entire exchange shows incompetence, lack of transparency, and outright sharp practices amongst uniformed men. For instance, when the caller says, 'Sir, I am under duress!' and Klint responds, 'Is that not the name of a condom?' When he says that the police, as 'men-in-uniform,' should come and challenge the robbers, Klint replies with a straight face, 'Put on your school uniform, disarm the armed robbers, and we will come and make the arrests' (NTL9 2006). Elsewhere, he plays doctor, wearing a lab coat, and pairing Lepacious Bose as his patient. Klint takes her up on her body size, using highly offensive terms such as needing a 'carjack' to lift her breasts and 'hire a crane from a construction company' to put her on the bed. As the patient rains insult at him for being offensive, he turns her statements into comedy. For instance, where she says: 'My God will judge you!' he replies, 'With goodness and mercy!' (NTL6 n.d.).

Song parodies have been used extensively by various Nigerian comedians to evoke laughter. Kehinde Peter Otolorin (Kenny Blaq) brings his own recorded song mixes, AY asks the DJ to play specific songs for him, while Klint does both singing with a live band when available and mechanically creating the beat he wants (NTL7 2005, NTL11 2007). AY is good at going down memory lane, calling up hit songs and singers that made waves in the past, such as Ras Kimono, Chris Okotie, and Alex O (AYL5 n.d.), juxtaposing past and present music preferences with the conclusion that more recent pieces have comparatively inferior lyrics. Klint's song parodies come in variations of the genre: popular American songs like Mark Morrison's 1996 hit song, "Return of the Mark" (NTL11 2007), imitation of the song patterns of different Nigerian ethnic groups (NTL4 2004), and he creates songs from scratch, for example, his satire about some reggae musicians who have no useful lyrics other than walking on the street and hitting their legs against a stone right after getting high on marijuana (Reel Nolly Studios 2017; Boss Blaze 2015). Kenny Blaq has made a more versatile progression with his song parodies in recent times. He speaks directly to popular singers in the audience about their songs (Trendtv Entertainment 2020), ridicules how different artists sing gospel and secular songs (Kenny Blaq 2019), and uses a medley of popular songs to create a two-hour long set of storytelling known as "The Oxymoron of Kenny Blaq" (Kenny Blaq 2017). The most recent edition of his event was a multimedia solo show incorporating dramatic comedy, joke renditions, video projections, and song parodies (Kenny Blaq 2020).

Self-denigration is another important device comedians deploy. It often comes as both real and made-up autobiographical narratives. It is evident in the excerpt of Forever's set in Figure 4. When satirising groups and individuals, they usually tell the stories as personal experiences to better mitigate offence. When Nigerian jokesters align themselves with ghettoised spaces, they create affinities with the weak, dispossessed, and lesser privileged members of society. Basket Mouth, for instance, talks about growing up in extreme poverty around Ajegunle (NTL15 2008; NTL19 n.d.). I Go Dye derogates his physical attributes, sometimes mocking his 'long neck', saying it happened because his parents continued having sex while his mother was pregnant with him. In another set, he states that the length of his neck is advantageous in exam situations where he can 'giraffe' his neighbours' works without scruples (NTL17 2009). I Go Dye also denigrates himself by talking about his naïveté and stupid choices on his first trip overseas (NTL11 2007, NTL20 n.d.), and Warri people in many ways, especially by claiming that when you say to a Warri girl: "'You are the sugar in my tea, the elastic in my pant." Warri girl go tell you, "That elastic go cut o!'"[14] (NTL15 2008). AY mentions his struggles, especially spending additional years at university because he could not pay his fees (AYL3 n.d.). For Klint, presenting himself as a drunk is an exaggerated form of self-denigration further deepened by using every opportunity to call himself stupid, foolish, and useless. In one event, after derogating himself repeatedly, he turns to the audience to say, 'And you are my friends … and they say show me your friend, and I will tell you who you are!' He further states, 'You cannot even arrest me because if you take me to court, I will say that I said it under the influence of alcohol' (Anitamuleya 2010).

Mimicry features prominently on the Nigerian stand-up stage. There have been mentions of AY's imitations of clergy people and other celebrities. In the mid-2000s, amidst bank recapitalisations and the resultant mergers and acquisitions, AY transposed uncertainties of the period to an imaginative joke narrative of different pastors being fused such as 'Mountain of Fire' and 'Reverend Kings' producing "Fire for Fire Ministries" (AYL5 n.d.). Here, AY imaginatively mimics the police and two Christian denominations by satirically evoking the different ways they deploy the term 'fire'.[15] Elsewhere, he transposes personality traits: running football match commentaries variously as popular Nigerian televangelists Chris Okotie and Chris Oyakhilome (NTL11 2007), playing police officers as Oyakhilome and the Nigerian singer, D'Banj (NTL19 n.d.), and making the musician Tuface preach like Oyakhilome (NTL20 n.d.). He has also experimented with cross-dressing for a role in his *AY Idols* (AYL2 2007). In all these roleplays, AY shows a sterling ability to represent characters accurately. Basket Mouth, for his part, draws on parallel behavioural patterns between people *wey wowo* (that are ugly) and the ones *wey fine* (that are beautiful), or *ajebutter* (the rich) and *pako* (the poor), as well as the mannerisms of specific individuals and groups. In one set, he compares film trailers for Hollywood and Nollywood. Using *Titanic*, he imaginatively mimics how it could be promoted as a Nollywood movie, in a high pitch, shrieking voice:

> Hei! Hei! See ship! See ship! Heei! Pepulu go kill me! Pepulu go kill me! See [...] See [...] See Leonardo! See ice block chook ship! Pepulu de fall! Pepulu de fall! I no go enta boat again! [louder] I no go enta boat again! [loudest] Wota! Wota, everywhere! See ice ...[16] (NTL15 2008)

He stops abruptly as the audience explodes into laughter and applause, pauses a little before performing how it is presented in Hollywood:

> He was born. And she was born. They were separated [pause] later on in future they met each other [echoes 'other']. They fell in love, and they got married. She called her mother and upon their arrival, she found out they were brothers and sisters. She cried. He also cried. Their mother cried. Their neighbours also cried. The landlady cried. Everybody cried. Mind you, watching this movie might also make you cry! (NTL15 2008)

Of course, this rendition does not have any resemblance to the movie *Titanic*, but the reality is that neither Basket Mouth nor his audience is in interested in veracity at this point, especially when the hilarity of the comparison is evident. Hence, Basket Mouth often tries to balance his mimicry by giving opposites, comparisons, and juxtapositions, as central techniques for his joke narration. Even when he claims to be advising men on how to lure women into their beds, he ends up turning on men, telling women in the audience to ward off such unwanted advances and how best to do so (NTL20 n.d.).

Furthermore, Basket Mouth also experiments with different styles, oftentimes employing techniques that may be considered unconventional for stand-up renditions. In the first instance, he laughs at his jokes while telling them. Laughing at one's jokes is sometimes considered offensive because it interrupts the narrative flow, and a joke performer is supposed to allow the audience to determine whether it is funny or not. Ordinarily, when performers laugh at their jokes, audiences may have nothing to laugh at, and the situation can deteriorate to the extent that the performer is embarrassed into leaving the stage. In Basket Mouth's case, he inserts guffaws intermittently as he builds up to the climax. By doing this, he instantiates the impression of someone who wants to tell a funny story but is unable to hold back laughter before completing the tale. With this technique, Basket Mouth prepares his audience, and it works because, by the time he is done with the narrative, he would have greatly heightened audience suspense and curiosity. Sometimes, his laughter and/or the way he tries to hold it back initiates audience laughter. He also deliberately dispenses with the formalities of having an introductory joke, building up to a climax, and leaving when the ovation is loudest. To achieve this, he gives the impression that his sets are unorganised and that he is giving the jokes as they come to him, not necessarily in a pre-planned order. In an event in Ibadan, he comes on stage with a piece of paper and makes a show of ticking each one off when the audience laughs, or not loudly enough, in which case he says: 'Dis one no work. Mek I try anoda one!'[17] (Globacomlimited 2010). Alongside this breaking of stand-up tradition, he has de-emphasised the regular way of leaving the stage when the ovation is loudest. At the end of his set, he starts a tale about people who tell their best jokes last so that while the audience is rolling on the floor in mirth, they leave the stage. He then tells the audience that he leaves the stage when he wants, drops his microphone, and exits. Sometimes it does appear that he will come back to finish up, but that never happens. This mechanic is a performance style that one considers uniquely Basket Mouth's because most of his colleagues neither leave the stage in this manner nor come to the stage with a script. This pattern of performance enhances the humour in Basket Mouth's presentations because it is primarily unusual. Live audiences mostly find it hilarious.

For his part, I Go Dye enacts numerous acts of imitation. He performs a narrative on rising armed robbery incidents in one set, demonstrating how citizens are being harassed on the streets (NTL13 n.d.). In another set, he questions why native healers fail to 'upgrade' to be more modern like evangelical preachers. To buttress his point, I Go Dye enacts a roleplay of the two groups, wondering why native doctors cannot use air-conditioned offices: 'Abi A/C de kill juju?'[18] This form of embodied representations frequently occurs in his acts because of their necessity in creating the right imageries with which he conveys his messages. Other stand-up artists also deploy mimicry: Helen Paul's child-speak (Channels Television 2015), Chigul's humorous imitations (FlipTV 2016), MC Aproko's (real name Gift Loveday Igbomgbo) impressions of Olu Jacobs, one of Nigeria's legends of film acting (T.A Media 2020), Mimicko's replication of speech patterns of Nigerian actors (Yaw Naija Entertainment 2017; MC Mbakara TV 2019), MC Tagwaye's roleplay of President Buhari (Channels Television 2018), among others. These examples show how both embodied and structural devices are employed and manipulated by various jokesters towards eliciting laughter from audiences. No device is used in isolation but is deployed to work simultaneously with others as one towards various goals, chief among which is that of entertainment.

Notes

1 This is discussed extensively in my forthcoming book on taboo, self-censorship, and the limits of humour.

2 Four of these challenges are discussed extensively in another work (Nwankwọ 2019, 102–104).

3 'Yabbis no case, first touch na offence' (meaning, '*Yabbis* is harmless, but laying a hand on another is the offence') is Fela's way of highlighting the innocuous, non-violent nature of *yabbing*. 'Kalakuta Republic' is the name Fela's shrine in Lagos bears. He referred to it as a shrine, but it is the venue where he performed live while he was alive. It is still being maintained by his family.

4 'People from Warri do not forgive easily!'

5 'Boma boys' were 'glamorized groups' of young men in the port cities of the Niger Delta, Sapele and Warri, who 'built their identity on two foreign traditions: cowboys and sailors' (Ojaide 2006, 46). Their influence over the region waned at the end of the civil war in 1970.

6 A transcript and discussion of the long narrative can be found elsewhere (Nwankwọ 2021).

7 'Basket Mouth got angry. Before he did, it was P-Square (and) D'Banj that went and purchased BMW Z5. It has a radio and refrigerator inside it. It also has an ATM. Basket Mouth was angry; you see him with dreadlocks, doing an advert for Malta Guinness. If you know how much he has. When Basket (Mouth) bought his, everyone became quiet. He bought, in one day, four different SUVs. No brand name on the cars. I only saw "B". They are customised. It was later that I saw "Mouth." If you see the car, it looks intimidating, as if it wants to apprehend someone. My people, that is why I said, I am a Warri boy, and they cannot intimidate me. Me, a typical Warri boy! What is the matter with them! That's why I got angry and said that I will go and find my own choice. That's why I angrily went on a search, and I found a very good-looking Infinity Jeep 2008 model. Black in colour. As I went on a further search, I saw another Infinity Jeep 2010 model. The white man said that the vehicle is too expensive. I insisted that it is the very one that I wanted. So, I closed my mind and purchased the side mirror of this Infinity jeep.'

8 Igbo [Sylvester Obialor (Odogwu), Johnmary Chukwumesiri (I Go Tuk, Ogbuefi Main Market Man), Emeka Smith, Pencil, and Funny Bone], Yoruba [Elenu, Seyi Law, and Broda Shaggy with his *alaye* (Lagos street boy) attitude], and Hausa [MC Tagwaye is currently the most prominent who plays this role].

9 Uche Ogbuagu is a Nigerian comedian who started on radio and selling audio recordings of his comedy around south-eastern Nigeria, popularly known by his favourite phrase,

'Bad condition'. D'Banj (Oladapo Daniel Oyebanjo) is a multiple award-winning Nigerian singer whose songs have topped charts around Africa and beyond.

10 AY's caricature of Genevieve Nnaji's song in his mock reality show, *AY Idols* (AYL2 2007; AY Comedian 2013), is a caricature of a reality TV show, *Nigerian Idols*, where he uses a song from popular Nollywood actress, Genevieve Nnaji's album "One Logologo Line" (2004) by EKB Records.

11 'I always imagine … something I imagine certain things that surprise me. Just imagine that ….'

12 'Anyone ugly tends to become a thief … like our current president,' a reference to President Obasanjo (1999–2007).

13 'Believe it or not, the frog must jump. The devil is an area boy (street urchin, or tout), and God is a godfather. A Warri boy can never be outwitted.'

14 'A girl from Warri will tell you that that elastic will cut!'

15 This joke narrative has two connotations at the time of its delivery: first, Mountain of Fire and Miracles Ministry, a Christian denomination, is known for aggressive prayers characterised by physical exertions and repeated calling of 'fire.' Reverend Kings is the head of another pseudo-Christian denomination in Lagos who is on death row following his conviction for burning one of his adherents to death. Second, 'Fire for Fire' was the operative tag word of the Nigerian Police then, which eventually became controversial because of the rising incidence of fatal 'accidental discharges' that resulted in the deaths of so many Nigerians at the hands of gun-toting policemen.

16 Part of what he says after 'See … see …' is not clear, but it appears he is referring to the other main character, Kate Winslet. English translation of his statements: 'Hey! See this ship! Hey! People will kill me! … Look at Leonardo (DiCaprio)! Look at how the iceberg pierces the ship! People are falling (off the ship). I will never enter ship again! Water! Water covers everywhere!'

17 'This one did not work. Let me try another.'

18 'Or does air conditioner destroy the efficacy of their talisman?'

4

Offence, taboos and themes

The social impact of Nigerian stand-up

By its nature, comedy requires 'certain referents, norms against which behaviors may be deemed humorous,' the absence of which makes its elicitation impossible (Auslander 2004, 107). For this purpose, joking relationships exist 'between two persons in which one is by custom permitted, and in some instances required, to tease or make fun of the other, who in turn is required to take no offence' (Radcliffe-Brown 1940, 195). These interactions occur within liminal moments that individuals can insult or satirise others without fear of censure, meaning that jokes can be taken wrongly outside such periods, leading to offence-taking and possible conflicts. Radcliffe-Brown further identifies two varieties of joking relationships:

> In one, the relation is symmetrical; each of the two persons teases or makes fun of the other. In the other variety the relation is asymmetrical; A jokes at the expense of B and B accepts the teasing good humouredly but without retaliating; or A teases B as much as he pleases and B in return teases A only a little. (Radcliffe-Brown 1940, 195)

Each of these two forms exists within stand-up renditions but in different measure. For the asymmetrical variant, jokesters insult audience members directly, and they, in turn, are not expected to retaliate. They do get rebuttals sometimes, which come in the form of a slight humorous jab, which often goes unheard from the stage, or which the individual can bear – even if a humiliation – good-naturedly. Symmetrical joking relationships are usually absent in stand-up situations due to the overwhelming power comedians wield, which suppresses that of the audience, especially during performance. However, there are situations where comedians are heckled and others where they instantiate forms of adjacency pairs. Within these, one finds instances of symmetrical joking relationship because there is an exchange between the stage and the auditorium. In earlier days, being present at stand-up events implies giving up one's rights to offence-taking, especially when the rest of the audience finds what has been said funny. More recently, however, due to increased sensitivities and consciousness of political correctness, the sphere of permissible joke materials and how they are handled has become more restricted than it has always been in various communities.

A third variant, dubbed the tangential joking relationship, has been identified. Taking off from the two forms Radcliffe-Brown propounded, Ibukun Filani postulates a variety in which 'the participants-of-the-joke do not have to make fun of each other; rather, their focus is on a third party who is not part of the joke exchange' (2017, 458). This accounts for the form of joking in which a third party, C, who is not physically present, is discussed. With the increased dissemination of the internet and satellite television, stand-up performances are now more available in locations outside their production contexts than before. Hence, the materiality of liveness, which privileged immediacy and on-the-spot criticism over post-mortem analyses, have dimmed in relevance. As such, joke materials are now subjected to wide-ranging measuring tools, many of which are at extreme variance with the subsisting circumstances and dynamics within their production venues. Nevertheless, while conceding the growing primacy of the opinions of the absent party in recent times, one accedes that the tangential variant does not qualify as a 'relationship' because it has no assigned role or mode of response for the individuals or groups it seeks to cover. Precisely speaking, unlike in symmetrical and asymmetrical variants where the roles of joking parties A and B are defined in each case, that of the third party, C in the tangential variant, is not stated. Assignation of roles here, in symmetrical and asymmetrical varieties, for instance, is to retaliate or not retaliate, respectively, in which case all participants are co-creators of the performance through their responses – exchanging insults or laughing at what has been said. These responses are essential to the sustenance of joking relationships because they do not endorse offence-taking and other more extreme forms of censure.

Considering the tangential joke relationship as a designation for 'joke targets' also does not help it become the third variant it is supposed to be because being the joke's object (a 'target') is neither the purpose of such categorisations nor is it a requirement for being a co-creator of humour. Admittedly, assigning specific roles to people who are not present in a joke performance is no mean task due to the boundlessness of its constitution and the unpredictability of the content of potential evaluation yardsticks. This diversity and boundlessness are evident in social media, where online presence has become as potent as *liveness* in determining how comedians produce and present jokes. Social media is an amorphous, unrestricted space, thereby allowing third-party audiences to subject jokes to conditions at variance with the ones prevalent during their production. Within online screenings, the cultural permissiveness and liminality of time within which gags are inoffensive lapse, exposing performers to denunciations. The scope of 'being absent' has been redefined by the growing primacy of online media dissemination and discourses, especially in the light of the COVID-19 pandemic. Two examples from the Nigerian stand-up scene underscore the intensity and altering effects of social media responses on comedy.

In January 2014, Basket Mouth shared highly offensive material on his Facebook page that suggestively endorsed rape. Though not an original 'joke' of his, the fact that he shared it drew the ire of many Nigerians, attracting all manner of clap back on him (Pulse Nigeria 2014, Hamada 2014). The bad press prompted Basket Mouth to make attempts at apologising for the act, but the damage had already been done. Five years after, owing to calls from different quarters, his name was dropped from the list of ambassadors of the EU campaign against sexual and gender-based violence in Nigeria (Augoye 2019). No doubt, the experience prompted Basket Mouth to stay off rape-related subjects both on stage and on his social media handles. The second example involves AY, who, in 2017, during one of his *AY Live* events, lined up all contestants of that year's Big Brother Nigeria (BBN) on stage, asking them questions and commenting on each individual's actions in the BBN house. In the course of the exchange, he made statements downplaying the sexual harassment against T-Boss, which led to the culprit, Kemen's disqualification and eviction from the house. On the same stage, AY advertently touched another contestant, Uriel, improperly (EbonyLifeTV 2017). His comments about Kemen's act and the way he touched one of the females on the stage set the internet ablaze with condemnations of his actions (Bellanaija 2017), forcing AY to offer an apology, resolving to be more sensitive in his future engagements with similar subjects. From these two examples, it is evident that long after the comedian's dominating voice over the speakers has died down, the absent party's participation and responses become emboldened and more vociferous and are, in most instances, condemnatory. As such, the idea of the tangential variant is not that of a joking relationship but that of a post-mortem evaluation which has been shown to differ from the enabling contexts of the joke environment. For being outside this milieu, it does not qualify as a joking relationship. Nevertheless, with the limitless, interminable, and individual-based nature of online audiences, even though the delayed (in terms of time) experience of the performance does not qualify it as a co-producer, its contributions are so powerful they affect the manner future jokes are produced. As such, the individuality of online *liveness* can quickly turn to a collective as opinions begin to coalesce and become more unitary and galvanised.

Nigerian comics broach sensitive, offensive, taboo, and political subjects, but their work has received little or no official clampdown or reprimand. As such, there is no recorded direct conflict with the government. It is my belief that non-confrontation is more a result of comedians not being taken seriously than a show of tolerance from the Nigerian federal government. Besides, comedians court government endorsement and sponsorship because that is where the big money lies. Nevertheless, successive presidents, including the one that supported stand-up comedy the most, Olusegun Obasanjo, was not spared direct personal attacks. He was roundly caricatured for being 'ugly,' excessively frugal and corrupt. Obasanjo seemingly took it all in good stride without reverting to his highhandedness as a military leader between 1976 and 1979, when he sent soldiers to attack Fela Kuti's 'Shrine' for his satiric song against soldiers titled, "Zombie," an attack that led to the death of the mother of the musician (Onishi 2015). While Obasanjo was still in office, Klint da Drunk once opened his set with a stern warning against people who say that the president is ugly, asking rhetorically: 'Don't you know he is a film star?' In the set, he pauses, scanning the faces of the bewildered audience, before asking, 'Do you know the film *King Kong*? Who acted the monkey?' To a surprised audience, especially given that he appeared profoundly serious when he started, Klint then says, 'What do you expect? He looks like the condition of the nation' (NTL4 2004). In this skit, it appears as if Klint is defending the president, then he ends up turning on him, and worst of all, attributing the bad state of the economy to the president's appearance. It is this tenor of ridicule that informs the criticism of comedians like Basket Mouth who spoke out of frustration: 'We jus' get money [in this country], everybody jus' de chop' (NTL15 2008), alluding to the general sense of displeasure amongst the populace about the Obasanjo era.[1] Elsewhere, he castigates Obasanjo for allowing Cameroon to take over the Bakassi peninsular (NTL13 n.d.).

Other more personal attacks include this one by Moye Idowu (Maleke), where he juxtaposed Obasanjo and Adams Oshiomhole (another politician ridiculed for being ugly).[2] Maleke narrates that Obasanjo visited Edo State and called on a church with the governor, Oshiomhole. Obasanjo quickly noticed two framed photographs of himself and Oshiomhole conspicuously hung on either side of a crucifix on the church's wall. He asks Oshiomhole what that means, and the latter says it is a mark of honour, to which Obasanjo retorts, 'You think I don't know that it means: "Jesus and the two thieves on the cross?"' He asks why his picture is on the left and Oshiomhole's on the right. In this joke, Maleke transposes the biblical tale of Jesus' crucifixion, using this narrative to call out these politicians, who were also feuding over personal interests and party affiliations, calling them 'thieves' in the process. From the position of the pictures, Oshiomhole is presented as the repentant thief that later went to heaven and Obasanjo, the self-righteous thief that did not make it to heaven.[3] There is a different version of the Obasanjo/Oshiomhole tale given more recently by the comedian Gordons, who tells that:

> [b]ecause of Oshiomhole, dem deny Obasanjo visa. Mek una hear o! [...] Obasanjo come collect visa, the woman said, 'You were here yesterday. We can't give you again!' (*audience laughter*) Obasanjo said, 'I've never been here.' Dem turn computer around (*miming the movement with his free hand*), Oshiomhole face show. Na 'im de woman say, 'Who is this?' Baba say, 'Dat's Oshiomhole.' Dem say, 'Eh? You change your name? Jus' because of ...' (*he is cut off by audience laughter*).[4] (JuvenisTV 2018)

71

Going by these and multitudinous other representations, Obasanjo and Oshiomhole are used whenever comedians want to characterise facial uncomeliness within Nigerian stand-up.

These caricatures of President Obasanjo, especially while he was still in power, elicited little or no apparent response from the government. This lack of official reaction is indicative of the relative freedom of speech and tolerance that the end of military governance and the democratic dispensation from 1999 engendered. Nevertheless, it is noteworthy that Obasanjo's support could have mitigated harsher criticisms of his government's ineptitude and foibles (Obadare 2016, 68) in a s/he-who-pays-the-piper-calls-the-tune kind of way. This supposition looks valid against the background of Ali Baba's admission that he tells his jokes about Obasanjo to him before going on stage with them (Olukole 2010), and one is not sure how often or how long this went on. However, it is undoubtedly an arrangement that did not apply to other comedians who roasted the president whenever and wherever the opportunity arose. Reportedly also, 'at a point the State Security Service (SSS) (now Department of State Services – DSS) surreptitiously muscled in to stop any further anti-President Obasanjo public jokes or *yabbis*. So, things are not always as harmless as they seem' (Ego-Alowes 2017, 46). This move was never advertised, and no comedian has admitted to being contacted to moderate their jokes. Aside from the usual social media trolling and name-calling over joke materials and the personal lives of individuals, there has been relative tolerance of even highly politically charged jokes in Nigeria.

Themes

Nigeria is the most populous black nation on earth, with over 200 million inhabitants and about 371 tribal groups of various sizes (News 2017), with individuals who adhere to various religious beliefs. The production and reception or repudiation of jokes are mostly tied to the vagaries of these partitions. Interestingly, these affiliations have been manipulated by the ruling elite for political gains (Agunwa 1997; Ukiwo 2003; Agbiboa 2003), often with significant fatalities across the country (Jacob 2012; Osadola 2012). Principally, there is an ideological difference between the south and the north of the country, with one being more liberal than the other. One way in which this difference has been shown in the arts is that despite the global reach of Nollywood, Nigeria's video film tradition, the northern part of the country has its parallel industry known as Kannywood (Adamu 2013; Ibrahim 2019), which conforms to the less liberal way of life prevalent in the north. Just like stand-up comedy emerged through the efforts of individuals within Nollywood, stand-up art in the north is, in the main, propelled by Kannywood actors such as Rabilu Musa, popularly known as Ibro (1971–2014), Aminu Baba Ari, Suleiman Bosho, Musa

Mai Sana'a, and Rabiu Daushe. These comedians perform in Hausa and stick closely to the more dramatic indigenous traditions of the *wawan sarki* and *'yan kama* mentioned earlier. Nevertheless, there is a significant followership of mainstream stand-up comedy in the south through various mediums. Opa Williams staged his *Nite of a Thousand Laughs* shows in Kaduna and Jos in the early 2000s in his quest to create a truly national brand. With the increase in the insurgency in the north since the 2010s, hosting stage events elsewhere in the north outside the capital city of Abuja has become very unattractive for events managers based in southern Nigeria.

Interestingly, despite differences in worldview, artistic exchanges between the two regions continue, especially among youths who share similar preferences in Afro-pop music and Nollywood films, mainly through social media platforms. As a result, even though most of the popular comedians performing in southern Nigeria do not operate in parts of northern Nigeria outside the capital, Abuja, they are also well known in that part of the country. With the emergence of English-speaking performers in the region, especially, more stand-up events in languages other than Hausa are frequently being performed, some of them with special appearances by those based in the south. It is worthy of note that there is a substantial amount of followership, in northern Nigeria, for comedians who perform elsewhere. For their privileging of the Hausa language, many of the jokesters in that part of the country are unknown to audiences from the south. Consequently, since humour is more readily evoked within local rather than national in-group situations, language and other aspects of culture possess significant relevance as to how themes are generated, articulated, and deployed within stand-up renditions. With the vast chasm of differences between a more conservative northern region and a liberal southern part, then entwined within the incendiary politics of ethnicity, religion, and class, humour generation in Nigerian stand-up art has mainly remained regional. There are similarities in satirising political power. The trapdoors of religious and ethnic diversity that readily create obfuscating group sentiments rather than a sense of national unity also exist. Thus, comedians are especially careful about the highly volatile subjects of religion and ethnicity when making jokes. They do use ethnic stereotypes but they often self-censor, particularly when they do not identify as members of the group they are referring to.

Described as 'a collective within a larger society having a real or putative common ancestry, memories of a shared historical past, and a cultural focus on one or more symbolic events defined as the epitome of their peoplehood …' (Schermerhorn 1978, 12), ethnicity is a significant feature in Nigerian stand-up jokes. Going by the sheer number of ethnic communities in the country and the condition that people readily identify themselves based on where they come from no matter how long they have lived in a different area, ethnicity is important to socio-political discourses in the country. As such, it is used most conspicuously in jokes, deploying stereotypes both real and contrived to enhance the imageries and believability of their narratives. Gags built on stereotypes and suppositions 'serve as an important strategy for defining ethnicity positively' because they elicit assertions of pride 'rather than serving merely to demean those who are marked as ethnically Other' (Leveen 1996, 29). Take, for instance, how I Go Dye pokes fun at his people, the *Waffi*, using specific typecasts and characterisations to 'play the audience ... by reappropriating a negative stereotype as a celebratory resource' (Adetunji 2013, 9). Though contestable given the potential for being politically incorrect, one accedes that ethnic jokes 'delineate the social, geographical and moral boundaries of a nation or ethnic group,' simultaneously defining belongingness and acceptable characteristics of membership (Davies 1982, 383–384).

In Nigerian comedy, ethnic jokes are mostly created from negative tags (Filani and Ajayi 2019, 151–152), but more specifically through replications of mother-tongue interferences on English language pronunciations. For example, there is the interchange of consonants /p/ and /f/, then /b/ and /v/ among the Hausa; /r/ and /l/ among the Igbo and Tiv; /l/ and /n/ among the Ijaw; and /s/ and /ʃ/ and the addition of /h/ before vowel sounds at the beginning of words and omitting same when /h/ begins words among the Yoruba. Other labels include the Hausa man's typical role as 'security guard' and *suya* or water seller, the Igbo man's love for and belief in the power of money, and the Yoruba man's 'cowardly' disposition and love for lavish parties.[5] 'Calabar' people are also roundly satirised for their favourite delicacy, dog meat (fondly called 404 after the Peugeot car model popular in the 1970s for its speed) and the supposed sexual prowess of their women. The Warri person, the *Waffi*, is considered confrontational and sometimes crime-prone, while the Bini person has 'Italian connection' and possibly practises witchcraft.[6] Essentially, jokesters depend on the shared knowledge of these assumptions and beliefs between audiences and themselves to use these traits judiciously to generate humour. Specifically, mother-tongue interferences, accents, and speech mannerisms of Nigeria's ethnic groups are easily recognised by the audience when enlisted by performers.

Comedians use such representations variously: imitating the habits of specific localities such as *Waffi* or *ghettoised* demeanours, using accents and speech patterns as seen in the acts of Federational Mallam (formerly known as Holy Mallam), Aboki 4 Christ and, more recently, MC Tagwaye playing Hausa/Fulani roles, and mixed acts wherein jokesters assume these roles briefly when talking about a specific ethnic group or saying something about them, like Akpororo talking about his friend who was flogged with *koboko* as part of Fulani marriage rites[7] (COZATV 2015). Akpororo here refers to the Fulani *sharo*, a traditional duel where young men compete for a girl's hand in marriage by flogging each other in public. For the greater public, the understanding is that whipping is part of Fulani marriage rites. Akpororo uses this traditional rite to erect a joke with which he enacts ludicrous bodily expressions of his friend's reactions to each stroke of the *koboko*. Furthermore, at a state event, the anniversary celebration of one of the south-western states, with President Buhari in attendance, MC, Ali Baba, used the opportunity of a slight delay in bringing the knife for cutting the ceremonial cake to say: 'Mr President, please give me your knife. I hear that all Hausa people carry knives with them' (Nwaubani 2018). In this example, asking the president to lend him his knife for cutting the cake is an allusion to a widely held notion among Nigerians that Hausa men are very combative and, as such, are always armed with daggers. This is thus potentially a more offensive stereotype, but the fact that on this occasion, the president laughed, the MC's effort at eliciting humour from such a seemingly off-hand remark hit its mark.

The 'Calabar' is another category of people who are often the subject of stereotypes and offence in Nigerian comedy. The widespread use of this stereotypical and offence-based portraiture came from the comic characters Bassey Okon and Clarus of the 1980's television comedy series, *The Village Headmaster* and *The New Masquerade*, respectively (Ekpang and Bassey 2014, 179). Specifically, Clarus's speech and personality traits popularised many of the stereotypes currently ascribed to 'Calabar' people in Nigerian comedy. In the words of Wilson Orhiunu (2007), 'of all the tribal stereotypes on offer in Nigerian comedy, the most politically incorrect and vicious lampooning seems to be reserved for the Calabar people.' Such representations are chiefly implicated in the accent and manner of speaking ascribed to ethnicities in that part of southern Nigeria. For example, I Go Dye says that it is difficult to differentiate between a preacher and the interpreter in Calabar churches because the person speaking in English uses the same sing-song inflexions as the one relaying their statements in the local language. He adds that when his 'Calabar' friend entered his long native names on the computer, it merely showed an error message because the machine could not handle the name (NTL1 2002). Another stereotype ascribed to people of the area is that their women possess special sexual prowess. This belief stems from the well-known tradition of fattening rooms for maidens right before marriage. For this purpose, the quintessential Calabar girl's (usually named Ekaette) personality is that of a buxom housemaid who would most probably sleep with her master without the knowledge of 'madam.' Alongside this character exists a male counterpart, Okon, usually a houseboy, who can be overtly foolish and possess some sexual prowess that ostensibly comes from dog meat consumption. On 'Calabar' and the love for 404 (dog meat), the comedian Koffi addresses Dan Foster, a popular American-born radio broadcaster in Nigeria (who died in June 2020) directly in a 'Calabar' accent, saying that on Foster's visit to Calabar, the announcement on the radio was: 'We hear one big dog is coming to Calabar!' (Naija Live Comedy n.d.), implying that the radio audience mistook the radio personality for a real dog.

Defining Foster in this light as 'meat' that could be consumed, especially given the radio broadcaster's body size, is a form of body shaming that eludes this performer due to his concentration on the 'Calabar' referent of his skit. Of course, for this audience, there seems to be no problem, but as the 'joke' circulates the social media space and is re-read in more decontextualised milieus, the offensiveness of this portraiture becomes more evident.

Igbo and Yoruba stereotypes have not escaped comedians' attention either, with several having made jokes around them. One of the most innovative uses of Igbo and Yoruba stereotypes available in Nigerian stand-up is from the young, emergent comedian AB-Jokes who uses names of Lagos suburbs, car brands and job preferences to describe each ethnic group to draw jocular parallels and similarities in Igbo and Yoruba penchants (AB Jokes Awhana 2020). Basket Mouth thinks that Osama bin Laden would have failed in Nigeria had he tried because the Igbo man would refuse to kill himself so that his family could get the payment. In an 'Igbo accent,' the comedian characterises what he believes the response would be: '*Nna*, give my family the bomb and give me the money'[8] (NTL13 n.d.). Klint demonstrates how different tribes sing their songs, especially how the Igbo seek to collect as much money as possible from the audience by singing the praises of well-to-do individuals among them (NTL4 2004). Elsewhere, he tells a joke of an Igbo man who was asked by armed robbers to choose between being intravenously injected with HIV or parting with his money. Due to his love for money, the man chose to be injected with the virus since he believed that the condom he had just secretly slipped on would protect him (NTL13 n.d.). In each example, the comedians designate the Igbo people as people that would do just about anything to get money. On the other hand, for the Yoruba, Seyi Law, who calls himself a 'proud Yoruba boy,' starts one of his routines this way:

> I tell people all the time that the Yorubas are not afraid (*pause*). We are not afraid of anything. It's just that we are always prepared (*audience laughter*). Because before it happens, we know! (De-9ja Music Ent. 2017b)

He proceeds to tell a series of jokes supporting his opening claim that the Yoruba are not necessarily cowardly but always prewarn themselves of danger to avoid being caught up in any. Audience laughter here comes from the knowledge that what Seyi says is antithetical to popular notions that the Yoruba are easily scared, cowardly, and afraid of bodily harm or death. He also uses other embodied expressions to counter his articulations of Yoruba 'fearlessness' and underscore the inherent sarcasm. Klint's retort to a lady who heckles him exemplifies the jocular use of Yoruba language interference in English expressions, where the sound /s/ replaces /ʃ/. He says to the woman: 'I love your *shoes*, not *sue* … *Sue* is what they do in the court!'[9] (NTL3

2004). There are inexhaustible examples from other ethnicities within Nigeria and beyond, far too many to be discussed here. There are representations of foreigners often characterised as *oyibo*, Indians, Chinese, Lebanese, and other Africans. *Oyibo* is characteristically the white person who is usually superior in many things but unlearned in local knowledge. The Chinese are recognised by how they speak and their production of cheaper and low-quality goods, while Indians and the Lebanese are projected as *fake oyibo* and with a predilection towards fraudulent acts.

Concerning discourses on religion, inviting comedians to church programmes has become normal practice, even though this affinity has not spared Christianity, its various denominations, clergy, and adherents from ridicule. The more frequent parodies and stereotypes include preachers' flamboyance, the sing-song drawl of Catholic priests, the preacher-interpreter pattern of evangelisation, and the overtly uninformed religious zeal of some people, which makes them susceptible to exploitation by charlatans. AY's imitations, for instance, metamorphosed from parodying Pentecostal pastors to dramatic enactments of 'white garment' prophets and seers. AY comes on stage with a retinue of acolytes in tune with heavy drumming and frenzied dancing in this new role. Then, following feigned gyrations of trance, he starts disbursing prophecies to individuals in the audience, especially celebrities, using factual stories about them[10] (AYL2 2007, AYL5 n.d.). With the right costume and body representations in this situation, AY engenders laughter mostly by ridicule rather than joke narratives. I Go Dye also derides people who allow themselves to be swindled by smooth-talking pastors, saying that these clergy people often use such monies to sustain their opulent lifestyles while the donors remain in poverty. He throws them a challenge, saying,

> Bible talk say, 'Greater work than I did, will you do.' Moses divide Red Sea, which Nigerian pastor don divide even gutter?[11] (NTL13 n.d.)

He states further that some preachers will just 'package themselves' so well that they can tell members to 'Give offering that will challenge God,' then asking in bewilderment: 'How somebody go give offering wey fit challenge God?'[12] (NTL13 n.d.). Through such observational commentaries, I Go Dye satirises the gullibility of individuals who easily fall victims to manipulations.

Religious criticism is not restricted to the stage but has also been expressed inside church auditoriums. In one of his church appearances, Ali Baba says:

> Beautiful church. Beautiful church. (*applause*) [...] This is the kind of church that you don't need to cast out demon. Place too cold. Demons go dey outside de wait for you. (*acts like someone who is feeling cold*) So una don close? Let's go home! (*audience laughter, applause*).[13] (De-9ja Music Ent. 2017a)

The reference to 'demons' waiting for some members outside the church is an allusion to the understanding that after the grandeur of well-built churches, the harsh realities of everyday living lounges outside, waiting for them to finish and return. Also, in a famous church in Port Harcourt, Gordons' jokes about a man who mistakenly transfers two million instead of two thousand naira to the church through online banking. The comedian mimics the man's disconcerted reaction as he realises his error via the debit alert he receives on his phone. Within this joke's risibility lies a parody of huge donations churches get from members, some of whom give out of inconvenience and discomfort (Siderz Entertainment TV 2019). Klint da Drunk has an example, too: in this Lagos church, he first refuses to climb the church's altar, saying that he is not spiritually qualified to do so. In his characteristic feigned drunkenness, Klint performs a very uncomfortable routine which culminates in his 'praying' for the church's leader in this manner: 'May the thunder of God's blessings fire you in Jesus' name!' (Liberation TV 2019). Even though the audience laughs, claps, and shouts, 'Amen!' to Klint's statement, the inherent satirical referrals are quite discomfiting.

For the very reason that comedians are more likely to make jokes about their religious affiliations or those they are more conversant with than they would when it comes to other people's faith, it is not commonplace to see jokesters in the south joking about other religions. Since there are few Muslim stand-up artists in mainstream practice, Nigerian humourists hardly ever joke about subjects related to Islam. Though certain stereotypes such as manner of dressing, mode of prayer, and particular cuisines and demeanours may be employed, there much more cautiousness in discussions about Islam than Christianity. Ethno-religious crises have usually occurred in the north, well before the infamous Boko Haram, and the present boldfaced menace of 'herdsmen' and armed bandits since the Buhari-led government came to power in 2015. For this purpose, southerners with little or no lived experience of the north often see the region as a hotbed of crises, blaming it all on religion and/or ethnicity, oblivious of the underlying politics that fuels the problems. This supposition informed Basket Mouth's set in a *Nite of a Thousand Laughs* event in the northern city of Kaduna in the mid-2000s, where he asked why religious crises persist in that city. In response, the audience heckles him, good-naturedly though, insisting that violence no longer occurs in their city (NTL13 n.d.). Osama Akpunonu (Osama) recently incorporates the fatal bombings in Abuja and Jos into his set. He mimics how they made people so conscious of their surroundings that they are in a perpetual hurry to scurry safely off the streets. The icing on the cake is where he dramatises how Yoruba priests conduct church services in a hurry, with the possibility of ending it abruptly if 'the outside is not clear.' Code-switching between Nigerian Pidgin English and Yoruba, he paints vivid pictures of how congregants note possible exit routes and make sure windows are not closed to enable them to see what is happening outside and mark their exit plans if something happens before they take their seats (AY Comedian 2015). In another event, Osama retells the joke, adding that in Abuja and Jos churches, 'The fear of boom is the beginning of wisdom …' (Juvenis TV 2016c).

The theme of religion comes up in Nigerian stand-up comedy, but there is a deliberate consciousness amongst promoters and practitioners to keep the art neutral, without the entanglements of unnecessary elicitations of provocation. It is noteworthy that the assertion, albeit erroneous supposition, of a Christian south and Muslim north, gives the impression that most southern cities' audience members are Christians. Rather than hinging the differences on religion, it is instead more of a language disparity, given that people in the south are likely to be more fluent in and more frequent users of Nigerian Pidgin English and English language than those in the north where Hausa is more predominantly used. Although insensitive comments and actions regarding religion have drawn ire and sparked deadly violence and retaliatory attacks across the nation, Nigerian stand-up comedy has not elicited any direct conflicts and rebuttals despite its potential for offence to groups or individuals when it comes to religion.[14] As such, comedians seemingly abide by an unwritten code that designates offensive religious themes as taboo, keeping them off-limits to many professional performers. They do this by remaining within subjects about the religious groups to which they belong or those with which they are familiar.

Ethnic jokes, unlike religious ones, are not considered offensive within Nigerian stand-up renditions. Ethnic stereotypes are easily appropriated for humour, but jokesters are more careful where religious stereotypes are concerned. It is possible to see comedians who are not Yoruba, Igbo, or Hausa make jokes about those groups, but somewhat difficult to have people of one faith make fun of others in mainstream practice. This may be due to the tacit understanding that people are more emotionally attached to their faith than they may be to their ethnicity. Hence, there appear to be no limits regarding who should use what ethnic stereotype, but comedians are still more likely to parody the ethnic group or region to which they belong or identify than they would do those of others. Akpororo and AY, for instance, make fun of Warri people even though they are Yorubas because they grew up in that region, and they do assert their *Waffi* identity whenever it is necessary for them to do so. As observed by Adetunji and Leeven above, stereotypes emphasise uniqueness, thereby creating the possibility of taking ownership and channelling them into group pride rather than shame. In the hands of Nigerian comedians, *otherness* translates into power instead of weakness, emboldening such usages by 'non-members' who are also careful not to dwell on one ethnicity in a routine so as not to be caught up in group bashing. In several cases, ethnic ridicule is engaged to deepen the understanding of a joke. When a comedian can produce an accurate replica of a particular group's mannerism or stereotype, the joke's meaning is enhanced since members of the audience are also aware of these typical ethnic demeanours. Hence, the comedian does not need to use long explanatory expressions to convey meaning to the audience. Thus, Nigerian humourists exploit the myriad comedic potentials of ethnic jokes far more than they would religious proclivities, especially when it concerns the two major faiths, Christianity and Islam.

When it comes to taboo subjects, sex features prominently in many cultures. Within discourses about sex are gender associations, sexual affiliations and relations, dating and marriage, and the way sexual intercourse is discussed. There have been instances of sexist jokes, including some dealing with rape. In his early days, a few of Basket Mouth's statements were quite offensive, such as saying that marriage is like having a DStv subscription with many TV channels, and the man is only allowed to watch just one of those at all times[15] (NTL3 2004). Other equally non-complimentary portraitures describe how men fight over women as the women helplessly watch the men quarrel over 'owning' them (NTL12 n.d.). Elsewhere, he talks about men unapologetically lying to their girlfriends because, 'A lie a day keeps the relationship going' (BMU2 2007). Some of these depictions are sarcastic, and he sometimes tries to balance his female portraiture with supposedly positive statements about women combined with attacks on the menfolk. For instance, he berates wife beaters and men who do not respect women (NTL12 n.d.), also saying somewhere else that, 'Women are ten times smarter than men,' qualifying the claim with a biblical reference to the Adam and Eve's story, emphasising that it was the woman who ate the fruit of knowledge first before giving it to the man (BMU2 2007). It does appear here that he is hailing women for being wiser, but the underlying suggestion sabotages the effort because Eve is portrayed as having hoarded her newly acquired knowledge and possibly amused herself at Adam's obliviousness to his nakedness for as long as she wished.

AY has also roundly condemned wife beating, but some of his gags appear to endorse the notion that Nigerian women are solely after monetary gains in their dealings with men. For example, he talks about school girlfriends dropping their poor boyfriends for richer 'sugar daddies.' He even has a prayer for them:

> All 'aristos' who will not let us meet our future wives; may their cars break down on top Third Mainland Bridge … Holy Ghost!' And the audience shouts, 'Fire!'[16] (AYL3 n.d.)

A prayer that Basket Mouth also repeats on another occasion goes like this:

> God go punish all de 'aristos' in Jesus' name! […] Una don marry una wives come de confuse our future wives. We go buy dem recharge card, una go buy dem phone. We go give dem moni for cab, una go buy dem car. Na who de babe wan listen to?[17] (NTL12 n.d.)

Both prayers tacitly endorse the supposition that women are after money and not love, and secondly, that women are incapable of fending for themselves. The inference is that women need the monetary support of older, wealthier men to survive, or at worst, they should settle for the prayers of their not-so-rich boyfriends to become relevant in life. These suppositions indubitably have roots in assumptions created by patriarchy and propelled, before now, by the fewer number of female comedians on the Nigerian stand-up stage. Even I Go Dye is vociferous in his representation of girls' dependence on men, to the point that women are shown to be duplicitous. To him, women are only interested in men's pockets, as shown in his narrative of his earlier days when he thought that the ability to speak English flawlessly would earn him a lady's love. He avers that he came to realise later in life that when a guy has money, women will flock after him: 'Girls don't believe in certificates, dem too like money!' he screams.[18] He further claims that girls become jealous that their men follow other women simply because the men in question are not rich enough. He thus claims that if the man is rich, he can have as many women as he wants, and all of them will gather around him without fighting, saying excitedly: 'Na our boyfriend o!'[19] (NTL16 n.d.).

Female comedians in mainstream practice often counter some of these negativities. In most of her sets, Helen Paul turns on the menfolk, ridiculing their misdemeanours and advising women how best to handle precarious situations with men. Using a story about her school lover who demeaned her for being a performer, telling her that he did not need a wife that would be a 'liability,' Helen Paul encourages young women to work hard to rid themselves of dependence on men (JuvenisTV 2016b). She also counters notions of female beauty by removing her wig on stage to reveal her natural hair as a way of encouraging women to be proud of their bodies. She once turned her stand-up set into a wig removal pageant where female audience members removed their wigs on stage to win (Paul 2020). Her commitment to countering sexist jokes and actions informs her confrontations with male comedians, as seen in her exchange with Gordons and other performers mentioned in the previous chapter. Princess has also taken opportunities to hit back at her male colleagues, thereby eliciting reprisal personal jokes against her (AY Comedian 2016a). Real Warri Pikin berates men for several misdemeanours to the delight of female members of the audience. In one event, she asks women what they are looking for in their men's phones, adding hilariously: 'Man phone dey like onions. E go mek you cry!'[20] (AY Comedian 2020b). Hidden within this likening of men's phones to onions is the allusion to infidelity and the multiple layers of the onions which are revealed after one is peeled off, on the one hand, and the supposed inability of men to stick to one partner implicated in the capacity of onions to water the eyes, on the other. Real Warri Pikin also uses her journey from grass to grace to encourage others to aspire to become more successful in life. In this way, she and other female comedians, especially in internet and social media humour enactments, are championing the rewriting of female portraiture in comedic expressions in the Nigerian stand-up industry.

Sexual explicitness comes up here and there within comedic performances, even though several events do not allow profanity and lewdness in deference to their sponsors who may want to use the show for promotional purposes on primetime television. Despite these restrictions, numerous randy and sexually suggestive jokes still find their ways into the public space through social media. Sexually explicit jokes can be farcical and funny but are often considered 'dirty.' Basket Mouth is adept at telling 'moderated sex jokes' where he uses innuendoes: suggestive terms, movements, gestures, pauses, and sundry verbalisations to nudge audiences into making sense of unsaid aspects of sex and nakedness. He does this effectively in his joke about Eve watching Adam walk about the Garden of Eden naked. From verbally creating imagery of how Adam's penis would have appeared by operationalising the term 'things will be moving' to evoke how it would be dangling, Basket Mouth draws parallels by imagining how male police officers, comedians, and even the president would look if they appeared naked in public. In the same set, he expresses frustration at how ladies' skirts and underwear have become increasingly smaller so that,

> Today, wetin we de see be say na rope dem de tie on top rope. Before, if you wan see nyash, you go open pant. Now, if you wan see pant, you go open nyash.[21] (NTL15 2008)

Elsewhere, he demonstrates breast sizes, saying that some are 'confident,' and others have 'low self-esteem' (NTL19 n.d.). In each of these examples, Basket Mouth does not get vulgar with his diction but stays within the bounds of nominal expression while nudging the audience to comprehend his intentions with part statements, pauses, and embodied expressions. For his part, Klint da Drunk reinterprets select popular Nigerian songs to discover their sexual explicitness in one of his routines, concluding the set with a joke about a court adjudication on the rape of a speech-impaired young lady by three men of different body and penis sizes (AY Comedian 2018b). This rendition grazes the borderline of political correctness, and is very unsettling, especially in how he broached the issue of rape.

More recently, comedians like Gordons use libidinous gags to evoke laughter. In one of such, he talks about the orgasms of Igbo and Urhobo girls, using the term 'soundtrack', which has been popularised in Nigeria as a synonym to vocal expressions during sexual intercourse. In this particular set, he talks about his Chinese experience where he says, 'Soundtrack be like guitar!' (AY Comedian 2016a). Gordons instigates humour in this rendition through his vocal replication of what he convinced his audience are the authentic 'soundtracks' of Igbo, Urhobo, and Chinese girls during orgasm. In another set, he turns to men, saying that there is no other time that a man looks more stupid than when he climaxes because the individual loses every form of control (JuvenisTV 2016a). MC Acapella is another Nigerian comedian that does not hold back, especially with suggestiveness and sometimes explicit mentions of sex and related subjects. In one skit, within highly charged political satire against President Buhari's government, he finds time to exclaim:

> If you go online now, women de buy vagina-tightening cream. Meanwhile, men de buy penis enlargement. As you de tight am, dem de open am […] Una two go die there o! (*audience applause*)[22] (Juvenis TV 2020)

The inference is that amidst the economic difficulties that have become the hallmark of the Buhari administration in Nigeria, people are still obsessed with their sex organs. As women spend hard-earned monies to make theirs firmer, men are paying to make theirs bigger. The sharp descent from talking about the impoverishment of Nigerians to this form of sexual explicitness is, at once, both hilarious and disconcerting. In a recent event, I Go Dye conflates the corruption in Buhari's government with deception by people, mostly ladies, who wear fake eyelids, breasts, and 'nyash.' Quite humorously, he adds: 'Person go cross road finish, *nyash* go still dey road!' alongside the embodied expressions of someone with more protruded buttocks[23] (Juvenis TV 2020). The word *nyash* is often not enacted in formal settings, even when Nigerian Pidgin English is being used. The accompanying embodied action is also ludicrous and somewhat lewd. In short, Nigerian comedians are freer to make vulgar jokes within mostly heterosexual relations but are still not free to endorse same-sex associations (AYL3 n.d., NTL8 n.d., BMU2 2007) in line with government regulations and what their audience currently endorses. Jokes continue to be mostly homophobic and offensive towards individuals of various sexual orientations other than heterosexuals.

Discourse on politics also features prominently, as already seen in the conflation of sex and government policies above. Nigerian comics dwell extensively on political satire, calling out the government of the day and its agencies for their many sins. However, humourists have been involved in praise-singing, as Basket Mouth did with the then gubernatorial candidate of Lagos State, asking the people to vote for him (BMU2 2007). When Fashola had already become governor in his next event, he asked the audience to applaud him for doing a good job in Lagos (BMU3 2009). Needless to say, it is the same Fashola who has become a much-criticised persona since assuming office as a minister in the Buhari government. AY it seems lampoons him in a joke created of a serial abusive husband who left Nigeria and tried to continue his evil enterprise with an American woman. Unlike her Nigerian counterparts, the latter pulled a pistol on the aggressive man, forcing him to run into and barricade himself in the toilet. From there, he called immigration officials to come and deport him. The joke's punchline is where he reveals the man's name to be

Fashola (AYL3 n.d.). One is unsure why AY used the name of Lagos State governor, but the association turned out to be quite humorous. Elsewhere, he ridicules the several botched attempts by his pastor, Chris Okotie, at becoming Nigeria's president (NTL11 2007; NTL13 n.d.), and some of the lampoons of Nigerian presidents, especially Obasanjo, have been discussed previously.

MC Acapella has an entire set where he enlists all the evils and foibles of President Buhari's government. It is an exposé that ridicules the claim of piety by the government, stating, for instance, the corrupt act of having fed horses on election duties with hundreds of millions of naira in one day, jokingly saying that we need to hear from the 'horses' mouths' to know the truth (Afroway TV 2020). Jokes on corruption also touch on parastatals and government institutions like the police, for example, where Koffi suggests that it might help if pockets are removed from police uniforms to deter them from collecting bribes, especially when they have to tell commuters to hold their money since their 'caps don full'[24] (Naija Live Comedy 2012). These samples are jokes created around individuals and institutions of government.

Class differentiation too features in stand-up jokes, as comedians juxtapose the lives of privileged and dispossessed members of society. Comedians talk about having a background of poverty, as expressed by Real Warri Pikin (JusticeCrack 2020). There are caricatures of those living in opulence, like Bovi's in the event where he refers to the nation's multi-billionaires, some of whom were in the audience, as his 'ordinary friends' (Ugboma 2020).

In summary, whatever theme is deployed, the objectives of Nigerian stand-up comedy entail creating a shared, unified culture of arts that bridges gaps and mends the country's multifaced crises-engendering differences. Humourists and their enablers thus exert conscious efforts towards creating a comedy tradition out of the various aspects of national life that are unlikely to create problems and confrontations. The industry has moved from the backwaters of *artistic* production, practice, and dissemination to become one of its greatest exports, especially to its diaspora in the west. Accordingly, it is increasingly employing globalised themes, especially those pertinent to the African diaspora in the west. Themes based on world politics and the many changing dynamics of everyday living across the continent and elsewhere also feature in Nigerian stand-up comedy.

Notes

1 'We have money, and everyone [meaning the politicians] is just taking as much as they desire.'

2 This joke was possibly on the *Nite of a Thousand Laughs* stage and was widely circulated on BBM in the mid-and late 2000s.

3   It is pertinent to note that Oshiomhole became governor in Edo State after Obasanjo's tenure as president in 2007. So, the narrative is a product of Maleke's imagination which is told in line with the ruling concepts about Obasanjo while he was in office and immediately after. At the time of this narrative, Oshiomhole was still held in high esteem for his labour rights advocacies during the military era, making people quite hopeful of positive change at his emergence as governor. In a decade and a half, the same Oshiomhole has emerged as one of the most hated politicians in Nigeria for his several choices while in office as governor and as leader of the ruling party under Muhammad Buhari.

4   'Obasanjo was denied a visa because of Oshiomhole. You should hear this! … Obasanjo came to collect the visa, the woman said … They turned the computer around, and Oshiomhole's face appeared … Then the woman said, … Baba (Obasanjo) said, 'That's Oshiomhole.' They said, 'What? So you changed your name? Just because of …'

5   *Suya* is meat kebab, sold mainly by people from northern Nigeria.

6   'Italian connection' refers to girls who go to Italy and other European cities for prostitution, most of whom repatriate much-needed funds to their family members back home, so that at one time it became a sort of prestigious venture for some.

7   *Koboko* is a long, light whip made from horsetail or cow skin.

8   '*Nna*' is the Igbo word for father, but here explicitly denotes 'my brother' or 'my friend.'

9   For some background, the lady ridiculed Klint by saying, 'I love your shoes!' It appears innocuous, but it is not because Klint's stage appearance entails wearing one pair of his shoes and holding the other under his arm or not wearing any at all.

10 'White garment' churches belong to a denomination of Christianity where adherents wear white flowing gowns, and they adopt elements of traditional religious worship which entails visions, prophecy, and mediumship.

11 My translation: 'The Bible says, "Greater work than I did, will you do;" Moses parted the Red Sea, which of the Nigerian pastors have parted even a gutter?'

12 'How can someone give an offering that can challenge God (when He owns everything in the world)?'

13 '… Demons will wait for you outside [the church] … Are you done? Let's go home …'

14 The killing spree, which official records put at 220 people dead and the *fatwa* pronounced on a journalist, Isioma Daniels, for her comments on the botched Miss World pageant slated for Nigeria in 2001 (Astil and Bowcott 2002).

15 A multi-channel pay-tv cable satellite television managed by the South African company, Multichoice.

16 Derived from 'aristocrats', it designates girls, mostly university undergraduates, who follow rich men for money. Aristo also refers to the rich men themselves.

17 My translation: 'God will punish all the "aristos" in Jesus' name! (…) You have married your wives and are now confusing our future wives. When we buy phone credits for them, you buy phones for them. When we give them money for a taxi, you buy cars for them. Who will the girls listen to then?'

18 '… they like money a lot!'

19 'He is our boyfriend!'

20 'A man's phone is like onions. It will make you cry!'

21 'Today, what we see is that they hang just ropes on lines. Before now, if you want to see buttocks, you open panties. Now, if you want to see panties, you open the buttocks.'

22 'If one gets online, you see that women are buying vagina-tightening creams, while men buy penis-enlargement creams. As you are tightening it, they are opening it … two of you will kill yourselves over it.' (The last statement is not meant in the literal sense. It is a way of emphasising the difficulty or seriousness of an issue.)

23 *Nyash*, also *yansh*, is a highly sexualised Nigerian Pidgin English term, meaning 'buttocks'. 'Someone will cross the street, and the person's buttocks will still be obstructing the road.'

24 'their caps are full (filled with the bribes they have collected)'

5

Language and accent

Language

Language is central to joke rendition as it involves both verbal and non-verbal expressions comedians enlist in relaying their narratives to audiences. From the 1960s up to the 1980s, there existed what was known as the 'language question,' which centred on disputations surrounding the issue of whether locally authored works in European languages can be dubbed African literature (Adejunmobi 1999, 581). The belief is that works written in foreign languages are often devoid of 'blood and stamina,' dispossessed of 'means of self-enrichment,' and ultimately unavailable to local people who do not know the foreign language (Wali 1963, 13–14). The choice of language in artistic expression is thus a political act because it is an expression of the artist's preferred target audience(s): 'his[/her] country[people], who share a language with him[/her] or, readers outside his[/her] country, with whom he[/she] shares a foreign language' (Riemenschneider 1984, 78–79). This language question, which elicited numerous disputations over five decades ago, appears to have been answered by the linguistic choices of African stand-up comedy. Unlike literature, stand-up comedy has adapted itself to creolised, derivative, more popular languages, slang – pidgin English in Nigeria, Sheng in Kenya, and a rise in *vernac* comedy (indigenous languages) in South Africa. Thus, it restricts itself through its linguistic adoptions and its appropriation of local motifs in the generation of humour, becoming exclusive to specific groups and locales. In this manner, stand-up comedy enables local ownership of its production and consumption.

There have been overabundant linguistic enquiries on Nigerian stand-up art. Emphasis has mostly been on its use of Nigerian Pidgin English and other linguistic devices. Put more succinctly, Ogoanah and Ojo aver that the focus has been 'mainly on identification, characterisation, and description of linguistic and pragmatic techniques employed by comedians in their routine' (2018, 41). Ibukun Filani has also written extensively on comedians' expressions of linguistic strategies (2015a, 2015b), including in utterances about their identities (Filani 2020), and expressions of ideological leanings (Filani and Ajayi 2019). Other works enumerate the pragmatic strategies comedians deploy, especially towards co-opting audiences into their stage work (Raheem 2018), the interactional context of exchanges between comedians and audiences (Adetunji 2013), and the presentation of models for evaluating humour through the prism of pragmatics (Kehinde 2016; Nneji 2013). One major drawback of these and other linguistic appraisals is that they scarcely consider stand-up comedy as a performance. Take Filani (2016), for instance, who presents an excellent engagement with mimicry in Nigerian stand-up art, but by extrapolating standpoints from linguistics and postcolonial studies, it occludes reading mimicry as an aspect of performance. By paying attention mainly to the verbal aspects of comedians' communications with the audience, most of these studies reduce the enactments' performed aspects to mere 'paralinguistic' additives. Specifically, embodied actions within stand-up acts have been merely called 'movement of hands and legs' (Lamidi 2017, 127) and 'nonverbal cues' (Filani and Ajayi 2019, 141; Filani 2015b, 77). This predilection strips stand-up comedy of its other aspects such as the dynamics of performance-audience interaction, movement, facial aspects, costume, stage paraphernalia, and performance aids, and the ways these and other non-verbal components affect joke renditions. For this reason, there is widespread extraction of jokes without contexts and references to when and where they were performed, often with little or no citations for retrieval purposes. There is no overstating the importance of these background details because joke excerpts become dispossessed of their accompanying contexts for meaning-making without them.

Consequently, the over engagement with the verbal subsumes the gestural and complementary non-verbal enactments in speech. This condition creates the impression that the accompanying performed aspects of stand-up comedy are just appendages when, in actuality, they play overtly complementary meaning-making/-altering roles to the verbalisations. Specifically speaking, what comedians do, how they do it, the performance venue and ambience, and the subsisting dynamics of performer-audience interactions are equally as important as what the comedians say and the linguistic formulations they deploy towards their utterances. One common misreading is that comedians' speeches are sometimes taken at face value, such as a discourse analysis of how comedians construct 'national identity' through what they say on stage (Filani 2020). Here the expressions of the artists are treated as if they are their personal opinions and convictions when, in fact, they are just part of their imitative acts. The implication thus is that what they say may not amount to their true ideas about 'national identity' or any other political view. Hence, despite the primacy of speech in stand-up renditions, the stage humourist is fundamentally an artist who uses speech and other embodied representations. These words of Eugenio Barba reinforce the notion of comedians as performers:

> The performer's different techniques can be conscious and codified or else unconscious but implicit in the use and repetition of a scenic practice. Transcultural analysis shows that it is possible to distinguish recurring

> principles in these techniques. The recurring principles […] produce physical, pre-expressive tensions. These new tensions generate a different quality of energy, they render the body […] 'believable' and manifest the performer's 'presence,' […] attracting the spectator's attention 'before' any form of message is transmitted. (Barba 1995, 9)

One surmises that comedians do not intend that much of what they say would be believed *in toto* except to the point where they elicit the laughter. It is tied to Ajaye's 'honesty' already mentioned in Chapter 2. In joke performances, what matters is the elicitation of humour, and the level of audience laughter determines how funny the joke is (Limon 2000, 12). It is factual that 'in joking situations, speakers report the speech or action of other individual hearers' (Filani 2015a, 42), a tacit agreement that what stage humourists do is roleplay, a performance. However, his reference to them as 'speakers' rather than performers or actors underscores the ongoing discourse about the stripping down of stand-up performances to language. Thus, jokesters are disembodied by this privileging of what they say over what they enact with their bodies alongside.

It is undeniable that language encapsulates thoughts and conveys the same to audiences within stand-up renditions. The predominant language used in Nigerian practice is pidgin English. There are also code-mixes/switches involving other Nigerian languages, dialects, slang, and formal English depending on the location, the audience, and the humourist's linguistic capabilities. Nigerian Pidgin English has become quite useful primarily because most Nigerians are not multilingual. The majority are likely to speak only English and the language of the area where they were raised, in which case, they may not speak their 'mother tongue' quite fluently. Also, pidgin English has evolved as the language of choice for stand-up comedy, popular culture, and broadcast media, thus becoming ingrained in the national fabric. It has also been rightly described as one language that

> has come to stay with Nigerians and is acquiring new roles in every facet of the country's economic and socio-political life. It is no longer seen as the restricted mode of interlingual communication with limited lexicon but as a language with its own vitality and essence. (Mensah 2011, 213)

Though still mostly oral, pidgin English has been attracting scholarly attention in recent times.[1] It has also become part of youth culture and a marker for Nigerian authenticity in mostly informal settings. Nigerian pidgin variants also exist for different parts of Nigeria, with the significant distinction being code-switched or adopted terms derived from specific local languages. As stated previously, comedians from the Niger-Delta like I Go Dye, Gordons, Julius Agwu, and even AY build their acts around recognisable inflexions and registers popular with people from that area.

Performers who do not possess unique pidgin English proficiencies codeswitch to Yoruba (Seyi Law, Elenu, Helen Paul) or Igbo (Acapella, Klint da Drunk, Funny Bone). A few characterise their acts with accents, not necessarily a specialised use of pidgin English, especially the Hausa manner of speaking (Aboki 4 Christ, Holy Mallam, Gospel Alhaji, MC Tagwaye). Adetunji avers that Nigerian comedians' use of pidgin English is 'an affiliative resource, an index of a desire to speak with, rather than to, their audiences' (2013, 6). Thus, it indicates the performers' intention to present their renditions to a broader audience, which would not be possible when using one indigenous language or standard English.

Although there is validity in the assertion that the use of pidgin English makes stand-up comedy accessible to more Nigerians because it is widely spoken and understood (Adetunji 2013, 6; Filani 2015a, 45), this conception is likely to be an exaggeration. There are no statistics to show Nigerians' proficiency level in local languages, but as someone who grew up in southeast Nigeria and worked for a couple of years in northern Nigeria, I can attest that people in the north are more accustomed to Hausa than pidgin English. Those who do not speak and understand standard English quite appreciably may also have the same problem with pidgin English itself. Nevertheless, pidgin English is used extensively, especially in more cosmopolitan areas like Lagos, Abuja, and other multi-ethnic cities, such as Calabar, Port Harcourt, and Warri. In this way, pidgin English is indeed an 'urban language' and the 'semi-official language of the police and the army' (Wilkinson 1986, 616–617). However, referring to it as a language 'spoken mostly by the less educated members of society' or a 'vulgar' language (Wilkinson 1986, 618) leaves much to be desired, especially considering how far pidgin English has come in its present elevated status within popular culture. This supposition is a product of two factors: decades of belittling and inferiorising the language and its speakers, and the lack of any effort being exerted into recognising it as a pervasive language capable of featuring in more formal situations. As such, characterising it as a language of 'uneducated people' is misleading in the light of present realities, as well as offensive.

The principal usefulness of Nigerian Pidgin English to stand-up comedy is its humorousness and malleability, inherent in its rendering, specifically domestication (what some may call bastardisation) of English words. For instance, there is a difference between a comedian saying, 'As I walked into the house ...', and its Nigerian Pidgin English equivalent, '*As I waka enta de house ...*' or between, 'You can imagine how hungry I was ...' and '*You fit imagine how hunger de waya me ....*' In the Nigerian Pidgin English translations, a dramatisation invoked by the terms 'waka enta' and 'de waya me', which have no equivalents in the English language, is observed. The ability to steer narratives in inventive ways comes naturally with Nigerian Pidgin English's unboundedness, a treasure for stand-up comedy. This pliability makes it a melting pot for several indigenous languages from which it unapologetically pillages terms, rendering them in whatever ways it sees fit. In this wise, English terms are static, while Nigerian Pidgin English is performative, with a predilection for drawing out words and creating imageries. English language, at the hands of Nigerian comedians, lacks the capacity to bear the entire gamut of representations required for joke performance. Furthermore, stand-up comedy and Nigerian Pidgin English share the trait of straddling formal and informal speaking spheres, capturing thoughts, formulating ideas, and voicing impossible words in more formalised settings. With this capacity, Nigerian Pidgin English encapsulates social critique (Akande, Adedeji, and Robbin 2019). Wilkinson rightly avers that,

> Pidgin is used, like a deformed or outsized feature in a caricature, not only to mark out the character as belonging to a type or class but in order to foreground an eccentricity, a deviation from a norm; thus the Pidgin speaker is presented as not only mangling and distorting the accepted linguistic norm but as violating the rules of behaviour and decency. (1986, 621)

This assertion also underscores the work of a typical Nigerian stand-up comic. By performing in Nigerian Pidgin English, local jokesters loosen the strictures of formality often upheld by the regularity of standard English and thus enable criticism, satire, and questioning of the *status quo* through an equally transgressive language. With the increasing 'gentrification' of Nigerian stand-up, especially with its manifestations in glitzy and elitist locations, there is a juxtaposition of the officious and the banal, the city and the ghetto, the privileged and the underprivileged, in both physical performance settings and the ambience of joke narratives.

I Go Dye's experience buttresses the point made earlier that Nigerian Pidgin English is not spoken as widely as earlier thought. He tells of his early days and how he found himself in stand-up practice:

> It all started when I was in the village with my grandmother. When I was 16 years old, I realised that my grandmother was not my real mother, so I felt very sad. So the first time I was in Warri, I [could] not speak the normal pidgin English that the Warri man speaks, I only spoke Urhobo and [that] made me a laughing stock. Funnily (sic) enough, my mother had a shop in our compound and I was put in charge of the shop to sell provisions. So what do you expect from a salesman who don't (sic) know how to speak English? Comedy, of course. Because a lot of people came to the shop and I could not speak simple 'wetin you wan buy?' I was like a comedian then. So the story spread around Warri that there is one big boy who cannot speak simple pidgin, a real Urhobo boy. (Nigerian Films 2009)

It is instructive from this assertion that he only spoke Urhobo at first as someone who grew up in an Urhobo-speaking community. However, this excerpt advances a vital explanation for I Go Dye's peculiar use of Nigerian Pidgin English: that he did not grow up using the language. He had to learn it after moving from his village to the city of Warri. Hence, he speaks a unique Nigerian Pidgin English with a definite Waffi piquancy. Apart from the characteristic use of Warri registers, I Go Dye's language specificities include wrong verb inflections and unusual tautology. For example, he could say things like, 'I will *broke* the yoke of poverty in your life!' Alternatively, when referring to an individual, he can be heard to say. '*Only you one* will …' instead of 'Only you …' or 'You alone …' Furthermore, there is the use of Nigerian Pidgin English terms within what is supposed to be standard English: 'I be *Togo*' ['I am Togolese'], 'Excuse me, I am *Kenya*' ['Excuse me, I am Kenyan'], 'Sing your own *sing*' ['Sing your own song'] (NTL20 n.d.), and elsewhere, ' … to *barber* my hair' [' … have a haircut'] (NTL12 n.d.). It is not apparent whether these are deliberate coinages because they are not syntactically correct even within Nigerian Pidgin English expressions. His word choices instigate hilarity in audiences; whether it is for the jokes or the language in which they are expressed, it is difficult to determine which one gets the most laughs.

Klint da Drunk uses an equal mix of standard and Nigerian Pidgin English in his renditions, sometimes ridiculing individuals who speak 'bad English.' He also deploys puns and rhyme in twisting statements and words in humorous ways. For example, he lures his audience into saying things to him, and then responds with his comedic interpretations of what they say. In one of his sets, he starts by saying, 'When I went to France …' then he pauses, then challenges no one in particular, 'You say na lie? (*pause*) Oya, speak French mek I interpret it for you.'[2] Then the audience takes up the challenge. He tells the first speaker, a girl who reels out a French sentence: 'I asked you to speak French not "Calabar" mixed with Idoma.' Then, to the ones he wanted to hear, he gives hilarious misinterpretations: 'Comment tu t'appelles?' becomes 'Comot your tooth and put it in a pail,' while 'Ça va?' means 'served her?', and for the avoidance of doubt, he spells it out, 'Have you served her?'[3] He exploits this approach, using for example, 'Bonjour' which he says refers to someone 'born in June,' and 'au revoir' means that, 'You must be a smuggler: that is the short cut to Côte d'Ivoire,' while 'merci' implies a girl's name, 'Mercy,' adding, 'Is that the girl you want to spend your life with?' in order to entice increased involvement of the audience (NML n.d.). Klint's language play also extends to English where, for example, he tells the audience that if 'Give her her book' is correct, then it follows that 'Give them them book,' 'Give us us book,' 'Give we we book,' 'Give him him book,' and 'Give I I book' should also be correct. He even turns it into a call and response rendition with the audience (NML n.d.).

Another significant specialised use of language in Nigerian stand-up is in the double acts of the duos: Sam and Song and Still Ringing. As mentioned in

Chapter 2, these humourists build their acts on the preacher-interpreter model of Christian churches and missionaries, where the principal performs in English, and the other translates into a local language. Their subjects are also mostly church-based, where the humour comes with misinterpretations of familiar biblical texts and statements. Apart from being part of the repertoire of traditional performances, as mentioned earlier, this form of rendition featured in *Icheoku* (Igbo language word for 'parrot'), the 1980s and early 1990s weekly television comedy programme on Nigerian Television Authority (NTA), set in an Igbo community during colonial times. The main characters are a British colonial administrator known as Nwa DC (District Commissioner) and his interpreter-court clerk, Williams. Much of the action centres on the settlement of disputes within the community, whereas humour is elicited through a series of misinterpretations and disagreements between the British officer and his court clerk. While the court clerk speaks Igbo to the people, he uses the smatterings of English of a basic speaker in his interactions with Nwa DC. Despite Williams' scant English language proficiency, Chiji Akoma describes him as a subversive persona because he questions colonial impositions in very subtle ways (2009, 93). For Sam and Song, Song's interpretations of Sam's English statements are either into Igbo or Nigerian Pidgin English, depending on the audience's composition. In the case of Still Ringing, the interpreter's speech is rendered in Yoruba. Their acts have been described as 'code pairing,' a merger of two texts with different meanings combined to create a new humorous text (Lamidi 2017, 116). One difference between the acts of the duos is that while,

> Still-Ringing's interpreter engages in wittier, subtler and more regular conveyance of punchlines to the audience, the interpreter of the Sam and Song's group, Sam's major comedic technique is through exaggerated dysphemia which makes him stutter excessively and oftentimes is not able to complete his sentences. (Osuolale-Ajayi 2022 , 128–129)

Still Ringing enjoys an advantage when performing in spaces where the audience is made up of a significant number of Yoruba speakers, making it easier for the interpreter to speak extensively in Yoruba. To elicit humour, the interpreter uses similarity in sound and rhyme to designate equivalents to what the main speaker says rather than interpreting English words based on meaning. For Sam and Song, performing in locations with many non-Igbo speakers makes them engage in drawn-out dramatic enactments, and sometimes wordy exchanges. Sam's use of feigned difficulty in speech, often expressed through distended stammering, does get somewhat offensive. Their mode of stand-up rendition is not built on joke-telling but on misinterpretations and accruing arguments between the two performers for the two groups. For Sam and Song, such disagreements are sometimes unnecessarily extended, while Still Ringing does not dwell on theirs, moving quickly to the next rendition, creating the impression that the main speaker is mostly oblivious of the interpreter's error-prone rendering of his speech.

In Sam and Song's performances, Song, the 'preacher,' often opens before introducing his partner. In their appearance at AY's London show in 2017, Song turns to the audience after appreciating the person who introduced him:

> I won't say anything tonight without appreciating someone so special to me. This person came into my life, and my life changed for good. Ladies and gentlemen, I'm talking about somebody I respect so much. She is the love of my life – the wife of my youth, my strength, my pride. Please, appreciate my wife. (*with his right hand extended to a side of the auditorium*) Please clap for my wife (*the audience obliges him*). Clap for her. Please, appreciate my wife. Appreciate her. She is the shy type. (*audience realises he is not referring to anyone in particular and starts laughing*) Yes, she is not here with us (*audience laughter; he moves to centre stage*), and we have not met (*more laughter*). She is somewhere with her mother, maybe East Africa or North Africa. And I believe, one day we will meet. Please appreciate her once more in advance (*audience laughter, without applause*). (AY Comedian 2018c)

In this opening statements, Song speaks in English with a heavy Igbo accent. It is obvious from the excerpt that he does not code-mix. It is his interpreter, Sam, who switches from Igbo to pidgin English, and sometimes to English. Once Sam comes on stage, they start with arguments about what Song said in introducing his interpreter. From then on, Sam assumes an oppositional stance to Song both in language use and the subjects of their discussions. In the same London event mentioned above, the duo has several such exchanges, one of which concerns whether Sam is a university graduate or not:

SAM: (*facing Sam, emphatically*) I be graduation.

SONG: You are not a graduation; you are a graduate!

SAM: (*calmly, but emphatically*) Na your graduation? (*audience laughter*)

SONG: Okay, Sam, if you say you are a graduate, can you tell us. Which school did you graduate from? Tell us.

SAM: No vex … Which school wey you go like mek I graduate from? (*audience laughter*)

SONG: But you said you are a graduate?

SAM: Ehen na, since you dey interested for the graduation, which school you go like mek I graduate from now? (*audience laughter*)

SONG: Okay, Sam. I want you to graduate from the University of Ekpoma.

SAM: Nna, naa! (*waves his palm in rejection*) I no like that name. (*audience laughter*)

SONG: Why?

SAM: (*stressing the first two syllables*) EKPOma!

SONG: What's the meaning of that?

SAM: (*In Igbo*) Ị maalụ ihe ọ pụtara na Igbo? [Do you know what it means in Igbo?] (*audience laughter*) EKPOma, in English, 'Masquerade knows!' (*in a contemplative manner*) EKPOma! Nna, you will graduate there, not me o! (AY Comedian 2018c)

Comedians often use 'bad' English to elicit humour, casting the speaker in a mould of an illiterate. The first statement from Sam in the excerpt is one of such endeavours. 'I be graduation' [I am a graduate] is incorrect both in standard and Nigerian Pidgin English expressions. As Song does, correcting him is a way of highlighting the lousy syntax, which Sam heightens with the query: 'Is it your graduation?' In this manner, Sam signals differences in their personalities, thereby underscoring the clash of ideologies that make up their stage acts. This oppositional stance between the two is like a contest of cultures, which Akoma (2009) has identified between Nwa DC and Williams in *Icheoku*. Also, like Williams, Sam code-mixes Igbo, Nigerian Pidgin English, and standard English in his presentations. For the sake of playing mostly to mixed audiences, he ensures he translates some of his Igbo statements into English.

Apart from these verbalised conversational aspects of their acts, the duo speaks to audiences via highly symbolic and visual actions, a form of performance language. In most sets, Sam comes on stage with various things related to either what is going on in the event or relevant to other salient happenings in society. In two church events where members celebrate their spiritual leaders, they bring goats on a tether as birthday gifts (SamTV 360 2018), adding yam tubers to a goat on another occasion (Flow Entertainment 2017). In the latter event, Sam conveniently links their gift to observances in traditional Igbo societies where animals and tubers of yam are usually used for sacrifices and gifts. At the *AY Show* in London mentioned above, Sam wears layers of winter jackets which he dutifully peels off on stage while highlighting his unpleasant experience of the icy weather (AY Comedian 2018c). With his attire and attitude, he can draw parallels with the popular Nollywood film, *Osuofia in London* (2003). In another *AY Show*, Sam brings a ladder onto the stage, asks Song to drop his Bible and hold it up from the other side. Song obliges him, and Sam begins to climb, holding the microphone in his left hand and using the right one to steady himself. On the third rung, Song asks him why and where he is climbing to:

SAM: Sebi dem say dollar don rise? (*audience laughter*) [Did they not say that dollar (to naira exchange rate) has risen?]

SONG: Yes, dollar has gone up.

SAM: Dem say fuel don rise? [They said that (the price of fuel) has risen?]

SONG: Yes, there is increment in fuel.

SAM: (*stuttering*) Dem say even tomato don go up? [They said (the price of) tomatoes has gone up?]

SONG: Yes …

SAM: I de go meet dem. (*audience laughter*) Hol' am! Hol' am o! [I am climbing up to meet them … Hold it, Hold it!]

SONG: You want to go and meet dollar tomato?

SAM: (*stuttering*) I de go meet dem anywhere dem dey. (*pause*) Hol' am o because if I fall now, 'e go rise pass. [I am going to meet them wherever they are … Hold it because if I fall, their (the prices) will rise the more.] (AY Comedian 2018a)

Here, using comedy, Sam and Song underscore the haplessness of Nigerians in the face of inflation and its exacerbation under the Buhari regime. Without becoming overtly political, the duo dramatises a highly symbolic semblance of Nigerians' fruitless efforts in the face of a general sense of abandonment by a government that has failed woefully in every promise it has made the people. Two other examples emphasise the subtle political subversiveness inherent in the performances of the duo. In the first one, Sam comes on stage wheeling a travel bag in tow. He explains that he has just arrived and that he is late because he had to take the night bus when the 'planer' (pilot) of the flight he was supposed to take to Lagos said he was not making a stop in Benin City so that he could eat before proceeding to Lagos (AcapellaTV 2017). The second is a church event where Sam comes on stage with a basket filled to the brim with onions, to wild applause from the audience, and his colleague is hailing him as the richest man in Nigeria. Song offers to help him with the load, and he says, 'Dem no de help onions now. Na onions de help people now.'[4] They brought the onions as gifts for the pastor's wife: 'If anybody tell onions say for 2020 'im go blow, 'e no go believe.' He uses the onions crisis in Nigeria to relate to the herdsmen and farmers' crisis that has been ongoing in Nigeria for quite some time (Sam and SongTV 2020). The inadequacies of social amenities with a tacit suggestion of government culpability are highlighted in each example. The night bus experience refers to the lack of a reliable transportation system across the country, while the onions drama alludes to the scarcity of onions, mostly in southern Nigeria following the brutally repressed #EndSARS movement in late 2020.[5] In each of their presentations, they deploy verbalised and enacted languages in eliciting humour and running salient, recognisable commentaries on the nation's state of affairs. For me, by using visuals they augment one thing their performance lacks, which is, something Still Ringing has: the capacity to interpret into a local language.

Still Ringing, for its part, brings an interesting comparison, the most extensive use of local language in Nigeria's mainstream stand-up stage. The interpreter is consistent in using Yoruba, with allusions to current affairs, individuals, and other significant aspects and materials of contemporary living. Using rhymes, puns, and homonyms, the interpreter outrightly renders English words in Yoruba, as seen in the excerpts below:

MAIN SPEAKER: For who can come to the Father except He draws him?

INTERPRETER: *Ta lo le fi ofada je draw soup?* (*audience laughter*)

MAIN SPEAKER: (*faces Interpreter*) Draw him!

INTERPRETER: *Ko le rhyme now ko ni dun.* (*further laughter*)[6] (StreamComLive 2016)

In this example, 'father' and 'draws' are translated into 'Ofada rice' and 'draw soup,' from which the interpreter creates a counter script from the main speaker's: while Main Speaker talks about God, Interpreter is more concerned with food. Then, the conversation continues to the point where Main Speaker says: 'The Lord shall help you expressly,' and the interpreter's rendering is that Road Safety officials will not be able to stop 'the people' on the 'Express.' This response prompts Main Speaker to emphasise the word 'expressly' and Interpreter to issue a retort, enforcing his script, as seen below:

INTERPRETER: *Ehn won le dawa duro, a mo Jagaban.* [They cannot stop us because we know Jagaban.]

MAIN SPEAKER: You know when Daniel held the keys to mouth of the lion den.

INTERPRETER: *Woni Kiss Daniel gan ko ni fe korin ni waju lion.* [You know, Kiss Daniel will not want to sing in front of the lion.]

MAIN SPEAKER: You are too 'bam' to be ensnared.

INTERPRETER: *Woni e fe ma se bi bado snie. Lai se Olamide.* [You will not want to behave like Olamide]. (StreamComLive 2016)

Unlike Interpreter's, Main Speaker's script is consistent with its Christian theme and focus. As in the former excerpt, Main Speaker continues to speak like a preacher, but Interpreter enacts a counter script which references an influential politician, Bola Tinubu, popularly referred to as 'Jagaban,' and two singers, 'Kiss Daniel' and 'Olamide.' There is no gainsaying that these mentions have no direct relationship with what Main Speaker is saying except through elicitations of similarities in how the words sound or as an offshoot of a previously made statement that the interpreter chooses to pursue. Nevertheless, through this second performer's acts and responses, the duo catalyses much of its humour. Main Speaker's contribution to this is creating a more consistent statement, which fashions the basis for Interpreter's comedic deviations. Additionally, Main Speaker's feigned obliviousness of the misinterpretations that are going on is used to reinforce what Interpreter has said, thereby evoking more laughter. Still Ringing uses Yoruba and English extensively together with code-mixes of these two and Nigerian Pidgin English. Nevertheless, using vernacular expressions is something comedians keep to the minimum as much as possible because there are tiny opportunities to translate what has been said within the little time they have to make their most impact.

It is noteworthy that there are performances in mainstream Nigerian stand-up comedy presented in English. Forever does much of his rendition in standard English, as seen in the previous Chapter. Chigul too, but she brings a difference with code-switching to Igbo at specific points in her renditions. Her autobiographical one-person stand-up event in 2019, *Chigul Entertains*, has a mix of all her talents, including singing, impersonations, and initiating bouts of laughter in her audience with stories about family life when she was younger (Omeruah 2020). A couple of other comedians perform to local audiences in standard English while the rest, more accustomed to Nigerian Pidgin English gigs, transit to the standard variant when doing shows abroad.[7] Joke-telling thrives on liminality, breaking norms, and altering reality for laughter. Nigerian Pidgin English offers such opportunities better than its standard variant due to its inchoate, permissive, and accommodating matrix instead of the other's rigidity and strictness in form. In Kenya, Sheng, a derivative of Swahili and indigenous languages, performs the same function as pidgin English in Nigerian practice. Even in places where other languages aside from English are used, the slang, marginal forms of such languages are preferred, as seen in the emboldening of the South African *vernac* comedy variant in recent times. Nigerian Pidgin English is the most dominant language used in Nigerian stand-up comedy. This reality is growing rather than diminishing, thus positing the language as an inalienable aspect of the practice.

Accent

Accent is defined as 'the product of the interference of one linguistic system (sounds, grammar [...]) with another language system' (Dobrow and Gidney 1998, 112). It is further described variously: first, as a labelling element used by a 'listener' to assess the 'the sounds of the talker in terms of his (or her) own background' (Chreist 1969, xvii); second, as a complex body of linguistic systems 'which characterise a speaker of a foreign language as non-native' (Jenner 1976, 167); and third, as 'phonological cues ... which identify the speaker as a non-native user of the language' (Scovel 1969,

38). The second and the third characterisations aver that accent delineates between natives and foreigners, while the first highlights a salient, albeit negative, aspect of the deployment of accent as an identity marker. Chreist's designation of accent underscores the negativity of an evaluation done from the perspective of a 'listener' who is judging non-native speakers on how they are speaking a foreign language to them. It then follows that accent can best 'be understood and defined if there is something to compare it with' (Lippi-Green 2011, 45). Accent is one salient aspect of stand-up art put to diverse uses by comedians to elicit humour. It can imbue and elicit preconceived, often stereotypical notions of group identities and characteristics. It also creates associations with which individuals include or exclude others from their (non-)belonging concepts.

In stand-up art, audiences easily recognise accents; consequently, accent is often deployed for the purpose of avoiding the use of elaborate joke setups. Thus, instead of using words to create contexts, humourists deploy accent in characterising individuals and groups within joke narratives, accompanied by peculiar word registers that best describe their referents. Different ethnicities possess identifiable accents and, unlike character stereotypes, speech variants are more undeniable because they are often very evident in interpersonal exchanges. In Nigeria, accent differentiation can be understood at two levels. The first is recognisable in mother-tongue interferences on the English language expressions of different ethnicities. In this sense, people speak the English language with Hausa, Ibibio, Igbo, Tiv, or Yoruba accents, and these are recognisable in everyday conversations and within popular culture. It is noteworthy that people who belong to the same ethnic group may not speak in the same way, but there are recognisable registers, tone, and manner of speaking for specific ethnicities and groups. These kinds of identifiable peculiarities in English expressions are generally used to make specific representations in stand-up comedy. The second variant entails approximations of American or British accents by Nigerians often seen in broadcast media, Nollywood films, and everyday exchanges, referred to as *phoné* or *foné*. Omoniyi describes it as 'a label for a prestigious standard English variety often used to describe the highly educated or native-speaker-approximating performance of a nonnative speaker' (2009, 113). The term, *foné* comes from *phonetics* and is specifically used to portray sophistication. Within Nigerian Nigerian Pidgin English usage, *foné* conflates with 'speaking with accent,' when an individual wants to show off, adorn a form of superiority over others and assume foreignness. In this context, it possesses 'an implicit accusation of inauthenticity' (Heyd 2015, 676), a falsehood often ridiculed by jokesters.

Many Nigerian comedians represent different ethnicities through imitations of their accents or equivalents of how different groups sound when speaking English. They use ethnic accents to characterise individuals within their jokes with minimal words. Accents are, therefore, shortcuts towards portrayals of individuals and groups without overburdening the joke setup. Such representations are often signalled with names of individuals, places, type of food, or all of them together to call attention to character transitions within individual narratives. Some of the following examples have been made previously under other uses, but are here repeated to show ways in which accents also form part of the representations of individuals and groups in stand-up comedy. Chigul is a good example, given the way she represents the Hausa, Igbo, Indian, and various forms of British and American accents in her stage and online presentations (Resuss TV 2019). Basket Mouth and Klint present 'Igbo accent' in two different jokes: where an Igbo man responded to Osama bin Laden when asked to become a suicide bomber, and the characterisation of a foolish Igbo man who thought he is safe from intravenous HIV injection because he is wearing a condom, respectively (NTL13 n.d.). Also, in the example cited earlier, where Klint demonstrates how different tribes sing their songs, he uses accents attributed to differentiate the Hausa, Igbo, and Yoruba singers (NTL4 2004). Some performers characterise other ethnicities such as the *Waffi*, the 'Calabar', and the Bini person. In each rendition, humourists strive to elicit registers, like *nna* for the Igbo, *Osanobua* for the Bini, *mbok* for the 'Calabar', and *kai* and *shege* for the Hausa. Comics like MC Tagwaye, Aboki 4 Christ, and Holy Mallam have more sustained depictions of the Hausa ethnic group. Some others imitate Indian, Japanese, and other foreign accents, while jokesters like Helen Paul make voice impressions of a loquacious young child, known as Tatafo, running commentary on social life from an impressionable young child's perspective.

Ali Baba uses Hausa 'accent' to characterise a gateman to Dan Etete, a one-time influential politician from southern Nigeria, who he claims had a lion in his house in Port Harcourt. According to the comedian, Etete returned home one evening and found the door to the lion's cage open. The gateman's response for this, on his boss's enquiry, given with stereotypical inflexions and body action, catalyses the entire gamut of beliefs about the Hausa person's *laissez-faire* attitude to life (Laugh Angle 2017). Elsewhere he performs impressions of how Yoruba, Hausa, Igbo, and Warri men respond when someone asks them what the time is. Specifically, according to his narrative, the Hausa man's response would be 'about pour,' whether the time is 'to four' or 'after four.'[8] To him, everything is 'about.' The Warri boy would say: 'Dem de craze. Na Rolex na!' accompanied by gleeful arrogance[9] (De-9ja Music Ent 2017c). In the Yoruba and Igbo examples, he code-switches into the respective languages. Towards the end of the same event, he narrates his encounter with former President Obasanjo, where he (Ali Baba) was invited to an event on Obasanjo's recommendation. He claims that after introducing the president, the latter walked up to him to ask for his share of the appearance fee he (Ali Baba) has been paid. In his replication of how he introduced the president, Ali Baba switched to a different accent, a more officious way of speaking which is not essentially *foné*. He signals this transition by calling the audience's attention to what he referred to as 'the voice', with which he does MC work. It is worthy of note that a substantial part of this performance, held in a Lagos church, is done in standard English, making it one of the few events where comedians code-switch. In more regular situations, comedians use Nigerian Pidgin English primarily between standard and pidgin English and other indigenous languages, depending on the humourist's capabilities. Most importantly, he switches speech mannerisms, some of which amount to a change in accent, throughout his set.

One component of *foné* is 'blowing grammar,' described by Mensah as 'the ability to impress people with high sounding English words [...] without the ability to solve simple practical problems' (2011, 222). It is instructive that in Nigeria, speaking *foné* and 'blowing grammar' often empower individuals because of the impression of knowledgeability they confer on the speaker. However, both can be ridiculed within stand-up acts and portrayed as fake, unimpressionable, and ludicrous. Most Nigerian humourists have little or no talent for using various accents, perhaps because they are largely monolingual. Many play one- or two-character stock persona or imitate a wide range of personalities within their narratives to augment this shortcoming. Polyglots are better at accent imitation, like Chigul, who speaks a couple of Nigerian languages and two European languages apart from English. Her *Chigul Entertains* has the most diverse use of accent impressions in mainstream practice in Nigeria. Chigul's characteristic narrative voice is that of a partially educated Igbo lady trying to impress the audience with a bad imitation of the British accent. Within the context of this accent, she uses words like 'Amrika' (America), 'makeeti' (market), 'seelf' (self), among others, and she gets the audience to repeat after her, thus highlighting their ludicrousness (FlipTV 2016). She creates affinity with the audience by setting out a call-and-response, asking in a thickly accented voice, 'You get it?' with a heavy emphasis on the consonants, and the audience responds, in the same tone, 'Yeah!' Her accent is identifiably Igbo, with sprinklings of English language terms which Chigul uses to impress. She has other laughter evocation techniques, but 'You get it!' has become a trademark for her performances. Due to its overabundant use, audiences endeavour to respond with the same Igbo accent for which she is known. Given that accent is one of the many speech mannerisms within performed jokes that one cannot easily transcribe in a meaningful manner, it is impossible to write down the texture, tone, and quality of accents. However, audiences are knowledgeable, especially in recognising accents and understanding the several ends to which comedians put them.

Comedians deploy *foné* towards meaning ends. Mention has been made of AY's imitations of two evangelical pastors: one speaks *foné*, and the second 'blows grammar.' He also transposes recognisable speech mannerisms of the preachers and other celebrities he mimics into situations that are at variance with their usual selves, like making them run football commentary (NTL11 2007) and characterising Pastor Oyakhilome and the musician D'Banj, as policemen at a checkpoint (NTL19 n.d.). Okotie uses 'big grammar' to talk about his political ambitions within the context of live football commentary, claiming afterwards that his congregation often comes to church with dictionaries and Bibles, in that order, because they will need to find the meanings of the unfamiliar English words their pastor uses. Oyakhilome, on the other hand, is presented as a *foné* speaker, and D'Banj is recognised in AY's narrative by the use of the lyrics of his popular song tracks. AY mimics each of the duo, stopping commuters, searching their vehicles, and querying passengers. Elsewhere, he imposes Tuface's non-western accent on Pastor Oyakhilome, asking a childless woman who is looking for a miracle baby to switch on her Bluetooth and take children while simultaneously moving his waist in a sexually suggestive manner[10] (NTL20 n.d.). There is yet another of AY's contrast of *foné* or 'blowing grammar' and local accent/ low diction English language renditions in gigs where he intermingles imitations of these other preachers and that of Prophet T. B. Joshua who speaks differently from them. Within these representations, wide-ranging speech mannerisms easily yield themselves to humour when brought to the stand-up stage, and AY greatly exploits these qualities. Before moving his renditions away from imitations of these men, in recent times, AY developed a reputation for not just mimicking them but also for transposing them into situations that are at variance with their real-life activities.

There are two narratives by Koffi that show interesting ways ethnic accents and *foné* are used without giving many details about who the characters are:

KOFFI: Has Mopol slapped anybody here before? You know there's a difference between police and Mopol. A teacher was asking some kids.

TEACHER: What's the difference between the regular policeman and the mobile policeman?

KOFFI: (*flails free hand in imitation of* ajebo *gesture.* Foné *is engaged, mixed with a child's voice*) Smart kids from VGC ...[11]

KID: The answer is their uniform. The regular policeman wears black, black, black, black, black (*touches shirt, trousers, shoes, cap indicating pieces of clothing that are black*) as though he is mourning his salary. But, but the mobile policeman wears green, green beret, green khaki (*touching his head and his right leg*).

TEACHER: Put your hands together for him.'

KOFFI: One small boy wey God help 'im papa e don go VGC. Na from AJ 'im grow. With annoyance ... [One little boy that

	God recently prospered his father that the family moved to VGC. He grew up at AJ]
BOY:	Teasher, it's a lie! (*audience laughter*) The difference between regular police and Mopol is the slap' (*shows his palm to the audience; audience laughter*).
KOFFI:	He said …
BOY:	When regular police comes to meet you, you are in the process of the offence. He will warn you.
POLICE:	Oga, don't do this. If you do that next time, I will slap you. [Sir, do not do that …]
KOFFI:	But Mopol, e no concern am o! Na you and your guy Efe, na 'im get *gbege*. Wey una de provoke, na 'im 'e go just show from nowhere … [But the Mopol has no business in the matter. It is just you and your friend, Efe, who are quarrelling over an issue. Both of you are angry, and that is how he appeared from nowhere …]
MOPOL:	(*Hausa accent*) Kai, chai (*concurrently kicks and slaps*) *Shege*! *Dan bura uba*! I don slap me before?' (*audience laughter*). [*Hausa exclamations and expletive*. Have you been slapped before?] (Naija Live Comedy 2012)

This first part of the narrative is given solely by Koffi. I have used character names to make the voice transitions more evident. The name, KOFFI, characterises the narrative voice, which code-switches from standard English to its pidgin variant, and back. TEACHER is named once and then differentiated in the two places she is enlisted with a subtle *foné*, separate from the 'smart kids from VGC.' The use of *foné* here, coupled with the location marker, VGC (Victoria Garden City), a prestigious suburb of Lagos, accentuates the depicted personality. The narrative then moves to BOY, whose father recently became so privileged that the family moved from Ajegunle, a Lagos ghetto, to VGC. This character gets a local accent but spoken in standard English. Rather than 'teacher,' he says 'Teasher,' which is an instance of mother-tongue interference experienced by a couple of Nigerian ethnic groups. His tone is less polished, harsher, and quite confrontational. His Mopol (mobile police) experience is entirely different from that of the child who spoke before him. The reason for that is subtly relayed by Koffi's mention that his family had recently moved to VGC from AJ. Then, Koffi brings in another ethnicity, the *Waffi*, through the name Efe and the accent he uses here. The Mopol, who enters to intervene in the quarrel between the Warri boy and his friend, Efe, has an unmistakable Hausa accent. No question asked, no mediation attempted, Mopol goes into kicking and slapping the two friends, asking him, 'I don slap me before?'[12]

Koffi continues into the adjoining narrative maintaining both the Mopol theme and the Hausa accent. It is truly fascinating seeing how he weaves in and out of different personalities without marking them out with names and explications, but merely by using appropriate accents. The following excerpt continues from the preceding without any break:

KOFFI:	On Ozumba Mbadiwe here, three months ago, and you know they love *koboko* very well, MOPOL? So, some of these boys selling in traffic, Gala, CD, pirated things, was selling *koboko*.[13] So, from nowhere, the MOPOLs parked. They just hailed the guy.
MOPOL:	(*raises his hand to indicate how they did that*), Kwobokwo, kwom! [*Koboko*, come!]
KOFFI:	The guy thought that he has seen a durable market, na 'im him jog, happy. [… that was how he jogged, happy]
KOBOKO:	Hey, I don hammer today. Hei! [I am going to make huge money today]
MOPOL:	Kwobokwo, come. How much be dis ya kwobokwo? [*Koboko*, come. How much is your *koboko*?]
KOBOKO:	One thousand naira, sir.
MOPOL:	Kai, one thousand? Dis kwobokwo wey be like de horse no die beta? (*audience laughter*). How much last? [*exclamation*, one thousand naira? Is that the price for this *koboko* that looks as if the horse from which it was made did not die well?]
KOBOKO:	Okay, oga pay five hundred. [All right sir, you can pay five hundred naira]
MOPOL:	Five hundred? Okay, where I go test the kwobokwo? [Five hundred? Okay, where can I test if the *koboko* works]
KOBOKO:	(*Walking away in fear*) Ah-ah! Oga, when you reach house, you test the *koboko* na! (*audience laughter*). [*exclamation*. Sir, when you get home, you can test your *koboko*]
KOFFI:	From nowhere, *shaa* (*imitates the sound of the whipping, reacts accordingly too*).
MOPOL:	I say how much last …? [I am saying, what is the last price]
KOBOKO:	Oga, pay three hundred. (*another stroke, reaction*)
MOPOL:	I say, how much last?
KOBOKO:	Oga, pay two-fifty. (*another stroke, reaction*).
MOPOL:	I say, how much last?
KOFFI:	As he was decking de guy, one other guy selling cutlass on

the roadside was laughing (*guffaws, imitates Mopol seeing him suddenly*). [As he was flogging the guy …]

MOPOL: Cutlass, *kwom*. How much be ya own cutlass? [Cutlass, come. How much do you sell your cutlass?]

CUTLASS: (*Cutlass seller places everything on the ground*) Oga, de pick am dere, na free, I no de sell. [Pick anyone from there, they are for free, I don't sell them] (*runs off, audience laughter*) (Naija Live Comedy 2012)

In this second narrative, Koffi reinforces the Hausa accent while also underscoring the rascality of some mobile police officers. He is still consistent with the Hausa accent. Here, the two men selling *koboko* and cutlass, respectively, are presented as street hawkers who mostly speak in Nigerian Pidgin English, frequently without any identifiable accent. The way the cutlass seller puts down his wares and takes to his heels is hilarious, more so, the unsaid suggestion that he must have imagined his cutlass being 'tested' on him the way the Mopol tested the *koboko* on its seller. Koffi's capacity for eliciting laughter through these enactments is implicated in the mishmash of accents, language alternation, and embodied actions. They work together in the narrative to create the right imageries, believability, and authenticity, without which audience laughter would not have been possible. It is pertinent to note how he transits from one character to another through changes in language, accents, speech mannerism, and embodied representations. It then follows that even though Nigerian Pidgin English is the basic language of Nigerian stand-up comedy, humour is also generated through code-switching/mixing, combined with the deployment of accents and body language discussed in the preceding chapter.

Notes

1 See Ndolo 1989, Jowitt 1991, Elugbe and Omamor 1991, Mann 1993, Faraclas 1996, Deuber 2005, Deuber 2006, Gaudio 2011, Dibie and Robert 2018.

2 'Did you say it is a lie? (…) Then, speak French and I will translate it for you.'

3 'Remove your tooth and put it in a pail (metal bucket).'

4 'People do not help onions nowadays. Onions help people.'

5 There is so much to unbundle here in terms of the politics behind the 'onions politics' (as I call it) and the venue of Sam and Song's performance. Based on their comments at this event, it is obvious that the duo was referring to President Buhari and how he has empowered his clans people, the Fulani, in blatant indifference to the plight of other Nigerians. Apostle Suleiman, the church pastor where they enacted this drama, is a known opponent and critic of the president and the notorious, yet-to-be unmasked 'killer herdsmen.'

6 'Who will eat Ofada rice with draw soup?' 'It will not rhyme and will not be delicious.'

7 Basket Mouth easily comes to mind because he has performed extensively in Anglophone Africa, including neighbouring Ghana, South Africa and much of East Africa.

8 'About pour' is 'about four', meaning a few minutes to four o'clock. 'pour' is an example of the Hausa speakers' interchange of the sound /f/ with /p/.

9 'They are crazy. It is a Rolex.' 'Dem de craze' is a highfalutin pidgin English expression with which individuals express consternation and disbelief.

10 Here, AY uses speech properties to impose Tuface's notoriety as a philanderer on a charismatic preacher, thus imaginatively creating a stupendously comical character: an Oyakhilome speaking like Tuface and vice versa. Oyakhilome's *foné* is legendary. He is one of the foremost evangelical preachers to develop a reputation on his 'oyibo' looks, which others have tried to copy so unsuccessfully. On the other hand, Tuface is equally successful in the music industry, with little or no pretentiousness to his personality. He is regarded as a core streetwise person who climbed to national acclaim for his diligence and talent. However, he is often regarded as a poster boy for sexual promiscuity for having children from different women.

11 'Ajebo' is short for 'Aje-butter' [someone who eats (with) butter]. It is originally a Yoruba expression now subsumed in pidgin English, and the closest English equivalent is 'someone born with a silver spoon in his/her mouth. The opposite is Aje-pako. 'Pako' (chewing stick), is here contrasted with 'butter'. One is eating 'butter', another is chewing stick: used to depict living in wealth and in penury, respectively.

12 Within Hausa language interferences in English expressions, 'you' is often replaced with 'me'. So ordinarily, the question should be, 'Have you been slapped before?' or in pidgin, 'Dem don slap you before?'

13 'Koboko' is Hausa term for a type of whip made from horse hide or that of other animals, usually long and twisted, and sometimes with two or more strands. It was a favourite of the military and Mopol (a militarised police unit) especially during Nigeria's long years of military rule. The term is widely used across Nigeria and has become part of the pidgin English lexicon.

6

Audiences, venues and events

Audiences

The Nigerian stand-up audience is categorised into two: live spectators that throng to performances and mediatised consumers. Live audiences gain the initial experience of the performance and access the raw dynamics of being present and seeing events as they unfold. Mediatised ones only see the portions of recorded live events that film editors allow them to access. This book has concentrated on the second group for two significant reasons. First, the video formats of these shows are quite readily available, which means that more Nigerians have access to them than to live shows. And second, comedians have become more renowned through recorded performances (which are disseminated widely through online mediums) than live shows, often staged in Lagos or Abuja, with a limited audience in attendance. Nevertheless, live audiences to date have been quite varied, including front-row spectators comprising special invitees and others who can afford the rather steep entrance fees. One ingenious means that events organisers have devised to generate income from the audience is that they now now provide expensive group tables where individuals who want to be together can sit at one table. The cost of such luxuries has moved from around fifty thousand naira in the mid-2000s to tens of millions naira in 2019 and early 2020 before the Corona pandemic lock-down.[1] They are often booked in advance and are the preferred sitting positions of major patrons and sponsors. Apart from the tables, there are positions for VVIPs and VIPs, offered at various steep prices. While campaigning to become the governor of Lagos State, Raji Fashola attended *Basket Mouth Uncensored 2*. At other shows, attendees range from politicians to film stars and captains of industry to leaders in Nigeria's entertainment industry. Attracting influential clients with deep pockets is an excellent source of funding for stand-up comedy. Promoters have been sufficiently innovative to provide a range of seating arrangements with varying pricing to cater to the tastes of different classes of people. By doing this, live stand-up comedy has been made attractive to socialites and those who can afford to pay entrance fees. For others, who cannot attend because they live too far away or for whatever other reason, the recorded versions are a sufficient experiential proxy for the performance.

The presence of a live audience gives stand-up comedy one of its most significant affinities with theatre. Just as a theatre audience endorses the authenticity of the theatrical experience, stand-up spectators determine the pulse of every performance since its response or lack thereof determines the rate and strength of delivery. Within Nigerian stand-up, there is extensive use of theatre devices and technology to enhance performer-audience interactions. The functional and mutual exchanges between humourists and their audiences are desirable because the progression to humour starts from jokesters' activation of the baseline of knowledge common between them and their audiences. Where such shared cultural cognitions do not exist, it behoves the comedian to find commonplace subjects to predicate their jokes. It is on such pedestals that the familiarity which enhances plausibility is engaged. Therefore, by their nature, familiarity with the subject is essential for both the humourist and the receiver(s) because jokes work primarily with incongruities and distortion of the expected. As such, spectators need to be conversant with the nominal version of a specific context before its alteration can amuse them. Essentially,

> (t)he [joke]teller thereby relies on the [audience] for approval-through-laughter, and not merely for psychical release. The joke listener's involvement in the joke act also includes an ego investment dependent on risk, because the surprise element of the joke structure implies a relational vulnerability. The joke listener allows her/himself to be duped by the joke teller, to play the fool; in order to participate in the surprise of the joke punchline. The [audience] must trust the teller to not exploit the assumed gullibility that operates within the joking relationship. At the same time, the joke listener is complimented by the 'offer' of the joke and, as listener, is elevated to the level of judge. If the joke act is successful, the joke listener benefits by the immediate gratification of entertainment. (Leveen 1996, 31–32)

Outside of this form of connection between comedians and their audiences, the full extent of a joke's risibility may not be attained. Put more succinctly, when comedians tap 'into popular culture … to tell a joke' they 'wager that their audience will also hold some knowledge of the tangential cultural references that they call upon,' and when 'the audience does not understand the reference … the joke will be ineffective' (Blank 2016, 186).

Contextual devices that enhance audience-performer interactions within stand-up enactments also include stage set, lighting, auditorium-stage relations, and the way comedians appear. In many ways, these have a direct bearing on how gags are delivered and received because they 'mark the stand-up comedy experience as separate from informal joking, […] more than the stringing together of a series of jokes, […placing] it within a particular social frame' (Rutter 1997, 69). Audience presence and participation (in the production of its laughter) deepen live stand-up gigs. Even in less obvious situations, stand-up performers depend almost entirely on audience response to gauge the best way of delivering every succeeding line of their set. Unlike storytelling, where the narrator needs to provide expansive details, stand-up comedy requires brevity and minimal narration, while the audience fills in the parts left out by comedians. As such, audiences are co-performers who complement the acts of jokesters by recourse to their socio-cultural experiences. There is no dormant audience in stand-up shows because its response or repudiation determines the rate, tone, and intensity of joke delivery. Furthermore, extant anthropological theories on joking relationships underscore the socio-cultural milieu within which potentially offensive subjects are rendered humorous and inoffensive.[2] Radcliffe-Brown (1940) discusses how specific social conditions and relationships enable the exchange of insults bereft of recourse to offence-taking while the duo of Gluckman (1963) and Turner (1969) concern themselves with differing modes of momentary inversion of power relations in traditional societies, which engender questioning of the *status quo*. This condition empowers comedians, with other community members' permission, to momentarily assume authority over others. Consequently, the fundamental enabling component of performer-audience interaction is the existence of an unwritten/informal licence that allows comedians to broach taboo subjects, and insult and castigate individuals and institutions, within the bounds of culturally permissible deviations, without fear of offence or backlash.

Like Blank's view above, John Limon (2000) holds that laughter is the sole purpose of stand-up comedy, and more importantly, that laughter, once given, cannot be withdrawn. Post-production reviews, criticism, and individual afterthoughts may not retroactively correct responses given on the spot. Hence, once the audience laughs, it is usually taken for granted that whatever the comedian had said is funny, at least within the subsisting circumstances of the performance. Audience appreciation or otherwise is instantaneous as spectators do not need to wait till the end of the performance to know whether they have understood specific jokes. Herein lies stand-up comedy's uniqueness: the audience does not rely on post-mortem evaluations to make sense of presentations but on instant evaluation. Acceptance and endorsement are shown through giving or withholding laughter. Michael Billig refers to the repudiation of a joke, exemplified by the audience's refusal to laugh, as 'the rhetorical opposite of laughter,' named 'unlaughter' (2005, 177). Thus, unlaughter is an indication that the audience is powerful in the moment of the performance because, by its response, the comic is forced to make appropriate changes to gain the desired objectives. Other forms of elation accompany laughter – clapping, whistling, standing ovations, and catcalls; unlaughter comes with its acts of rejection ranging from disruptive noise to throwing stuff at the performer to get him or her off the stage. It is for this purpose that performer-audience interaction is at the centre of stand-up art. Therefore, when laughter comes, the comedian relaxes and receives additional impetus to continue. However, when it is withheld, failure is inevitable, and the more the comedian persists in trying to force the audience to understand the joke, the more he or she aggravates the situation. Consequently, when a joke fails at the first punchline, professionalism demands that the comedian changes track and moves to another narrative to save him- or herself from embarrassment.

It is not easy to obtain a recorded example of embarrassing situations on the Nigerian mainstream stand-up stage because videos are only released after being thoroughly edited. However, there are two joke examples from which one can be acquainted with how such situations may arise. The first is a narrative from I Go Dye, where he describes a wet-behind-the-ears comedian whose set failed dismally because he smoked marijuana before going on stage. For the conflicting inspirations going on in his head concurrently, he ended up making a fool of himself and left the stage shamefaced (NTL19 n.d.). Basket Mouth tells a similar story, but in his version, the said comedian is uninformed about how best to make jokes work, not that he was high on marijuana (BMU2 2007). In each of these examples, the comedian failed because he could not create a workable rapport with his audience. Creating a working rapport with the audience is something that comedians handle differently. Basket Mouth and others like him rarely allow audiences the opportunity to heckle them. There are yet others such as I Go Dye who induce responses from the audience with short call-and-response words like 'Area' and Chigul's 'You get it!' However, comedians like Klint da Drunk build their entire stand-up sets around audience responses.

Klint usually ensnares his audience by asking them questions that elicit either specific or a range of answers to which he has prepared reactions. He then builds his subsequent acts on such responses, typically catching the audience unawares. Unlike most comedians, he uses direct insults to evoke laughter, specifically deploying *yabbing* and *wording* in inventive ways. In the *Nite of a Thousand Laughs* event in Kaduna mentioned previously, Opa Williams arranges a raffle draw to increase ticket sales. One of Klint's opening statements at the event is, 'How many of you came to win something? Raise your hands.' A good number of people in the audience, perhaps believing he will be announcing the winners and give out prizes for the raffle, raise their hands. Instead, he says, 'So you people don't have TV at this age?' As soon as Klint says this, some members of the audience try to walk back what they said, making varying statements of denial, thereby falling into another of his numerous traps. He picks on an individual who said, 'Don't mind them!', and fires a retort in the direction of that voice,

> This man that said, 'Don't mind them'… you bought four tickets for one person. (*pause*). This man that just spoke, I don't understand his lifestyle. The other day, he went to his office with his towel […]. It takes him five minutes to start to think. (NTL11 2007)

This excerpt is a typical practice in *wording*: you say something, the opponent comments, then you make the person see the folly in what has been said, the individual attempts to walk it back, and then comes the main hit, the punchline. This man wanted to make others look foolish by saying, 'Don't mind them!' at once, attempting to be on the side of the joker and making all others look foolish for their choices. Then, the humourist he thinks is on his side hits him unexpectedly hard to amuse those he had mocked earlier. The joke works this way, and it goes round because no one is spared the ridicule, including the performer. Already, Klint has presented himself as a drunk person, very unsteady on his feet, and everything he says becomes permissible and humorous. In another event, Klint's handling of the audience shows a rush of negative emotions as he misreads what someone in the audience says. At first, he thinks the person said, 'You are crazy,' to which he replies without prompting: 'And you paid to come and watch me?' Then, while tongue lashing the speaker, he hears this person repeating himself more clearly now, saying 'You are impersonating.' At this point, Klint checks himself and makes a conciliatory comment in a bid to mitigate his earlier attack on this member of the audience. This individual's comment is a reference to Klint's costume on that occasion because he came on stage dressed in a police uniform (NTL9 2006). Klint's initial response here indicates that comedians are not immune to offence-taking themselves. This example is also proof that much of Klint's stage act is in reaction to audience responses, seen also in another set where someone makes an off-handed comment that he (Klint) is making a fool of himself, and Klint replies, 'You paid to come and watch me make a fool of myself. What does that make you?' (NML n.d.). In yet another example, he throws a massive barb back at another heckler: 'You are *losing* hair? At this age? You think it is evidence of riches? It is lack of vitamins. When was the last time you ate pawpaw?' (NTL4 2004).

Nevertheless, not all of Klint's performances are rooted in direct insults and audience abuse. For example, in a performance in Ghana, he hoodwinks the audience into believing he is insulting them. As he walks onto the stage on being introduced by the MC, Klint says loudly: 'You are very stupid! You know that you are a very foolish person!' Embarrassed, the MC tries to laugh off the insult as the audience watches in bated breath. As the MC is about to hand the stage over to him, Klint turns to him and says: 'I was on the phone, what were you saying?' before removing the small Bluetooth speaker in his right ear, which was out of the MC's view. Of course, he feigns ignorance of the MC's discomfiture at his earlier statements. The MC could not help but shout: 'Ah! You got me there!' Klint then tells him and the audience that such devices make people look mad and foolish in the street (Anitamuleya 2010). In this instance, Klint lures the MC and the audience into believing that he is insulting everyone but eventually uses the situation to create impressions of how invisible earphones frame people in public. In this event, he does not rail insults but does song renditions, another speciality of his, within which he also encourages the audience to sing along with him.

For his part, I Go Dye does more observational comedy, drawing the audience into acquiescence to the things he says. He dwells on the ordinary aspects of reality for the evocation of laughter. Even while being overtly offensive, especially in his castigation of femininity, I Go Dye observes his audience to know when to pull the brakes and then divert to ridiculing men. He says in one instance that women are uglier than men because when they shave their heads like men do and remove all their wigs, their heads will reveal the true ugliness of some of them. Specifically, he says that some heads will be like bicycle seats, others like the map of Africa, and if rain falls on some, water will not run off their skulls (NTL16 n.d.). Elsewhere, he talks about musicians, saying that when American performers like R. Kelly throw singlets into the audience area, people will rush to grab them. However, in Nigeria, D'Banj can throw in his boxers, and the audience will not mind, but if Tuface does that, girls will take to their heels because the boxers can get them pregnant (NTL19 n.d.). It is noteworthy that this set was performed before R. Kelly's conviction in September 2021 for sexual crimes against minors. These jokes are part of the repertoire of renditions in which the performer courts the audience's understanding for the narratives to make their greatest impact. I Go Dye's facial expression shows this deference to the audience. The smile playing at the sides of his lips when broaching subjects on the borderline of permissibility and offence indicates his awareness of the unsettling atmosphere and feelings engendered. More importantly, it is an indication of acknowledging the supremacy of the audience in both the co-production and appreciation of humour within his performances.

Live audiences, for several reasons, are not likely to activate unlaughter in most Nigerian stand-up comedy situations. First, there is very little time for such critical appraisal of what comics say for those who are physically present because they would not want to lose the next joke while dwelling on the preceding one. It is a different kettle of fish for audiences who are viewing recorded versions because they have more time for multifarious analyses and post-mortem evaluations. This is the primary reason why live audiences most likely find almost all jokes funny, so long as others are laughing. The second is the sense and feeling of community that arises within the performance environment. People feel like they belong together, especially when the performer knows how to work this form of unity into their renditions. The third reason is that most mainstream comedians in Nigerian have attained celebrity status, and some of them evoke laughter even before the first jokes are presented. Some people pay for shows just to see specific jokesters perform. In this context, laughter, especially the initial, could be due to an appreciation of the humourist's oeuvre and not necessarily because of what he or she has just said.

Furthermore, one can add three other significant reasons for the continued absence of unlaughter in mainstream practice. The first of these is that front row seats/tables are the most expensive positions and are mainly reserved for patrons, other comedians, Nollywood film stars, and elites who are unlikely to make a scene in public by showing disapproval for a joke. In addition, event organisers reserve some of these seats/tables for gratis allocation to special guests, whom they hope can use these front seat/table positions to influence the way other people in the auditorium respond to joke renditions. The next is that Nigerians are accustomed to the traditions of *wording* and *yabbing*, within which it is improper to take offence when ridiculed or satirised. As such, individuals join in the laughter even when they find what has been said to be highly offensive. Consequently, the response of the majority (or the more privileged members of the audience, seated at the front) ends up being that of the rest of the people present. The comedian, Destalker says this occasionally in his set:

> If you know say de thing wey I de say de touch you, mek you follow others de laugh o, mek dem no think say na you I de talk about![3]

Then the final reason is that comedians always fashion their jokes in ways that put them on the side of their immediate audience. In this way, they create a form of in-group affinities with sections of the audience before presenting specific jokes. For instance, comedians often ask for specific groups to identify themselves if they are in the audience. In the Nigerian situation, when the narrative is about Warri people, the humourist often starts the set by shouting, 'Area', and when it is about Igbos, he or she shouts something like, 'Igbo *kwenu*!' These are ways of self-identification with the group that is about to be discussed. From this posture, performers play down possible offensive aspects of what is coming next by either calling the joke character a friend or making the joke about themselves. The aim is to find a connection, no matter how remote, that ties the jokester with what he or she is about to say. These methods of self-identification have worked very well in Nigerian stand-up comedy.

Nevertheless, some people in the audience might feel offended by one bad joke or the other, but the performer aims to keep the number of this group to the barest minimum. It is safe to say that the general Nigerian live audience is still very forgiving, and this disposition comes from the harsh reality of living in a country where everything is already complicated and challenging. The permissiveness of Nigerian audiences does not come from ignorance of what the limits of humour or political correctness should be; it is rather a choice to laugh despite the difficulties that people encounter in every area of their daily lives. Stand-up comedy provides an avenue for laughter, and in the 'suffering and smiling' mode of the Fela Anikulapo-Kuti era, people take their time to laugh. By being an avenue for poking fun at power, stand-up comedy has provided Nigerians with latitude for keeping their sanity and assuring themselves that despite the deceptions and lies from politicians, they still have their wits. As such, people are in no way hoodwinked by the shenanigans of corrupt politicians. Regrettably, it is due to this form of permissiveness and tendency to easily forgive that politically incorrect renditions concerning women and minorities persist.

Venues

Performer-audience interaction further concerns itself with the size, distance, and relative position of the stage to the auditorium, where the audience is seated. It entails explicitly taking cognisance of the types of stage used, the invisibility or visibility of the stage set, whether the performer makes any use of the audience area, and how all these affect joke renditions. The performance venue's physical features often determine relationships between the stage and the auditorium, directly influencing how comedians communicate with audiences and vice versa. For Nigerian stand-up art, the choice of performance venues at prestigious centres in different cities has increased the possibilities of having a wealthier and more influential clientele. The relevance of these venues to the stand-up event is that they are naturally the preferred hangout spots for the elite, where they feel safe enough to be after work hours. Undoubtedly, the relative safety of these locations has aided event managers to circumvent the challenges of the lack of security and unsafe streets at night, which are some of the reasons adduced for empty theatres in the late 1980s. By moving to posh areas where security is ordinarily tight, attendees are assured that their lives and property are secure throughout the event and that they can easily get to their homes or find suitable accommodation in the same vicinity afterwards.

Various stage patterns have been used, with the proscenium-thrust variant the most frequent, perhaps due to the need to create greater rapport between the performers and audiences. The proscenium setting is used often for stand-up gigs because it gives everyone in the audience a good view since comedians need to focus only on one direction instead of moving to the various stage areas so that all sections of the audience can see them face on. Some shows like Bunmi Davies' *Stand-up Nigeria* consistently use arena staging where jokesters perform inside a boxing-ring kind of stage. This form of staging, where the performer needs to turn to different sides of the auditorium, is not favoured since comedians need to keep audiences in focus to determine how best to deliver succeeding jokes, especially in terms of the rate of delivery and timing. Comedians' preference for the proscenium stage is largely based on the fact that they use facial expressions and not only words. As such, spectators need an uninterrupted view of their faces for the entire duration of the enactment. For this reason, most jokesters stand as close to the audience as possible, parallel to the footlights, no matter the stage used.

Jokesters rarely use the entire stage since joke performance is a one-person show and expansive stage movements could be more distracting than functional. Additionally, rather than use upstage spaces, some comedians prefer downstage positions and often enter the audience area to gain greater access to specific individuals in the auditorium. AY is an excellent example, especially when he is playing the role of Prophet AY. In his maiden *AY Live Show* in the UK, he comes on stage with the Nollywood duo Chinedu Ikedieze and Osita Iheme (Aki and Pawpaw) and the comedian Elenu as his acolytes and interpreter. He jumps down from the stage after a frenzied ritualised dance to heavy drumming and picks on members of the audience for his satiric 'prophecies'. Compared to a similar Lagos performance, AY does not go into the auditorium but stands on the stage and names both individuals present in that audience and others who are not but are well-known. For instance, he mentions Aliko Dangote, saying: 'The Lord says that you have been complaining for a long time about your grasses [referring to the man's expansive estate]. The Lord says that you should give the man of God your grasses!' (AYL5 n.d.). As such, his going into the auditorium for the London event is an ingenious way of making up for the knowledge gap between local and diaspora audiences. While still on stage, AY calls out 'Segun', asking him to stop sleeping in train stations and head home if London does not favour him. Though he refers to no one in particular, the audience finds this funny because it is a sarcastic commentary on Africans who live abroad, even when they do not have any meaningful means of sustenance. The only person he acknowledges directly in the audience is the Nigerian footballer, Osaze Odemwingie, whom he jocularly warns to be careful with 'London women' to avoid repeating the mistake he made in Russia. He then turns to another lady and tells her that the Lord says she should 'loose' (sic) her weave-on and let it go! (AYL London). If AY had done these from the stage, the impact would have been different because standing there and pointing out targets in the audience without calling their names would not be as effective as his coming down and putting his hands on their heads. What is immediately apparent here is that the use of audience space in Nigeria's stand-up comedy is often restricted to moments when it becomes necessary.

Stages are meant to elevate performers above the auditorium floor as a means of emphasising them. Most event organisers use staging platforms available at performance venues, sometimes with little adjustments. There is no dedicated performance space and no specialised physical requirements for stand-up performances. As such, comedians decide how best to use the stage available to them for their artistic goals. In performer-organised presentations like the *AY Live Shows* and *Basket Mouth Uncensored*, there is often no deliberate attempt to change the stage. Even in an outdoor event like *AY Live 7*, held in Port Harcourt, where the stage is constructed, it is just a simple platform for elevating performers. In this gig, AY moves into the audience to enhance his interaction with it. However, for the initial three series of *Basket Mouth Uncensored*, proscenium-thrust stage is used, though the arm projecting into the auditorium does not extend far enough into the audience seating area to be of much effect. Such extensions help performers be closer to the audience and remain elevated, unlike when they must come down from the stage to get closer. The preference for a sparse stage set aims at not situating the performer in a fixed environment due to the fluidity of themes, locations, and situations within individual routines. Considering that humourists are going on stage in quick succession, it would be impractical to have a stage set that caters to individual performers and their specific jokes. Since there are no directors and group rehearsals (at least, to public knowledge), the physical contexts of intended joke narratives to be enacted are known only to the comedians. Furthermore, many stand-up renditions are generated from interactions with audiences and are therefore not scripted. These aspects of performances come from spur-of-the-moment decisions made by comedians in choosing their cadences of delivery.

A substantial part of every rendition is given to speech, with minimal facial expressions and gestures. For artists who do not go into serious embodied actions, comedy is specifically a stand-up affair, and the appropriate use of the microphone is paramount. Hence, a microphone is a primary set requirement. Nigerian practice has mostly dispensed with the microphone stand. Whether this is for cost-cutting purposes or another reason is unclear. However, what is certain is that the absence of stands must aid stage mobility, ensuring that comedians can move freely from one part of the stage to another and into the audience area as required. The absence of microphone stands too enables the liberty to use more elaborate gestures as well as other body and spatial movements for emphasis and appropriate (re)presentation of jokes. Most shows have their titles emblazoned on a banner placed on the wall behind performers for the backdrop. In recent times, large screen projectors are increasingly being used to create altering montages while comedians perform. AY uses these screens, fusing stage and video images in seamless transitions to stage action. Thus, performance venues have become better organised in acoustics and visuals, mostly deploying multimedia means, especially sound effects, song cues, screen projection, and lighting.

Scene design in Nigerian stand-up productions is increasingly becoming innovative, with significant improvements in recent shows. AY's events, for instance, have shown great advancements in scenic properties ranging from animated backdrops on projector screens to sometimes futuristic three-dimensional stage décor. There are minimal stage props, feedback speakers, and footlights at some venues, making *AY Shows* more theatrical in design than earlier *Nite of a Thousand Laughs*, where regular backdrops bearing the event's name were used. In recent shows, disc jockeys (DJs) have been used in place of live bands. For *AY Live* shows, it is always a medley of acts – stand-up routines by various comedians, live song or karaoke performances by popular singers assisted by celebrity DJs, film projections, and choreographed dances by professional troupes. Special effects are achieved through purposeful lighting, sound, and other visual cues such as smoke simulation and the use of red-light gel in creating a surreal atmosphere within which the dance group, D.N.M.T, leads Prophet AY onto the stage. Through interspersion of coloured and bright lights as the stage action moves from dancing to a secular song to trance-like gyrations in tune with the succeeding sombre religious hymnal, and back again; a sense of alternation between the spiritual and the banal is successfully created on stage with the aid of lighting and sound effects (AYL5 n.d.).

Commonly, there is general lighting for both the stage and the auditorium, and then more intense lighting for the stage for visibility and emphasis of performers. Keeping the audience area lit enhances performer-audience interaction because comics can see the ways people in the audience respond to their jokes. Unlike in the early days, the mid-1990s specifically, when matinees were preferred to save costs and ensure that people would attend, present-day performances are held at night and mostly indoors. With the growth of night shows came the demand for better lighting. There have been instances of poor lighting at some point, like *AY Live 7* held in Port Harcourt and *Basket Mouth Uncensored 1*. In these recorded versions, one encounters low visibility, and uncoordinated follow spots, which leaves sections of the stage in semi-darkness even when performers in great need of illumination are standing there. Since then, there have been improvements on all fronts for both AY and Basket Mouth shows. The *AY Live Invasion* series in Abuja and Lagos exhibit AY's staging capabilities as shown in innovative lighting, animated backdrops, and enlivened staging. The *Basket Mouth Uncensored* series and other brands produced by the comedian have also significantly improved in staging, video recording, and presentation techniques. These advancements in both production and post-production packaging of events are now evident in most mainstream recorded stand-up comedy packages disseminated online in recent times. It is noteworthy that comedians in several other cities are floating their events, taking mainstream performances to places they have not been hosted before.

All events are produced with an eye on distributing them, on VCDs and DVDs, and more recently through satellite television and online media networks . There are professional film crews, complete with cranes and multiple camera positions around the performance venue. Special care is also taken with sound capturing, ensuring that it is recorded with as little interference as possible. AY gives an interesting example of the use of sound cues in one of his events where he tells the audience that if they had not 'shouted' in acclamation of his entry, he would have surprised them by playing recorded applause for himself. He then wonders why Nigerian spectators are often very reserved in their appreciation of artists, noting that if the show were overseas, people would even faint when just seeing their favourite artists, rueing that no one has done that for him. AY asks the DJ for his version of applause, and a tumultuous ovation comes over the studio with the voice of the announcer: 'It's AY!' Then another voice cuts in over the hubbub, in panic, 'Somebody has fainted!' (AYL 2011). The sound is so real and convincing that the live audience gives an equally loud endorsement. At the turn of the 2010s, most productions had better video and sound qualities than previous ones. From earlier efforts, like using a lone camera perspective interspersed with shots from a poorly filmed unsteady camera in the making of *Basket Mouth Uncensored Volume 1*, there are now multi-camera recordings with outstanding audio quality. It is evident that things are different nowadays as almost all shows have since caught up and much of what is distributed on social media has better audio sync and less ambient sound.

Costumes

Costumes are vital in stand-up comedy but are often ignored in favour of the things the comedian chooses to talk about. Although they may not have the same functions in stand-up comedy as in theatre and film, where they characterise the wearers, they are essential, especially for comics who rely on them to instigate specific audience responses. It is for its subterranean usefulness in stand-up art that costume is discussed under this section rather than in the earlier chapters. Like scenic properties, lighting, and sound accompaniments that are quite subtle in their influence on stand-up routines, costumes have a salient but quiet effect on the stage presence of humourists. For Nigerian comedians especially, costumes are deliberately selected to highlight and emphasise performers. It is noteworthy that in the use of costumes, performers do not necessarily dress up to play the different roles that their jokes elicit but to extract as much comicality as possible. As such, there is as yet no extended or characteristic use of cross-dressing and stylised costuming on Nigeria's stand-up comedy stage.[4] What obtains is a general sense of corporate dressing because comedians believe that it is one way they and their business can be taken seriously. AY tells of one experience where he was invited to perform, and while waiting backstage, one of the organisers approached him and asked if he had seen the comedian. He said he was the comedian and the man was surprised because he expected 'a hungry-looking person' but found someone who looked like a business executive (AYL3 n.d.). Consequently, in terms of dressing, Nigerian comedians have imbibed the general Nigerian mentality that 'the way you are dressed is the way you will be addressed.' Having come from a background of denigration of humourists, most performers take special care about the clothes they wear when performing. Even those just starting out in the business often make the effort to wear suits and ties, dressing up as if they are going to business meetings. They believe this will make people not look down on them, especially when they need to charge exorbitant fees for their services.

Basket Mouth does not have a consistent costume style, evidenced in the wide variety of dress he wears on stage, which ranges from the informal to the very formal. In *Basket Mouth Uncensored Volume 3*, he sports a pair of shorts, a T-shirt and long glittering necklaces just like American rap artists. Here, Basket Mouth starts with rap before going over to his comedy routines. In other shows, his costumes have no specific patterns to which any particular purpose can be ascribed. He once allowed his hair to grow into dreadlocks which he shaved off recently. I Go Dye, on the other hand, dresses quite differently, and was referred to by Helen Paul as the best-dressed comedian in Nigeria in the event where she had fiery exchanges with Gordons (Kilarigbo Live 2015). I Go Dye is almost always overdressed and often puts on very outlandish necklaces, bangles, and ornamented waist belts. The first thing that audiences notice about I Go Dye whenever he mounts the stage is what he wears. It is seldom commonplace. For instance, he wore a white shirt, a black waistcoat over the shirt and then a kilt, complete with shoes and stockings (NTL8 n.d.), to an event held in Nigeria and not Scotland where such costumes are familiar. His predilection towards 'dressing to kill' is not in doubt. Even early on in his career in the industry, his clothes were outstanding in their unusualness. He has commented on them, indicating that they are worn to make statements often incorporated into his skits. For example, in one event where he wears a suit different from his black trousers, he seemingly downplays the importance of his choice of clothes by saying,

> The trouser no reach na 'im we sew only the top. All na suit. Even di body sef, I tell tailor mek 'e find pieces do the pocket.[5] (NTL15 2008)

In another event, where he is dressed in a white T-shirt, jeans, and long shiny necklaces, he says that if there are Warri boys in the audience planning to waylay him, they should not bother themselves because the trinkets are fake. He hits one of the ornaments on his microphone for emphasis, saying they are just iron (NTL9 2006). There is yet another instance where he dresses like a militant: a black T-shirt with the picture of a skull on the front, a denim jacket over the shirt, and a red bandana for his head. He also has dark shades across his eyes and a pair of jeans covering his legs (NTL11 2007). On this occasion, he does not say anything about his clothes. However, multiple statements can be deduced from the chosen attire, given that the event happened at the peak of the Niger Delta militants' confrontations with the federal government, and such costumes are known to be common among the militants. Although the precise message that he wishes to convey with his choice of dress is open to debate, his identification with the Niger-Delta area, from which he hails, is unmistakable.

In the 2000s, AY imitated flamboyant Christian clerics, which rubbed off immensely on his dress sense. As a result, it is a kind of character costume that transforms him into the people he is imitating, especially when he must adorn their diction and mannerisms. Moreover, in his shows, AY makes two presentations: a dramatic roleplay of a white-garmented church prophet, followed by the stand-up part. He also cross-dresses at one event where he satirises Genevieve Nnaji's song and makes unsalutary comments about homosexuality (AYL2 2007). Generally, AY's stage apparel is innovative, enhancing his stage presence. In his appearances as Prophet AY, he wears a white flowing gown and cap to match. He gradually eased away from wearing suits and ties for his stand-up roles, starting from an almost indescribable costume he wore to his 2011 event. In this show, he has a blue fitted low neck T-shirt, a waistcoat, and deep blue baggy trousers that almost look like a flowing skirt beneath (AYL 2011). This stage dressing is a sharp contrast to his usual corporate wears in preceding events. To signal that this particular dress is part of his show, AY later infers that his costume responds to people who often try to intimidate others by 'throwing' names of international fashion designers (AYL 2011). Hence, AY overtly incorporates his costumes into his performance: whether dressed in a suit or sporting an outlandish pair of trousers beneath a weightlifters' shirt, he makes his audience pay attention to his clothes. The various components of his apparel also call attention to themselves as part of his comedic acts because they come either in unique colours, sequined and shiny, or as white flowing gowns in which he plays religious roles.

Costuming also forms a significant part of Klint da Drunk's stage acts. He dresses for his part – the persona of a drunkard on stage. Specifically, Klint usually attires himself in a suit, with a shirt underneath, perhaps a tie, and a pair of trousers. These dress components are never worn in the usual fashion; for example, the shirt is often unevenly buttoned, and the suit hangs comically from his body. The trousers are either rolled up on one or both his legs, and he sometimes comes on stage shoeless, though there are occasions when he wears one of what is supposed to be a pair of slippers. He seldom wears anything appropriately, and his appearance often complements his inebriated movements and speech pattern. This is because the way he dresses depicts him as a true drunkard who takes no notice of what he wears to benefit those who have paid to watch him 'make a fool' of himself, like he characteristically says. Therefore, he is very definite and consistent in what he wears to the stage because it helps him define his character. He uses his appearance to make many statements. His entry elicits comments from the audience due to two basic factors. The first is his dress, and the second his gait and posture. In addition to his dress pattern already described above, Klint sometimes has an empty bottle of beer clutched protectively under his armpit, which he is almost always ready to defend so no one can take it away from him. He does look unsteady on his feet as he tells his joke, rolling his eyes and index finger in a seemingly helpless bid to coordinate his thoughts. Essentially, Klint's stage performance is a true-to-life replication of drunkenness enacted as accompaniment to his picking on people and making silly comments about them.

Klint's inebriated appearance is deliberate and, as such, forms part of his stand-up act. He does not aim at any smoothness; neither does he appeal to any gentlemanly disposition. His entry immediately elicits a certain kind of baseness, surreptitiously dismantling all social strictures of decorum and instituting a reign of 'anything goes'. As mentioned previously, a drunken fellow, just like a mad person, is often not considered seriously, and what he or she says is typically dismissed. Taking up this role, for Klint, is like being in a state of unassailability from which he can address society pointedly without fear of censorship or reprisals. Appearance is everything for him because it gives him a mask of permissiveness that other comedians do not have. For instance, where others use the caveat: 'Na joke I de do o' [It's just a joke] to signal jocularity, Klint depends on his dishevelled appearance to do that for him. For example, he is the only Nigerian known to have danced with a president's wife because he asked Obasanjo's wife, Stella, to dance at a state function, and she obliged him. It is this demeanour of his that also made the late former first lady sing his praises at an event (Radiopalmwine 2009).

Nevertheless, by the 2010s, comedians had started gradually discarding suits, ties, and the general sense of corporate dressing. Emergent comedians like Destalker do not dress as though going to a business meeting. In one event, he walks onto the stage in a white shirt, shorts, and trainers. His shirt has a black stripe, sewn in the usual 'safari' design typical in the Niger-Delta area (AY Comedian 2020a). Elsewhere, he wears shorts again and white canvas shoes, but, this time he sports a gold-coloured shirt, with a black design on both the shirt and the shorts (Gold Edge TV 2020). His clothing choices have little to do with his renditions but are chosen to reinforce a casualness that augments his mostly calm, calculated delivery pattern, suffused with wise sayings, which he often attributes to his father. The most regular of them all is the statement, 'Person wey buy poison, and still de wait for change, never make up him mind to die'[6] (AY Comedian 2020a). Destalker also characteristically introduces himself as a 'very funny' comedian. He then says that if any member of the audience cannot laugh at his jokes, that person needs to be taken to 'Synagogue' for prayers.[7] Afterwards, he swears an oath that whatever he is going to say is a lie and that if his statements are similar to what anyone is experiencing, the person would do well to laugh so that their neighbours in the audience would not know that they are currently mired in such situations. Nevertheless, the gradual disappearance of corporate attire has not reduced the exhibition of flamboyant costumes for several performers like Gordons, I Go Dye, AY, and the women, Real Warri Pikin and Helen Paul. The act of wig removal, which Helen Paul always enacts on stage, forms part of her disavowal of needless cosmetic beauty to encourage women to take pride in their bodies and their natural looks.

Distribution

Part of the uniqueness of Nigeria's stand-up art lies in its eclecticism and straddling of different genres. It started out as a stage art, but also, mainly due to the influence of Nollywood, has been recorded and distributed on VCDs/DVDs, and, more recently, on streaming platforms and satellite television. Then, for marketing purposes, in the first decade of its emergence, most events were packaged as variety shows featuring popular musicians and professional dance groups who perform interchangeably with the comedians. In this way, comedy aligned itself with the equally successful Afro-pop music, the other popular art apart from Nollywood for which Nigeria is known. This packaging catered to the preferences of audiences who are more accustomed to mishmash performances than just solo stand-up comedy. Next, stand-up events combined theatre staging devices, on the one hand, and essential film elements (mostly implicit in set arrangement, attention to the dictates of cinematography, and post-production editing), on the other. Though Nigerian stand-up shares several characteristics with live theatre and Nollywood, it is a more contemporaneous with live art where the performer talks about prevailing circumstances without first doing a script, sourcing funds, casting, and rehearsing before going into performance. Thus, it is a relatively cheaper expressive art within which the performer seeks to entertain audiences primarily through the evocation of laughter.

There are live and mediatised audiences for Nigerian stand-up, made up of spectators who throng to performance venues and those who watch recorded VCD or DVD versions, respectively, or on satellite or social media platforms. Each group experiences stand-up differently, but live audiences' experiences are more direct than those of mediatised ones because they (live audiences) are co-creators of jokes with the performers. Nigeria's stand-up comedy has taken a tortuous and rigorous path to arrive at its present height. In its early years, comics merely performed as poorly remunerated MCs at social events. From this humble background, the art form has steadily grown to become one of Nigeria's most lucrative entertainment genres. At inception, practitioners took advantage of its low-budget nature to fill the gap that the country's dearth of live events had created. The industry has followed and mostly stayed close to Nollywood's distribution channels, which has recently moved to internet streaming and social media. This form of dissemination has continued from the VCDs/DVDs eras to present-day satellite television and social media use.

Through these mediums, both stand-up comedy and Nollywood have become widely known in Africa and globally. Since the mid-1990s, when stand-up comedy emerged professionally in Nigeria, events have been increasingly being held during festivities and holidays, and at social, political, and religious gatherings. The emergence of newer events and opportunities for comedians has significantly reduced the monopoly that Opa Williams' *Nite of a Thousand Laughs* had in the 1990s and early 2000s.

Moreover, just like stand-up comedy, Nollywood went through its peculiar challenges. For example, it was roundly criticised for its use of videotapes. At the time, African scholars bemoaned the death of celluloid filmmaking in Nigeria, calling it a tragedy, and referring to Nollywood producers in uncomplimentary ways (Ogunsuyi 1999). Specifically, Abiodun Olayiwola opines that,

> The point is worth stressing that 90 percent of those who straddle the video film industry in Nigeria today have no formal education [...]. They are only involved in a game of trial and error, leading to shoddy productions. Most films are poorly directed because the present practitioners think that all it takes to be a movie director in Nigeria is money and a handful of people. Armed with a camcorder, you are already in the business. Better still, wait until your face appears in a couple of home videos and you will be instantly transformed into a star director. In essence, the actor-producer-director practice of the early pioneers still reigns supreme in Nigeria. The rare combination of talent and training that make a good director is yet to be understood by the Nigerian industry. Present day filmmakers lack the technical know-how needed to direct a film (the same could be said about those working in other parts of the industry). (2007, 59)

More recent positive reviews and the tremendous success of Nollywood have dispelled this form of negativity. Evolving in Nigeria from an environment of pessimism and sundry socio-cultural upheavals, Nollywood and stand-up comedy have catalysed similar practices in other parts of Africa. Together, both artistic genres have augmented the shortfalls experienced in celluloid filmmaking and live theatre, respectively.

Though Nollywood films were initially distributed on videotapes, initial stand-up events were recorded on VCDs and DVDs, especially those of Opa Williams' shows. The VCD/DVD format at the time was more convenient and less cumbersome than VHS tapes, and marketers quickly embraced this emergent technology. One peculiar trait that trailed the use of VCD/DVD from Nollywood to comedy was breaking one production into several parts. It worked successfully in filmmaking, where scenes were purposively and easily elongated to make room for post-production editing. The cut-offs for each part of the films were made at suspenseful points to provoke audiences' curiosity and desire to obtain the subsequent parts of such movies. Mac Collins Chidebe's *Nkoli Nwa Nsukka*, released first in 2004, ran for a total of 20 sequels called 'seasons' till 2007, and all were released on DVDs. This format encountered difficulties for stand-up comedy because the recordings are for disparate live performances, mostly by different individuals. Since stand-up events are not created from single, linear plots whose scenes can be easily drawn out and cut as desired, the primary producers at the time, AY and Opa Williams, had little or no order in which events were packaged. For instance, each VCD/DVD comprises a medley of roughly edited stage performances, often in a disjointed manner because there is no adherence to location, date, or event. There is often little or no sense of order in the arrangements, given that stand-up events at different locations and times could be merged into one 'edition'. Aspects of specific individuals' renditions are sometimes cut abruptly with the interjection of another comedian's performance or the same performer in another location. Furthermore, some of the VCDs/DVDs do not have production dates in their credits, perhaps in a bid to enhance their marketability over a more extended period. The aim was not to maintain historical accuracy but to maximise marketing opportunities: the producers selected routines and talents based on their idea of what would make each 'episode' of the VCD/DVD sell. Hence, no other detail mattered in the editing process or the packaging of the versions they wanted to sell. Before the 2000s, it was mostly *Nite of a Thousand Laughs* produced by the Nollywood film producer and marketer, Opa Williams. By the time comedians like AY created their own events at the turn of the century, they initially followed the established patterns enumerated above. By the 2010s, video dissemination shifted from VCDs/DVDs to online and satellite television channels.

The internet and satellite television brought newer dimensions to the distribution of Nollywood and stand-up comedy. Multichoice, a South Africa-owned media company, has been at the vanguard of screening movies and stand-up programmes through its Africa-wide satellite television, DStv. In the early 2010s, DStv initiated comedy programmes like 'Comedy Club Live in Lagos' and 'Comedy Club Live in Kampala,' with different hosts, live audiences, and comedians featuring in every episode. Stand-up comedy was disadvantaged in airtime allocation because, unlike video films with multiple dedicated channels, its airtime allocation was continually reduced. This disparity stems from generic differences between stand-up and movies in that the former is better produced and consumed in more public spaces than the latter. The implication is that video films have retrieval value and can be watched repeatedly, whereas stand-up accumulates a diminishing value with every repeated viewing, which directly and adversely affects the marketability of its recorded versions. Much more than satellite television, the internet has assisted in giving the dissemination of Nigerian stand-up comedy a decisive boost. Talents and their enablers have appropriated various social media platforms towards popularising their acts. At one time, BlackBerry Messenger (BBM) aided the distribution of snippets of stage events. Today, other platforms have taken over completely – YouTube,

Instagram, WhatsApp, Facebook, and TikTok, to mention but a few – affording comics innovative ways of disseminating stage and online comedy. Specifically, WhatsApp and other private short message exchange services like Telegram, Signal, and IMO are deployed to exchange memes and short versions of these events, especially by consumers in the same way BBM was used in the 2000s. Apart from the exchange of short videos and memes, there is also the circulation of links, statements, and other forms of information concerning performances, performers, and materials that comedians themselves use in their jokes.

Instagram, Facebook, and TikTok provide jokesters with the possibility of sharing shorter video content over a longer period, with the capacity to host live online events for a restricted period within which they can have one-on-one discussions with their fans. There is also the provision to elicit and maintain larger followerships on these platforms. As of May 2021, AY and Basket Mouth had the highest number of followers among Nigerian comedians, with 10.6 million and 7.5 million on Instagram, and 6.9 million and 4.3 million on Facebook, respectively. Real Warri Pikin has about 2.1 million and over 600,000 followers on Instagram and Facebook, respectively, while Helen Paul has 2.8 million on Instagram and a substantial following on Facebook. Comedians who upload their work on social media have large followings, to the extent that a relatively new entrant like Akpororo has 2.8 million Instagram followers compared with Ali Baba's 1.1 million. Comedians also make good use of Twitter for commenting on social and political issues across the country. YouTube provides the greatest enabling environment for comedians because they can host channels where content is distributed much more easily than via other channels, with enhanced protection of copyright of the producers. Many comedians now have YouTube and Instagram channels to distribute their videos. There are other official and unofficial channels featuring stand-up videos of Nigerian humourists all over the internet.

The most significant aspect of the proliferation of social media presence and activities for Nigerian comedians is the additional income they receive from their content and visits to their pages. Proceeds from visits and adverts on these pages, which now form part of the industry's income, are not made public.[8] It is important to note that social media has all but ended the distribution of stand-up comedy on VCDs/DVDs and other retrieval formats, which were previously prevalent. This is also true for Nollywood as it is increasingly being distributed on streaming platforms like Iroko TV, Netflix, and satellite television. Of course, stand-up comedy has taken a different, more appropriate route. However, apart from the money, popularity, and glamour it has bestowed on Nigerian comedians, social media also serves as a veritable feedback mechanism for producers and consumers of humour. It is not just about followership but also about engaging with most people in real-time and over time. Judging by the number of followers, comments, and views that have been exchanged on the social media handles of numerous Nigerian comedians, it is evident that people are airing their opinions about the stage work and real-life activities of comedians. One example where this engagement became obvious recently was during the (anti-police brutality, anti-government mass action) #EndSARS movement in 2020, where the actions of several artists were reviewed, questioned, and censured, forcing some of them to account for their actions and inactions. Others had to quickly state where they stand – with the government or the people – with some appearing at the protest venue and others making cash donations to people both at the site of the protest and online.

Before the COVID-19 lockdown disruptions, live performances were held with greater frequency each year. Live audiences have increasingly become made up of the *crème de la crème* of society, ranging from serving political officials to business moguls and other celebrities. Corporate bodies like Glo, a locally owned mobile phone services provider, has its show called *Glo Lafta Fest,* which is still being hosted in various major cities. Rhythm FM Lagos hosted *Rhythm Unplugged* in the 2000s, while banks and other businesses invite comedians to perform at their annual general meetings. They are also involved in patronage, and the financing and sponsorship of specific events, such as *AY Live Shows,* often supported by banks and other business entities. There has been growth in the proliferation of newer gigs in formal and informal settings and the emergence of newer performers. Invariably, stand-up artists appear to be more financially empowered than Nollywood actors and actresses. One significant reason for this is that the stand-up structure allows individual humourists to become entrepreneurs in charge of the production processes and thus able to benefit directly from the proceeds of their creative output. However, in filmmaking, where performers are the most visible of all those involved in the industry, the bulk of the proceeds go to producers and 'marketers' who are often unknown to the public. On the level of affluence that Nigerian jokesters have been gathering, Augusta Okon (2010) writes that,

> Fame and fortune have accompanied these comedians with some being engaged as comperes (sic) in corporate/social events, and also endorsing companies (sic) products by way of adverts. [...] Corporate bodies even sponsor these stand up comedy shows. A better life has been guaranteed for comedians who possess the laughter medicine and are skilled in administering sufficient dosages of it to the audience. Besides the creeping threat of re-cycled jokes which some comedians are kicking against, and the need for other states to become beneficiaries of the laughter sphere, stand up comedy has not done badly in the Nigerian entertainment circuit and with certitude is here to stay!

This excerpt underscores some of the successes stand-up comedy has recorded in Nigeria. Notably, it mentions one of the salient challenges of contemporary practice:

joke recycling and plagiarism. Efforts to create a comedians' guild, just like Nollywood has successfully had for over two decades now, have serially proved abortive. For the lack of industry regulation, comedians and event organisers are free to practise however they deem fit, but this engenders a more debilitating problem: plagiarism. Comedians borrow joke materials without acknowledgement and pass the same off as theirs. The second challenge is that mainstream live events are restricted to specific cities, especially Lagos, Port Harcourt, Calabar, and Enugu in the south, and Abuja in central Nigeria. This is gradually changing post-COVID-19 lockdown, with comedian-events managers taking their colleagues to smaller cities than the main ones across southern Nigeria. With the negative impact of the COVID-19 pandemic and the attendant lockdowns globally, online performances have become quite regular. Online events like Okey Bakassi's Independence Day *Laughter on Lockdown*, *AY Live Lockdown*, and *Bovi on Fire Again*, among numerous others, were staged on different social media platforms as the effects of the lockdown on live performances became more and more evident.

Without any doubt, stand-up art has evolved as a pervasive entertainment genre mostly because it provides much-needed laughter in the face of continued socioeconomic upheavals in the nation. It has thus adapted itself to be appropriately relevant for the long haul, prompting Onyerionwu (2010) to opine that,

> [f]rom the assertions of these mostly young Nigerian men drawn from almost all sections of the Nigerian nation, it is apparent that humour can be ground out of everything Nigerian. It is also crystal clear that being a successful stand-up comedian in Nigeria imposes the prerequisite of multi-varied talent. That is why almost every Nigerian stand-up comedian is at the same time an excellent dancer, a consummate singer, a polyglot, an actor, a poet.

This points to the overabundant array of talents existing within Nigerian stand-up practice. Some comedians are singers and dancers, like Chigul, Kenny Blaq, Klint da Drunk and Akpororo. Others are adept at voice impressions, character imitation and dramatic comedy, like Helen Paul, MC Tagwaye, Koffi, AY, and Basket Mouth. Yet others have excelled in events management, displacing pioneers like Opa Williams. These include, for example, AY, Ali Baba, Julius Agwu, Basket Mouth, and Pencil, among many others. Deserving of mention here is the inclusion of popular music and musicians during live shows. Every stand-up event in Nigeria is staged with popular musicians who mount the stage to perform karaoke versions of their songs to the audience's delight. In recent times, Nigerian music has become immensely popular and successful. Thus, many music stars have become as popular as their peers in the comedy and film industries. Hence, when they perform at stand-up events, they thrill the audience not necessarily because of their performance but with their presence. Some musicians get the audience members screaming just by their introductions on stage, and when they sing recorded songs that the audience knows, it turns into a sing-along affair. Consequently, a communal feeling is created, not just through laughter but also from singing together. Nevertheless, where the singers thrill audiences with the same songs they have played repeatedly, comedians maintain their relevance and good standing with their fan base by avoiding the repetition of jokes or telling ones that others have already used. In other words, comedians who have attained and continue to retain foremost spots in mainstream stand-up practice in Nigeria do so by providing fresh jokes. It follows that despite its affinity with these other popular art genres in Nigeria, stand-up comedy continues to retain its major essence as a medium for eliciting laughter and doing so with freshness in perspectives and joke formulation.

Notes

1   In 2000, the official exchange rate was 85.98 Nigerian naira to 1 US dollar, and 105.00 to 1 US dollar on the parallel market. In September 2021, it is 410 to 1 US dollar officially, and 575 to 1 US dollar on the parallel market rate.

2   See Alfred Radcliffe-Brown's postulations on 'joking relationships,' Max Gluckman's 'rituals of rebellion,' and Victor Turner's 'liminality.'

3   'If you know that what I am saying affects you, kindly laugh while others are laughing so that people will not think that I am talking about you.'

4   One instance of cross-dressing that this writer has noticed is AY's. In the early days of his *AY Live Shows*, he appeared in a mock stage reality show, "AY Idols," dressed as a lady.

5   'The clothing material was not enough to make the trousers and the jacket. It is still a suit. Even for the jacket, the material was not enough to make it, and I told the tailor to use pieces of clothes he could find to sew the pockets.'

6   'A person that buys poison (to kill himself) and waits to get his change back is not yet ready to die.'

7   The Synagogue Church of All Nations, led by Prophet T. B. Joshua till his demise in 2021, is a well-known site where people go for prayers and to receive all manner of help. It is also popular with celebrities and people from different parts of Africa.

8   A *Daily Trust* publication of June 2021 gives estimates of earnings by Nigerian online comedians (https://dailytrust.com/nigerian-entertainers-earning-big-on-youtube).

7

Diaspora performances

African outposts

With the understanding of popular culture as 'expressions – music theatre, fiction, songs, dances, pictures, poetry, jokes, sayings – [that] emerge from everyday life […], precipitated by new historical experiences' (Barber 2017, 2), Nigeria has over time exerted significant influence on the emergence of popular genres across Africa. From Nollywood to music productions, the successes of stand-up practice in Nigeria have rubbed off on other African countries, giving rise to similar traditions elsewhere.[1] There have been exchanges between Nigerian comedians and their colleagues from other parts of Africa, with local jokesters performing in various African countries and their counterparts from elsewhere also featuring in shows within Nigeria. Uganda's Salvador has performed at Basket Mouth's *Lord of the Ribs* and *Glo Lafta Fest* in Lagos a couple of times, while AY has hosted South Africa's Thenjiwe Moseley in his Lagos and London shows. In terms of mobility, Basket Mouth has performed in more African countries than his colleagues, having featured in stand-up events in at least 11 African countries outside Nigeria.[2] He is followed closely by Klint da Drunk who has taken his acts into over five other African countries.[3] Also, after a decade and half of the successful hosting of stand-up events across Nigeria, Opa Williams took his *Nite of a Thousand Laughs* abroad, specifically to Kenya (from 2011), Uganda (from 2012), and Ghana (from 2010). Year after year, these productions played successfully to audiences with a blend of Nigerian, subregional, and local comedians in those countries. In Rwanda in 2014, comedians from Burundi and Kenya played on the stage in Kigali alongside home-grown favourites (Times Reporter 2014), for example, thus enhancing interregional cooperation amongst comedians on the continent.

It is safe to say that in anglophone Africa, the Nigerian stand-up industry's successes have catalysed professional practice in diverse locations, in both the emergence of talents as well as their discourses. Examples include comedians like Kenya's Eric Omondi's serially elicit Nigerian stereotypes and themes (Ndinda 2019), and the emergence of comedians who use their part-Nigerian personalities to evoke humour in their native homes, such as Ghana's Jacinta Ocansey and Kenya's Oga Obinna. Ocansey grew up in Nigeria, became a professional comedian under Buchi's tutelage, and avers that 'Ghanaians were first exposed to Nigerian comedy so that was the standard' (Buckman-Owoo 2018). One of Oga Obinna's parents is Nigerian. He has embraced that part of his background to bring to life the typecasts popularised by Nollywood films among Kenyans and other East Africans.

The development of stand-up comedy in Africa has been restricted to the three main colonial language blocs on the continent – anglophone, francophone, and lusophone. Due to the pre-eminence of language in stand-up renditions, there is a fair amount of mobility of comedians across borders of nations that have the same colonial languages. Consequently, for example, Nigerian practitioners naturally gravitate towards featuring in shows in English-speaking countries on the continent. Therefore, unlike Nollywood, which has exerted influence across the whole of Africa, irrespective of language barriers (Ryan 2015; Okome 2019), the spread of Nigerian stand-up comedy is, to a large extent, limited by language. Despite these challenges, performers have garnered much social capital, becoming some of the most recognisable comics across the continent. Their recognisability in other African countries is not necessarily for their funniness but for their Nigerianness, a concept that Nollywood has popularised. The propagation of 'Nigerianness' across Africa's socio-cultural sphere comes from the proliferation of Nollywood's films into various parts of the continent (Şaul and Austen 2010; Krings and Okome 2013; Onyenankeya, Onyenankeya and Osunkunle 2017). Thus, in its transcultural sojourn across Africa, Nollywood has distilled stereotypical mannerisms now attributed to Nigerians. Comedians thus elicit jokes based on existing (mis-)conceptions about Nigerians wherever they perform on the continent. These stereotypes can be found in Eric Omondi or Oga Obinna's comedic characterisations of Nigerians for Kenyan audiences and Salvador's replications of same for Ugandans and Kenyans (Churchill Show 2017b).

For their part, Nigerian humourists also tap into these labels in their renditions in other African countries. For instance, Basket Mouth has a characteristic joke he used in some of his performances in East Africa for a couple of years. At one of his appearances at the *Churchill Show* in Nairobi, Kenya, he starts,

> I've been wondering what's been happening with Africa. You know we are diverse, like you know […] we have the Nigerians, Ghanaians. We have different behaviours. Like Nigerians, we know the answer to a question (*audience response*), but we will ask you (*audience laughter*) regardless. Like, a Nigerian man saw me, and said, 'Hey, Basket. You are here?' (*audience laughter; takes a surprising look at himself, with a bewildered expression*). I said, 'Yes' (*audience laughter*). But sometimes, I try to be sarcastic when some people come and say, 'Hey, Basket Mouth, so you are here?' I will say, 'No, am sleeping at home' (*audience laughter*). (Churchill Show 2017a)

He uses this same joke in Tanzania, where he adds that Nigerians are always in haste 'to be late' at any event and that he was placed to perform last because the organisers expected him to be late (Daddyface Tv 2018). In each of these examples, Basket Mouth plays true to type, eliciting Nigerianness and using the opportunity of such enactments for self- or group-denigrating humour. In the Tanzanian show, he proceeds with a statement about different nationalities in Africa, briefly mentioning that Zambians are so slow, to the point that he once saw someone snatch another person's belonging in public. The thief was in no hurry to leave the scene, saying that his victim 'cannot catch up with him.' Then, contrasting Zambians with Nigerians, he tells the audience that the situation is different in his country. In both this joke and the preceding one, Basket Mouth draws on Nigerians' acclaimed dauntlessness both in everyday living and criminality. In each case, the audience's response shows that he is merely confirming notions they already have about Nigerians. Basket Mouth expresses this more succinctly in his next joke after the one cited above in his performance to a Nairobi audience. He narrates that he and his friends were out drinking after an event in the UK. Afterwards, they were so drunk that they chose the least intoxicated of them to drive the car. Then, the flashing light of a police car brought them back to their senses. The driver parked the car by the curb, and they waited with bated breath for the policeman to approach. At this point, he reveals to the audience that they were all Nigerians, and there were five of them. He does this so pointedly that he says,

> And the next thing, I thought about something. I'm Nigerian. We … You guys know (*audience responds in the positive*). (Churchill Show 2017a)

The point is that the audience agrees with him based on a myth that Nigerians will always find a way to get out of any situation, no matter how precarious or difficult. 'You guys know' is Basket Mouth's way of signalling to the audience that he is only saying things some of them already believe about Nigerians. This statement and the audience's endorsement of his claims give him the pretext he needs to conclude his story with highly implausible details. He claims that while waiting for the policeman to approach, he slid from the front passenger seat to the back seat. The driver also followed his cue, and so five starry-eyed adults were seated on the back seat when the policeman arrived at the side of their vehicle. Then, seeing no driver, he let them go and walked away. The basis of his story is a comparison of policemen in Kenya, Nigeria, and the UK. He first asks the audience whether the police in Kenya is 'nice.' They replied in the negative. He confirms that in Nigeria, the police is nothing to write home about. He then claims that the UK police is the best. Nevertheless, his story's conclusion shows negligence – a policeman seeing five drunk adults seated in a car with no driver, and he lets them go. This is one of the worst examples of a 'nice' policeman, but the audience is not interested in the story's veracity. It generally conforms to all they think and believe about Nigerians, which matters at the moment of the enactment.

Klint da Drunk is outstanding in his portrayal of a drunk person on the stand-up stage. There is the classroom setting and the teacher persona of Uganda's Teacher Mpamire and Kenya's Professor Hamo, which are unique in themselves. However, no comedian in mainstream practice has taken up a drunkard's role on the stand-up stage, thereby making Klint a unique comedian continent-wide. He brings his 'drunkenness' to bear in all his renditions outside Nigeria as well. In a show in Kigali, Rwanda, he tells the audience that he is happy to be in the country 'once again'. He pauses to count on his fingers the number of times he has been to Rwanda, with a facial expression that indicates deep contemplation. After counting almost all the fingers on both hands, he says it is his first time in Rwanda, something his audience finds hilarious. Klint opens with this as a way of easing the audience into his unique art. He then tells the audience that he is there to make a fool of himself, and that for paying to come and watch him being stupid they should clap for themselves. The audience claps for itself. With the background of 'stupidity' established, he turns on someone in the audience wearing a 'face cap,' wondering what the individual is covering when there is no sun on his face. With this setup for the entire performance, Klint successfully moves the audience into a realm where he can be as subversive as he needs to be regarding normative behaviour. Despite the need to break norms, he knows well to ensure that he first gets the audience on his side. This is something that comedians naturally do, getting themselves so acquainted with audiences that it appears that they are all on the same side. As a Nigerian, Klint entices his Kigali audience by praising them – from talking about how beautiful Rwandan women are to comparing their country and Nigeria. Rwanda comes tops for Klint with the present audience, the same way that the Tanzanian audience appeared better than the Zambians to Basket Mouth when he was performing at Dar es Salem. Klint says,

> I've gone round Africa, and I tell you … they said that Rwanda is a lovely place. I came here, and honestly, I'm not happy with your president (*audience, nervous laughter*). No, I'm not happy with him because he made everywhere so clean (*audience laughter*). It's so clean that it's irritating to we Nigerians. It is too clean … I can't even pass gas easily (*audience laughter*). You feel that your gas will have a colour when it comes out. I don't understand … (Igihe 2018)

Every society has its challenges. As such, every audience has several things that it does not like about its environment. Nevertheless, most people are pleased when a foreigner says nice things about their society, irrespective of the challenges they face. Hence, comparing Rwanda with Nigeria and saying explicitly that the former is better off in many ways is Klint's way of getting on his audience's side, at least for the duration of the performance.

Consequently, comedians self-denigrate 'Nigerianness' when performing to other Africans, breaking down the Nigerians' supposed invincibility. However, this is not done in any malicious manner. It is a way of taking ownership of one's foibles and humanising a group of people that have been (mis-)construed in various ways. This narrative pattern dots the entire length of Klint's Kigali performance. He continues with a highly dramatised skit about the Nigerian police compared to their Rwandese counterparts:

> Your police people are so wonderful. Put your hands together for your police (*audience obliges*). They actually greet. What! Police? Greet you, 'Good evening'? (*maintains an expression of shock; audience laughter*) Police? Good evening from the police, in uniform? (*to the audience directly*) Wait, do they carry guns here? Guns? The police? What kind of gun? Big one? And the small one? Our own even carry grenade (*audience laughter*). Just in case you want to run … (*he mimics the sound and action of someone unpinning a grenade and throwing it at another*) in front of you, so you run back (*audience laughter*). Our police are so rude; when they want to stop you … they don't know who you are. They don't care! What you hear is, 'PARK!' (*he makes a sweeping movement with his free arm to indicate where the driver should park*). 'PARK!' Even in the … see, when they stop you, first thing, 'Inner light.' You put it on (*to the audience*) even in the afternoon. 'Inner light' (*pause*) In the afternoon? They will stop you, tell you to come down. They search you, search your car, and after everything, they smile, 'Anything for the boys?' (*audience laughter*). It's terrible! (Igihe 2018)

Throughout this narrative, Klint uses extensive spatial and body movements as well as commensurate facial expressions as emphatic and demonstrative accompaniments. The narrative develops from the simple act of being greeted by the Rwandan police before delving into a tale of police brutality in Nigeria. There are exaggerations in both cases, especially with the overstated shock he expresses at the banal action of being greeted by the Rwandan police. Klint magnifies this action to the point that he can use it to draw comedic parallels. For the Rwandan situation, Klint's claim glosses over the existence of official government censorship on various forms of expression, something that does not exist in Nigeria. Specifically, Madelaine Hron writes that

> In Rwanda […], there is much skepticism towards humor, because disparaging and aggressive forms of humor were deployed in genocidal propaganda to shame, denigrate, and dehumanize Tutsis […]. Today, ironically, this distrust of humor is deployed by the current regime as a means of social control and censorship. Cracking a political joke could land a comic in jail or possibly worse. […] Thus, humor, potentially dangerous, is often (self-)censored in Rwanda, as it may be in other repressive regimes. (2016, 220)

Of course, it is not in Klint's best interest to take on the police or the Rwandan government on his first visit to the country and risk being arrested or barred from coming to the country again. In addition, since his audience is aware of the difficulties with authority in their country, they do not need a foreigner, let alone a comedian, to remind them of this. Owing to the nature of stand-up art, Klint needs to court his audience's acceptance, and praising their police or their women gives him the type of access required to win their hearts. Additionally, the exaggeration in the narrative is also in the way he characterised police harassment in Nigeria. Admittedly, the Nigerian police are notoriously unprofessional in their daily encounters with the public. However, it does not mean that what Klint describes in this narrative happens every time, everywhere, and in the same manner. Nigerian comedians can talk about ethnicity and other forms of divisions within their own country and still not be arrested by the police. They also speak to and about political office holders, and unlike in Rwanda, there has never been a reported case of official reprimand of any jokester.

The engagement of Nigerian comedians with audiences elsewhere in Africa does not only come with the form of 'feel-good' comedy that has been described above. In his set in Uganda in 2014, Gordons elicits laughter, covering subjects ranging from the secular to the religious and back. He spent a whole hour thrilling the Kampala audience using exaggerated tales, with little or no trashing of his native country. He begins by telling the audience that he feels at home because Nigeria and Uganda are similar, 'with the same infrastructure.' This last clause stirs laughter in the audience. Gordons develops the comparison by telling his audience that he has seen many cars in Uganda, 'including the ones that they do not produce anymore' (*audience laughter*), but that he is yet to see the most expensive car in the world. For a moment, it appears as though he will brag about things his native country has that Uganda does not have. By the time he is done with talking about the most expensive water bottle and wristwatch (where he quickly adds that he does not mean Rolex because 'it is for small boys,' and Omega, which is for 'mechanics'), it becomes evident that he is taking his audience on a cruise. He even makes the audience applaud God for being good to them, sounding like a Pentecostal preacher at that point. Throughout the rendition, Gordons steers clear of mentions of how bad things are in Nigeria and how they are better in Uganda (Pablo Live TV 2016a; Pablo Live TV 2016b). For the way Gordons handled the audience in this event, his performance received glowing reviews in Uganda, one of which reads,

> If last Friday's Pablo Live was a context, Nigeria's Godwin Omoneh (sic), aka Gordons would have deservedly carried the day. This guy's comedy flows naturally; he is not the type that has learnt to be a comedian. And he is not one of the usual clowns; no, Gordons is smart and funny and his heads-up humour is stand-up comedy at its finest. His is comedy that will make you laugh and at the same time make you think, because of the way he addressed life issues humorously. He joked about everything; at times sounding like a pan-

> Africanist, other times coming off as a born-again pastor. I don't remember how many times I shouted 'hallelujah' to Gordons' hilarious jokes. You could tell his inspiration comes from God. (Musasizi 2014)

This excerpt is indicative of the forms of glowing tributes that many a Nigerian comedian has received for their performances in other African countries. Though there are also instances where some of them have performed poorly, they remain sought after as main acts. Their characterisations of Nigerian stereotypes are part of the demand for their acts, but once at home, they begin to talk about ethnic differences, the government, and local materials familiar to home audiences. Here, there is no Nigerian label but that of the divisions in religion, ethnicity, political views, and other affiliations and proclivities occasioned by the overwhelming heterogeneity that has kept unity at bay.

Basket Mouth has been dubbed 'king of African comedy' for his numerous performances across different media both within and outside the continent. He may not be the funniest, but he is the most travelled given the number and variety of countries and spaces where he has performed. His popularity within the continent also stems from cable television features like hosting MTVBase *The Big Friday Show* between 2012 and 2016. The event featured comedy, pranks on celebrities, and other forms of entertainment aired to viewers across Africa. His big break came with his *Comedy Central Presents Basketmouth Live* hosting at Parker's in Johannesburg, South Africa, in April 2013. The feature was later broadcast across Africa on DStv in June 2013, bringing Basket Mouth continent-wide recognition. In 2016, alongside Thomas Gumede and Boity Thulo, Basket Mouth hosted *Ridiculousness Africa*, a programme also broadcast on DStv. Being the first Nigerian performer on these shows gave Basket Mouth an edge over his compatriots, advertising him to audiences beyond Nigeria. Since then, other Nigerian comedians have found opportunities to participate in several events on both stage and social media as well as cable television programmes. When looking at the continent-wide popularity of Nigerian comedians, this should be viewed in relation to the international recognition South Africa's Trevor Noah has garnered. Noah is undoubtedly the most recognised African comedian globally, basically for his work on the late-night American television programme, *The Daily Show*, and not necessarily for stage performances within the continent. The difference between Noah's popularity and that of, say, Basket Mouth is that the latter has had more performances in various African countries and a more overwhelming presence on African social media and cable television presentations than the former. Hence, unlike Basket Mouth and some of his compatriots, Noah has had limited face-to-face encounters with local audiences across Africa. The implication is that, unlike their colleagues from other parts of Africa, Nigerian jokesters are steeped in interregional stage appearances. For example, where Kenyan and Ugandan comedians perform mostly in East Africa, and South African comedians are popular in the southern parts of the continent, Nigerian comics are widely travelled and have participated in events in East, Central, and the southern parts of Africa, especially in countries where English is spoken.

Global outlook

There are two parts to Nigerian stand-up comedy's global outreach: comedians with a Nigerian background who perform for local western audiences and humourists who stage events in the west, catering mostly to diaspora audiences. Across the Global North, several comedians with Nigerian roots have emerged on the stand-up stage. Two examples are Stephen K. Amos and Nabil Abdulrashid. They were born in the UK in 1967 and 1985, respectively, to parents who had emigrated from Nigeria. Both comedians have spent much of their adult lives in the UK, although Abdulrashid returned to Nigeria when he was five, only going back to the UK in 2006. Their careers have taken different directions with Amos gaining much success and popularity from appearing on various television programmes as a TV host and compère, as well as an actor in a number of television dramas. In 2001, Amos took to the stage, featuring in events worldwide, specifically playing roles true to his nature of being black, British, and gay. For Abdulrashid, four years after his return to the UK, at the age of 26, he became the youngest comedian to perform at the Hammersmith Apollo. Since then, he has participated in numerous stand-up shows, using jokes to dissipate stereotypes about being Muslim or African. He also makes jokes about intercultural encounters, speaking variously about his marriage to a woman with Pakistani origins and other experiences of discrimination in the UK.

There is a strong presence of female comedians among Nigerian diaspora practitioners. Of those born in the UK, Gina Yashere and Andi Osho have garnered acclaim. Yashere was born Regina Obedapo Iyashere to Nigerian immigrants to the UK in 1974 but has since relocated to the US where she performs on stage, in television drama, and as a correspondent for *The Daily Show*. She sometimes draws on her Nigerian origins to create a substantial portion of her jokes, occasionally giving a very uncomplimentary view of the country and its people. She also at times deploys her characteristic British accent in discussing race relations, commenting explicitly on instances where she attracts unnecessary attention due to the fact that some people outside the UK are unfamiliar with the existence of black British people. The following excerpt from one of her performances shows clearly how she plays race and accent, especially with American audiences:

> What's up, New York […] I'll let you people get used to the way I speak. I really do speak like this. There are black people in England. Yes, there are!

Yeah! (*To a white couple in the front row, specifically to the guy*) Did you know, sir, did you know? (*he shook his head in the negative. She then, in a loud whisper*) We are everywhere! (*audience laughter*). Obviously, black people aren't indigenous to England. My mother is from Nigeria. [She then verbally paints a graphic image of how her mother chose to go to England, asking in a Nigerian accent] Where shall I go? [...] I am fed up with the sun [...] I want to go somewhere with a lot of drizzle and subtle racism [...] Cause the Brits have the best of racism. You don't know you are being discriminated against. [...] That's how good they are. They are fucking Ninja racists! (Yashere 2014)

Yashere does not only talk about her Britishness but also about her Nigerianness. She often starts her performances by establishing these backgrounds because they give her some leverage to speak to American audiences as an 'outsider' and authoritatively as a Nigerian and a Briton. In this narrative, the excerpt shows her narrative's thrust: speaking about being a minority and how she is affected by racism in the west. In the same gig, Yashere tells of how a 'red neck' colleague at her workplace inverted her name 'Gina,' calling her 'A nig.' Offended by this racist rendering of her name, she gets home to accost her mother, accusing her of giving her a terrible name. In her defence, the mother told her to confront the racist work colleague and tell him that her name is actually 'Regina' and not 'Gina.' The punchline of this jocular narrative which she emphatically reveals to her audience, is that when turned backwards, Regina reads, 'A niger,' which is even more racist than where she started (Yashere 2014). At issue here is not the name 'Regina,' but the characterisation of ways in which racism deliberately misreads materials based on skin colour, accent, and a couple of other *othering* traits that divide humanity.

This joke has a couple of significances, but the one most related to the subject of the discussion here is Yashere's characterisation of her mother in her renditions. She is often portrayed as a Nigerian woman who moved to the UK and has lived there for a long time, yet is still very rooted in her Nigerian ways, as seen in her obliviousness in how she defends her daughter from the 'red neck.' The main suggestion here is that she gives her child a foreign name without considering its racist implications. Yashere often uses this supposition to encase her discourses about Nigeria and its people jocularly. She speaks of one of her visits to the country, using it to talk about advance fee fraud tied to Nigeria-based online scammers and swindlers. She avers,

Nigeria was scary. I stayed in a hotel with white people. That's what I did. That's what I did. [...] It's a hustle [...] some of you might have received some of the e-mails from Nigeria. [...] You know the e-mails am talking about. (*changes voice slightly*) Hello, my name is Prince Obidapo Chukwuemeka. My father died, leaving me 26 billion dollars in his bank account. But I cannot get to it. I can't get to it. So, if you give me all your bank details and the PIN numbers for all of your cards, I will put the 26 billion dollars in your account and only take 10 dollars for myself (*audience recognition, laughter and applause*). You fall for that; you deserve to lose everything you own. [...] Nigeria is a scary place. (Boricua 2018)

Yashere's opening statement here is that she stayed in a hotel 'with white people' while visiting Nigeria. One considers this a way she signals her *otherness*, not being Nigerian and not 'white'. Thus, designating herself as an *other* enables her to critique criminality and its proliferation in Nigeria. This condemnation is more evident in another rendition where she deepens her critique of Nigerians through a dramatised narrative of how she was mugged while in a moving taxi on a Lagos street:

> Go to Africa. You'll see hungry thugs. I got robbed in a taxi doing 60 miles an hour. That, my friend, is thuggery. I was in a taxi. I mean, I feel am safe, am in Nigeria, am in Africa. [...] am on a freeway. I mean, what could possibly go wrong? So, I stuck my camcorder out of the window (*with right hand enclosing her right eye as if looking through the lens of a camera. So, she sweeps the 'camera' trained on the audience, slowly from stage right to left*) And am filming Africa. Suddenly, I felt *fftt* (*still filming in the opposite direction*), and my camera was gone! (*still filming*) and am left looking through my hands. This zoom is not as good as I remember. (Just for Laughs 2018)

With her sarcasm, she berates Nigerians for various crimes and her mother for sundry suggestions of naïveté. Her criticism is not just for the people but also for the Nigerian government and its perennial negligence and dereliction of responsibilities. For instance, she exclaims, 'We ain't get no CSI in Nigeria ... You can get away with murder in Nigeria except you are standing over the body saying that you did it!' (Cybertechproduction 2011). Nevertheless, despite the harshness of her tone, Yashere gains credibility to joke about Nigerianness by laying out her Nigerian 'roots' from the outset of her performance. In each of her renditions about the nation, she mostly commences or concludes the skit with variations of the following paraphrased statement: I went to Nigeria to find my roots and discovered that my roots are in the UK.

Andi Osho was also born to Nigerian parents in the UK in 1973. She also plays on accents, interspersing both Nigerian and British ones in characterising the different personae of her stand-up jokes. Osho has recently taken some time off from the stand-up stage, instead acting in television dramas, making podcasts, and publishing her first novel, *Asking for a Friend* (2021). Her accomplishments remain solid and substantial. Some of her stand-up comedy exploits as listed on her website include three national tours, appearances at *Live at the Apollo*, America's *The Late, Late Show*, as well as solo performances at the Edinburgh Festival, London's O2 Arena and Montreal's *Just for Laughs* (Osho 2020). She speaks about differences between British and American accents, specifically the advantages of a black person speaking like a

Briton in the US. She tells a story:

> I have to tell you: I love having a British accent over here. It is the best thing.
> This is how good it is: I got pulled over 'cause I ran two stops 'cause I was
> checking my phone (*mixed reaction from audience*). And […] yes, the officer
> came over, and he let me off, and I'm black. That is how good having a British
> accent is over here. That is it. As soon as he came over, I turned him to Mary
> Poppins […] (Locke 2014)

With the notoriety of violence and brutality against blacks in America which gave
rise to the 'Black Lives Matter' movement and other forms of activism challenging
racism in America, being a black person with a British accent is shown here to be
somewhat beneficial. Osho's tale here is a caricature of police brutality in the US, often
dubbed 'blue-on-black' violence. Her story shows that racism does not just target
skin colour but individuals who look, behave and speak 'black.' Without mentioning
it expressly, Osho carpets the American policing system here by stating that she has
a better life in the UK as a black person than in the US when it comes to policing.
The icing on the cake in this joke is the conclusion where the policeman who accosts
her returns to his partner in the car, and when his colleague asks him why he did not
arrest the 'black' lady who ran two stop signs. He replies, 'She is British!' This response
begs the question: does being British excuse the fact that this lady ran two stop signs,
endangering other road users' lives? Or does it mean that the reason she was stopped
in the first place was that she is black, and having a British accent meant she is not
the kind of black that should be stopped, no matter the offence? These are some of
the questions that expose the underlying intent behind this joke, which must be
made up – how else would Osho have heard what the police said to his partner while
she was sitting in her vehicle?

It is not all about Britishness for her. She also talks about Africa a lot like when
she narrates what could happen if there were ever a black British Home Secretary.
In mimicking this hypothetical government official's persona, she uses a thick accent
that comedians usually ascribe to Africans to say that the borders will be opened,
and that people should invite all their relations to come to the UK (ArseRaptor
2013). The reason for this blanket invitation is that there is work for everyone and
that people, presumably Africans, should come and take up these jobs. In playing
this role, Osho switches from her characteristic British talk pattern to a thicker,
denser pronunciation of English words and then back again to her typical joke
rendition accent. This change indicates a shift in character, from being her usual
British performer to roleplaying being an African-British Home Secretary. For her
and other performers, this thick accent has come to represent the manner in which
Africans typically speak. In an hindsight evaluation, however, why would an African-
British Home Secretary speak in an 'African' way when people like Osho herself speak

flawless British accent? Osho often talks about her mother and about being Nigerian, but not about visits to the country or how there are criminals everywhere, like Yashere does. Her concerns are mainly about the behaviours of relatives and how her strict Nigerian home contrasted with her British existence as a child (ArseRaptor 2010). Using this background, she comments on race relations and the challenges of being black in the UK, and as in the excerpt above, how her British accent distinguishes her from other black bodies when she is on a visit to the United States. Osho thus juxtaposes and switches realities to show how things would look when situations are reversed as she does in the following narrative about her name being mispronounced by some Britons. She narrates:

> The best example of people not getting my name clear is: I called a radio station to win tickets for a concert [...] and the DJ said: 'All right listen, you're gonna be on air very soon. Make sure you sound very excited. What's your name?' 'Yewande.' He went, (*a long pause*) 'Uh! I don't think I can pronounce that. Let's call you, Joe. (*a long pause*) What I really wish is the equivalent was happening somewhere in Nigeria: a little English boy calls up a radio station gets straight to the DJ (*audience laughter*). (*with an 'African' accent*) 'Ok, my friend, you are going to be on air very soon. Let me take your name and make sure you sound very excited' (*audience laughter*). And the kid says, 'It's Charles.' 'Cheese?' (*audience laughter*). 'No, it's Charles.' 'Chux? Ok, I cannot pronounce that. Let me call you Umar Farouk Abdulmutallab' (*audience laughter*). (ChortleUK 2011)

What Osho does here is to show how it feels when someone's name is mispronounced. She states at the beginning that Nigerian names are the easiest to pronounce because once you get one, the rest sound the same. To her, mispronouncing a common name like 'Charles' is the same as doing so for a Nigerian name like hers, 'Yewande.' The punchlines in this rendition are tied to two significations. First, the name is too long not to be mispronounced, especially for someone not accustomed to such names. Secondly, Umar Farouk Abdulmutallab is the name of the Nigerian associated with international terrorism, known as the 'underwear suicide bomber' involved in the failed attempt to bomb a US-bound plane in 2009 (Bunkley 2012). Osho talks about Nigeria as her homeland but in its defence and condemnation of maleficent excesses on the parts of the people and their government. Most importantly, like her colleagues, the joke content she explores centres around being female, black, and British.

Another Nigerian-British comedienne, Jocelyn Esien, exploits similar joke creation patterns as Yashere and Osho. Esien talks about her mother's numerous efforts to instil, with varying results, some 'Nigerianness' in her. Yashere, Osho, and Esien, in their respective performances, characterise their mothers, especially with somewhat exaggerated thick voice tones. This depiction pattern is a synecdoche for African parents in general and the varying ways they have mostly not adapted to the western pattern of life and their efforts to draw their children into living the Nigerian life even when they were born and raised outside the country. For these humourists, 'being Nigerian,' no matter how remotely, is a trademark. It is a distinctive brand that sets them apart from the throng of other comedians with whom they would ordinarily be sharing the same kinds of jokes if they were to assert their Britishness more than their *otherness* on western stand-up stages. However, their views of Nigeria represent the predominant conception of the country from western perspectives: a nation of e-mail scammers, unsafe streets, and one with a convicted would-be plane bomber, not to mention the stereotypically unnerving parents and family members that refuse to let Nigeria go even when they have lived elsewhere for a long time. For these and other diaspora comedians with little lived experience of Nigeria, their use of 'Nigerianness' is a way of gaining the pedestal and credibility needed to make jokes about the nation and its people without being considered politically incorrect. Their assertion of being Nigerian is thus a tool with which they prop up joke setups and punchlines in ways that their cohorts from other areas may not be able to do.

There are various comedians with Nigerian roots in the US and Canada who have made a mark in the stand-up industry. The youthful Opey Olagbaju and Ayo Edebiri, born to Nigerian parents who emigrated to the US, are gradually making their respective ways through comedy clubs and other events. Olagbaju makes jokes about being Nigerian and an immigrant. In one interesting joke, he conflates the Russian collusion case and Donald Trump's impeachment to suggest that Nigeria's President Buhari is a clone (Comedy Central Stand-Up 2020). To introduce the un-American side of his joke to his audience, Olagbaju explains how the president went missing on medical grounds for a long time, and when he returned eventually, there were rumours that he had died and a clone put in his place. Edebiri's stage work focuses on the complexities of her immigration background, making her jokes basically about being black, female, and considered an immigrant in the country of her birth and citizenship. She avers that working with NBC's *Sunnyside*, for instance, is 'really cool because the show is about immigrants [...] everyone in the writers' room is either an immigrant themselves, first-generation or married to an immigrant or connected to the immigrant experience in some sense' (Escandon 2019). Under the Trump presidency, with its anti-immigration stance, themes around *otherness* and identity became the major preoccupation of comedians from various backgrounds, including those mentioned here.

Two older comedians with Nigerian roots are Godfrey C. Danchimah, known simply as Godfrey, and Chinedu Unaka. They were both born in the US and thus are often caught up in the complexities of questions about their identity and *difference*.

Both comedians tell jocular biographical narratives about the same conditions their diaspora cohorts discuss. Godfrey talks about his parents, the home he grew up in, and how other kids (mis)understood his family, especially his father. He creates anecdotes that ridicule labels about Africans, as seen in the theme joke for his Showtime Comedy Special, *Regular Black* (Godfreychi 2018). In this one-person set, he sarcastically replays an awkward situation where someone referred to him as not being 'a regular black' because he does not have an 'accent' and did not grow up in Africa. He thus jocularly expands the narrative by hilariously interrogating the myriad implications of categorising people, especially delineating blackness into regular and irregular variants. Where Godfrey's jokes can be abrasive and farcical sometimes, Unaka's are more conversational and relaxed. He tells the same tales of his upbringing and contradictions of explaining his (not-)being Nigerian and American. He speaks most regrettably about his inability to speak the Igbo language, citing embarrassing situations he faces whenever he meets people who can speak it, especially when they tease him about having a name from a language he cannot speak (All Def Stand Up 2018). Somewhere within this joke lurks the desire to belong and be accepted as Igbo, especially since his name quickly gives him away.

Another comedienne with a Nigerian heritage is Aisha Alfa. Being the child of a Canadian woman, she grew up in Canada but spent time in Nigeria and different parts of the world. In her performances, she enacts a different form of remembering. For her, it is not always about her life in Nigeria, but that of her parent's relationships and the bi-cultural environment within which she was raised. Her characteristic enactment of how her parents met, alongside varying alternative narratives that would have resulted in her being different, always evoke laughter. She also plays on her name and how her identity is easily misunderstood because of assumptions surrounding it. Yvonne Orji, for her part, born in Nigeria and taken to the US by her parents while still a toddler, recently came out with an HBO special, *Momma I made it* (Lee 2020). In this latest outing, Orji creates the narratives around her Nigerian heritage – the pidgin English, Nigerian slang, customs, stereotypes, diaspora kids, and several dramas with her parents concerning career choice and getting married. She code-mixes accents to depict intercultural behavioural patterns between Nigerians, Americans, and Nigeria-Americans as she satirically comments on human eccentricities, excesses, and misconstrued labelling of others. The set's theme is her mother's dislike for her decision to become a comedian and how landing an HBO event dissipates much of her family's initial reluctance. In all her stage events, Orji indubitably foists her Africanness on American audiences, reiterating her dual identity as Nigerian and American.

A common trend among all comedians with (in)direct immigration backgrounds discussed in this chapter is that they first establish a premise of being Nigerian.

They then erect their acts mostly on autobiographical narratives, thereby making their jokes come from the perspective of personal experiences. From this position, a reiteration of their dual identity affords them the basis for 'punching up' against mainstream peoples and traditions, roundly problematising identity labels imposed on them by the dominant groups in their diaspora abodes. Above all, many of these diaspora performers' presentations designate a form of longing for belongingness because their present societies continuously remind them of ways in which they do not belong. Consequently, there is an ambivalence of attraction and repulsion for the homeland: a place they do not currently experience but are perpetually tied to due to the consequences of the prevalence of forms of divisiveness that continually designate them as outsiders and constantly remind them of how different they are amidst other groups in diaspora sites.

Local comedians, diaspora audiences

By the end of the 2000s, Nigerian comedians had commenced performances in Europe and North America, mostly catering to Nigerian diaspora audiences. Many such shows have emerged in the US, the UK, and Canada, but better known ones include *AY Live Show*, Basket Mouth's *Son of Peter*, and other events organised by him, as well as Julius Agwu's *Crack ya Ribs*, to mention but a few. Agwu's *Crack ya Ribs* debuted in 2006 and was the first home-grown Nigerian show to play to diaspora audiences in London (Olonilua 2018). In the second edition in 2007, the comedian came on stage with bruises he had sustained from being mugged in London the previous night, but undeterred and committed to continuing his pioneering work in taking live Nigerian stand-up to diaspora audiences (Molue Talk 2007). Between 2006 and 2010, the UK editions of *Crack ya Ribs* featured many Nigerian comedians, including Ali Baba, I Go Dye and Gandoki. Video recordings of these earlier events are not readily available on YouTube except for a few badly done versions, shot with camera phones by individuals who were part of the audiences. In 2010, *Basket Mouth Uncensored* and *AY Live Show* were added to the stand-up entertainment for Nigerians living in the UK. *Basket Mouth Uncensored* was held on 21 February and *AY Live* on 6 October the same year at the IndigO2 London. Both Basket Mouth and AY have been holding stand-up events in the UK since then. Julius Agwu and AY's shows have featured many comedians from Nigeria, allotting varying performance time within the events, while Basket Mouth's, in contrast, have followed more of the one-person performance format with more musicians and a sprinkling of side stand-up performers. For example, in 2010, Basket Mouth's London event featured Eddie Kadi, a Congolese-born UK comedian (MrCokoBar 2010). The fact that audiences comprised mostly Nigerians, comedians at these earlier shows performed in pidgin English drawing on the same modes and themes they are accustomed to in their routines in Nigeria. In recent times, it has become the practice for organisers to include comedians from other diaspora communities to expand their clientele beyond just having Nigerians, which has also influenced a slight shift towards using more standard English than the pidgin variant.

Furthermore, while AY has been consistent in using the same name for his brand in all his foreign and local shows, Julius Agwu and Basket Mouth have experimented with titles. Agwu has staged *Laff for Christ's Sake,* wherein comedians stick to a restricted subject range specifically devoid of expletives and non-conformist language and *Festivals of Love,* with themes revolving around family and relationships. Basket Mouth has presented events such as *Lord of the Ribs, Nigerian Kings of Comedy, African Kings of Comedy, Laffs and Jams,* and the more recent *Son of Peter,* with varying comedic personae and presentation formats for each of them. *Laffs and Jams* has more music interspersed with comedy shows, whereas *Son of Peter* and *Basket Mouth Uncensored* played more towards the one-person format. The rest involve various comedians both from within and outside Nigeria. Moreover, Nigerian stand-ups' encounter with diaspora audiences is not restricted solely to the UK. Apart from the UK, Julius Agwu's *Crack ya Ribs* played first at the Symphony Space Theatre in New York in September 2012 and later in Glasgow, Scotland (Jaguda 2012), while *Basket Mouth Uncensored* has seen action in both New York (SaharaTV 2015) and Atlanta in the USA, and Antwerp in Belgium (CreatedbyKelz 2018).

It is evident that there have been remarkable successes in holding Nigerian comedy shows elsewhere, but the UK remains the preferred choice of hosting diaspora events. Some promoters and organisers do much of the groundwork before the stand-up talents arrive from Nigeria. For instance, Ropo Akin of Cokobar has successfully run Basket Mouth and AY's events for years. Akinlolu Jekins has been working with Julius Agwu and briefly with Ali Baba to bring their events to UK audiences. London events often draw large audiences since other major cities in the country are conveniently close to the British capital, unlike in the US where major cities are so far apart that it is impracticable to attract sold-out crowds to any single city at any one time. Recently, though, comedians have been doing tours of cities outside London, even up to Aberdeen and Glasgow in Scotland, to reach out to as many potential audiences as possible. A UK tour presents lesser challenges than a similar endeavour in the US or mainland Europe. Hence, the UK remains tops in terms of hosting diaspora events. In short, however, a particular consideration when it comes to location choice, whether in the UK, the USA or mainland Europe, is the presence of a Nigerian community since it rather than the locals would be the target audience.

Performing outside Nigeria presents challenges both for the comedians and their diaspora promoters. Getting audiences, venues, travel plans, and other logistics together required to have a successful event is just one aspect of the required tasks. In the words of Akinlolu Jekins:

> 87% of [Nigerian comedians] have the craft, gift, skill but are not well experienced when it comes to the diaspora market and crowd. So working with us or partnering with my organisation makes it a safe haven. We educate, guide, and assist with paperwork. We also channel traffic, identify weaknesses and strengths, and use their gifts and skills (in skits/sketches, for example) to achieve successful shows. In most cases, we fly them in before the show to do press rounds, visit the venue, do ground testing and produce more pre-production content to be used in the event. Presently I have been lucky to deal with comedians/artists directly. That kind of takes away the stress of management/managers that may hinder swift productivity in most cases. But as promoters (I refer to myself as a strategist and event organiser/consultant). We have to understand the brand/client/comedian we choose to work with more, before embarking on such a project. (Jekins 2020)

From the preceding excerpt, it is clear that local organisers' input enriches diaspora performances in many ways, especially in aspects that the diverse artistic talents of visiting comedians are limited. The support provided by events managers like Cokobar's Akin Ropo and Akinlolu Jekins includes providing ticketing platforms and sourcing local talents and audiences, all mentioned in the excerpt above, for every event. Regarding differences between stand-up practice in Nigeria and what obtains in the diaspora, Jekins observes further that,

> We have a long way to go. We need to impact more race and ethnic minorities. We have less funding. We are not supported, unlike the others. In terms of securing venues, we are somewhat limited. Some venues play games and politics if the comedian in question is not known. There's monopoly too, that is, 70% of venues in the UK are owned by LiveNation. So, almost all the good dates are blocked out and not available. Checks are most times rigorous. We are tagged with noise, fights and indecent attitudes when in venues. But all that being said, we have our crowd – the population of blacks in the UK is estimated to be very high. So our theory is there's enough to go round. So with the ones we now put on larger venues. We do what I call a MIX and MATCH, which means, add a UK-born black comedian, other major comedians from an African country, and support from UK comedians of African or Caribbean descent. (Jekins 2020)

Jekins's Mix and Match has worked pretty well for diaspora performances. In one of AY's shows, South African UK-based female humourists, Thenjiwe Moseley, performed to the Nigerian London crowd (African Glitz TV 2018). Diaspora audiences are usually in need of slices of home in whatever measure they can get them. It is typically challenging to let go entirely and forget about home, as seen in the recurrent mentions of recalcitrant parents of diaspora-born children. Yashere, Osho, and Esien see this form of behaviours in their mothers, forming part of their stand-up jokes. Unaka and Godfrey find the same in their fathers. This idea of remaining 'Nigerian' even after spending a long time abroad, and the friction that arises from forcing children whose experience of that 'Nigeria' is within their homes in western societies, to live that kind of life always creates occasions for humour. In the same way, diaspora audiences need to be reminded of home. They desire the feeling and taste of home. They usually look for local cuisine, religious and sundry social organisations, and popular traditions with affinities to practices at home no matter where they are. The consumption of artistic pieces from Nollywood, Afro-pop music, and stand-up humour has become part of the culture of keeping in touch with Nigeria and is thus part of the selling points of these diaspora events. The basic validation for this claim is that even though there are other options available in their countries of residence, Nigerian diaspora audiences still flock to these shows presented by comedians from home.

Nevertheless, even in their desire for home, the audiences do not necessarily fall hook, line, and sinker for the comedians' narratives because their western sensibilities are ever-present to question everything. This is where the issue of content and treatment of materials come in. Given the socio-cultural differences between Nigeria and the west, cognitions of offence and taboo subjects often differ. As a result, comedians get caught in the web of controversial subjects which might sail through in Nigeria but are somewhat difficult for western audiences to absorb. Even when these audience members have Nigerian roots, some subjects tend to be insensitive and politically incorrect to them due to their different awareness and acknowledgement of reality based on their present residence. One instance is Klint da Drunk's performance of a girl with speech difficulties whom three men raped, cited previously in Chapter 4. During the court process where the men are being tried, she describes how they performed rather than being shocked and traumatised by the rape itself (AY Comedian 2018b). Klint establishes some baseline at the beginning of this story by stating that any man capable of raping a woman should receive the death penalty. There are moments of discomfort in the victim's designation: calling her 'deaf and dumb' and presenting her as a willing enabler of her rape by these three men. Rather than have an outright condemnation of the act, Klint presents a physically challenged person who describes her rape experience to a judge in terms of the sizes of her abusers' penises and how enjoyable or not each of them was. The story and Klint's performance conclude with the female judge declaring that the first two men should be locked up while the third, whom the girl professed to be the most sexually endowed, follow her to her chambers. Klint may have done a good job in downplaying the offensiveness of this narrative, but its unsuitability for his audience is evident in the facial expressions of members of the audience. Rape discourse and creating 'jokes' around it have become anathema and thus, largely not-humorous, especially when expressed by males and/or others who are not speaking from the perspective of experience. In his conclusion to this part of his routine, Klint trivialises rape. However, the mitigating statement which condemns rape in its entirety no doubt played a key role in tempering the offensiveness of this section of his act.

It is not possible to project meanings for evident instances of unlaughter in the preceding narrative, but the unease it elicited is not lost on live and mediatised audiences. There is no overemphasising how distasteful jokes created around rape and those erected around the unsettling discourses of race, religion, and ethnicity have become in both diaspora and local spaces. When a comedian is on the path to being politically incorrect, cheap laughter can be aroused, but the consequences may eventually be grave for the stand-up's career. For Nigerian stand-up to move successfully from performances to local and diaspora audiences to speak to those that are more globalised, it needs many modifications to some content and how certain subjects are treated. Such changes could however potentially deprive it of its uniqueness, making it fall somewhat flat with local and diaspora audiences, since, at present, these audiences – especially local ones – are more tolerant and forgiving of, and less susceptible to, offence than their cohorts elsewhere in the west. Diaspora audiences who come to see Nigerian stand-ups, largely know what they are coming to see. They are after that kind of humour which is different from what they are used to, the type of humour elicitation that conforms to western standards. It is little wonder then that successful Nigerian stand-up comedians can hardly find spaces to perform in Nigeria or to diaspora audiences beyond the country's borders. They are immensely popular among audiences desirous of their kind of work both within and outside the country. The marked differences in permissible subjects and the ways humour is derived are tied to the conservative, more traditional view of life among Nigerians. Just like Nollywood films which were seen, at inception, as degenerate and unworthy of scholarly attention until its fortunes turned later on, Nigerian stand-up comedy is a unique form, suitable for the environment where it evolved. It created its local audiences and succeeded in distinct ways, surpassing the attainments of the pre-existing joking traditions. Its difference in codifications of mechanisms for laughter generation does not make it inferior, but distinctive. It has its language. It has its audiences, and it is succeeding in aspects and places other forms of live humour entertainment have been less impactful.

Notes

1 In 2010, the BBC published a documentary about Nigeria's popular culture influence in parts of Africa, with respondents from different countries speaking about encounters with Nigeria, its popular culture, and people (BBC 2010).

2 Kenya (Muendo 2015), Uganda (Alinda 2019), Tanzania (Azam TV 2018), Ghana (Lequarrk 2008), Rwanda (Kagire 2019), South Africa (#JICF 2019), Zambia (Phiri 2012), Malawi (Sangala 2015), Ethiopia, and Swaziland.

3 Klint has performed in events in Uganda (Alex Muhangi Comedian 2019), Rwanda (Igihe 2018), Ghana (Anitamuleya 2010), to mention but a few.

8
Eyes on the future

One would have to be a soothsayer or of that ilk to predict Nigeria's stand-up art future. Nevertheless, its exponential growth and tremendous influence in and around the continent have shown that it will continue to be relevant for some time to come. Aside from its provision of much-needed laughter, it continues to reinvent itself in different spheres through the endeavours of its proponents, engagements with other expressive arts, and inroads made towards online presences. Stand-up's transition from marginality to the mainstream of artistic productions in Nigeria comes from the diligence and creativity of its practitioners without government or corporate body funding, especially at the beginning. Commenting on such movements by emergent traditions, Homi Bhabha writes,

> I do not mean, in any sense, to glorify margins and peripheries. However, I do want to make graphic what it means to survive, to produce, to labor and to create, within a world-system whose major economic impulses and cultural investments are pointed in a direction away from you, your country or your people. Such neglect can be a deeply negating experience, oppressive and exclusionary, and it spurs you to resist the polarities of power and prejudice, to reach beyond and behind the invidious narratives of center and periphery. (Bhabha 2004, xi)

Increased intercultural encounters engender these periphery-to-centre actions and equally enable the global shift in the locus of scholarly interests from hitherto mainstream to marginal expressions. At the same time, there has been an awakened realisation of interstitial spaces, which is the location of emergent artistic forms like stand-up comedy that, to no small extent, describe present-day experiences better than their more conventional 'others', such as theatre. These spaces referred to as 'the Third Space of enunciation, which makes the structure of meaning and reference an ambivalent process' (Bhabha 2004, 54), are spots that are betwixt and between; sites of 'negotiation' rather than 'negation.' Such locations and the expressions they foster hold products of interculturality and, as such, privilege intertextual and multi-layered expressions.

The meta-artistic nature of Nigerian stand-up comedy elicits the form of intertextuality described as calling 'attention to prior texts' while disavowing claims of 'autonomy' for any single text (Culler 1981, 103). As discussed in Chapters 1 and 3, Nigerian stand-up comedy situates itself within the formalistic appropriations of an intercultural range of joking relationships. Specifically, its constituent traits are assimilations of pre-existing indigenous forms, on the one hand, and bequests of past and ongoing western cultural influence, on the other. Therefore, it is neither 'this' nor 'that' because its form is constantly in flux, changing and adapting according to need and use. It is also neither 'here' nor 'there' in generic classification, especially given its extensive capacity to pillage forms and subjects from other expressive arts. Thus, rather than having boundaries, it is open-ended with possibilities for enhancements, extensions, and progressions into other realms of engagement with the joke subjects and audiences. Put more succinctly, Nigerian stand-up shows feature a constellation of humourists, musicians assisted by disc jockeys (DJs), and projected video shows, as well as the interplay of innovative live theatre design using lighting, scenery, and other aspects of stage sets. In addition, recordings of the live events parallel the shooting of live game shows and films, indicating the promoters' marketing intentions. Herein lays the intersections within Nigerian stand-up comedy shows – it is performed and viewed live like theatre, appropriates the embodied and spatial accoutrement of both performance and live theatre, borrows the personae and patterns of musical roadshows, and is then produced and distributed like video films. From *Nite of a Thousand Laughs, AY Live, Basket Mouth Uncensored, Rhythm Unplugged*, and *Crack Ya Ribs*, to more recently emerged ones like *Pencils Unbroken, Funny Bone Untamed, Akpororo Vs Akpororo*, and so forth, the videography and acoustics have become increasingly professionalised. Hence, there is an intrinsic fusion of theatre, performance, music, and new media in many shows. Specifically, *AY Live* has infused video projections, drama, and music into its stage presentations right from its early years.

There is no gainsaying that Nigerian stand-up comedy richly patterns itself with various artistic constituents that straddle almost all popular performance genres in the country today. However, just like its video film precursor, it is fashioned to be cost-effective, suitable for an economy that is as repressive as that within which it exists. In terms of survival, the bottom line is that Nigerian stand-up comedy practice is today patterned to make it affordable and adaptive to low-budget conditions. Thus, apart from its points of negotiating survival through hobnobbing with multiple performance forms, on one level, and artistic genres, on another, stand-up comedy in Nigeria also subscribes to multitudinous modes of distribution. It also finds expression in multiple media and has created a survival habitat betwixt and between these multifarious media. It is most probable that audience members would not find every performance enjoyable, but sections of a particular show are tailored to cater to the entertainment needs of sections of the audience. In more specific terms, stand-up comedy employs in its enactment myriad art forms, thereby subscribing to the tastes of not one individual but many individuals that make up its audience.

Thus, it inherently validates and upholds the notion that the 'existence of numerous particularities' within an internally heterogeneous setting 'does not negate the possibility or meaningfulness of shared experiences' (Flax 1990, 5). There is instead a negotiation at work here due to the intercultural nature of today's urban spaces. However, at the level where stand-up comedy disrupts conventional artistic forms, there is a negation at work. Herein resides the ambivalent nature of stand-up art: a form that negates and negotiates; one that also validates and disavows. Consequently, in consonance with Bhabha's postulations, Nigerian stand-up emerges as a hybrid art that straddles the generic interstices of various expressive arts, and is perhaps also at the threshold of a yet-to-emerge art form.

Despite the numerous bottlenecks it encountered in its developmental stride so far, stand-up comedy has become one of Nigeria's artistic success stories. In fact, of the three main emergent popular performance types in Nigeria in the past three decades, it has done the most in bringing all three genres together. Thus, stand-up comedy has become a melting pot for the arts, a more hybrid interstitial system, wherein comedians explore all humour-bearing and entertainment categories in satisfying audiences. Much of its collaborations with Nollywood have been discussed in the preceding chapters, and are shown to have been robust and mutually beneficial. In terms of its dalliance with the Naija-pop music industry, Nigerian songs have become an integral part of live shows either cued in by DJs or *karaoked* by the singers themselves. During shows, joke renditions are interspersed with song performances by popular Nigerian musicians like 2Baba (Tuface Idibia), PSquare, 9ice, Faze, Olamide, and Mo-Hit Squad, as well as those who have recently become popular like Burna Boy, Davido, Simi, Omawumi, Yemi Alade, and many others. The music artists engaged for most mainstream shows are those who are successful, and whose songs are topping the charts locally and internationally. Their stage performances mainly comprise singing along to pre-recorded background music rather than providing the more expensive live band renditions. With the aid of highly sought-after DJs, like DJ Jimmy Jatt and others equally successful, semblances of the recorded songs are provided while the singers sing along, sometimes with accompanying backup vocalists and dancers. Even for solo performances that Basket Mouth champions in his *Basket Mouth Uncensored* series, musicians are engaged to keep the auditorium lively, thereby creating a party atmosphere.

Interestingly, audience response to these songs is immediate, mostly coming from recognising the musician or the song, or both. Perhaps part of the fun is the recognition of the songs and the popularity of the artists themselves. As stated earlier, audiences often join singers vociferously in a sing-along fashion and dance steps to show their admiration for and appreciation of the performances. One supposes that this overwhelming participation by the mostly youthful audiences is buoyed by the excitement of seeing these music performers live on stage singing the same popular songs they are known for. There is however a sharp contrast between stand-up comedy and musical performances. Comedians are quarantined on stage, getting no help except when they have succeeded in making the audience laugh; musicians get all the help they need once their names are mentioned. More specifically, comedians do not get much help telling their jokes, but musicians get audiences on their feet, singing with gusto, once the first key of any of their songs comes through the speakers. Comedians get laughs from the audience, mostly when their jokes are new and full of the element of surprise, but musicians who sing unfamiliar songs get disheartened applause. This disparity has given rise to suggestions that being a stand-up artist is more complicated than being a musician. The latter gains popularity by repetition, whereas the former gets his or hers by being perpetually creative and new. Therefore, for humourists, applause does not come until they have earned it through a sterling rendition of a series of hilarious jokes. Some even need to compel audiences merely to welcome them with applause. Generally speaking, unlike songs, jokes need to be fresh (and funny) to elicit any favourable reception. Nevertheless, despite the contrast between these two entertainment genres, music performance has continued to be a regular feature in stand-up events. Rather than keep musicians away from the stand-up stage, comedians have co-opted popular songs into their renditions. Interestingly, the elicitation of popular songs always excites audiences the same way they do when the singers themselves render the songs. The difference is that when using such songs, comedians seek to enact parody or some other form of satirical interpretation of these songs. AY, Klint da Drunk, Kenny Blaq, and a couple of others immediately come to mind in this regard. As part of their performance style, they generate humour through song parodies and often play the songs they need before saying things they want to, about the singers or their products. They also make use of songs played by DJs or live bands.

Stand-up comedy's openness and receptivity also encompass its choices in mediums of expression. It is mainly a stage art but persistently seeps through cracks in the boundaries of the stage into other arenas. The first indications of its attempts at escaping the confines of the stage can be seen in earlier events like *AY Live 2: Lagos Invasion*. The innovative use of video projections and dramatic comedy epitomises some of the initial steps taken by this art form to incorporate performance spaces other than the stage. The seamless transition from AY sleeping in his bed and almost missing the show projected on the big screen, his numerous near delays by security and the likes, and his jumping onto the stage at the right time, all indicate this fusion of locations within stand-up comedy. Within Nigerian practice, stand-up comedy is much more than standing on stage behind a microphone and telling jokes to the audience, expecting to get applause at the end. It is no longer about individual performers telling individual jokes and taking their leave. It is about a total package, a variety show with joke-telling as the main course, with other forms of enactment equally served in varying measures. This practice accentuates Eugenio Barba's postulation that '(d)issimilar histories navigate a common river' even though every 'performing artist is different' due to their individual use of words, metaphors, and 'aesthetic or scientific orientations' (Barba 1995, 151). While the idea is to provide total entertainment that caters to the needs of different individuals, the purpose has been to enhance the social capital and relevance of stand-up comedy for audiences both within Nigeria and in the diaspora.

Besides appropriations of other entertainment genres within stand-up renditions, successful humourists have diversified into artistic productions in other mediums. For instance, AY has gone from presenting various shows, including *AY's Crib* and *Call to Bar*, to making feature-length comedy movies, in which he plays lead roles alongside other popular Nollywood actors. His MVP Lounge in Lekki, Lagos, which opened in 2014, is a plush exclusive club set up to cater to premium clientele in the commercial city. *AY's Crib* commenced in 2013, starring Alex Ekubo, Venita Akpofure, and Justice Nuagbe, who took his character's name, Ushbebe, to the comedy stage and hosted his events, *The Chronicles of Ushbebe Live* and comedy skits which he posts on his YouTube channels. His *Call to Bar* commenced in 2020 and stars comedians like Real Warri Pikin, Chigul, Buchi, and the online comedy sensation, Broda Shaggi. He has produced a number of films like *30 Days in Atlanta* (2014), *A Trip to Jamaica* (2016), *Ten Days in Sun City* (2016), *Merry Men: The Real Yoruba Demons* (2018), and *Merry Men 2* (2019). The exciting part of AY's filmmaking is that he opted to use cinemas for their screening rather than go the Nollywood way of distribution. These films belong to the top-grossing box office hits in the years they were screened (Bada 2019; Udodiong 2019). Most of these films are also being streamed on Netflix. For his part, Basket Mouth is well-known for his long-running television series on DStv channels, *My Flatmates*, in which he also stars as an actor. In 2019, the sitcom celebrated its 565th episode and six years on air, making it one of Nigeria's longest-running television sitcoms. The story of how the show came up from almost nothing, shut down for four years, and was revived with DStv's Africa Magic support is symptomatic of the kind of doggedness that has sustained stand-up practice in Nigeria (Ekpu 2019). He launched his comedy web series sitcom, *Papa Benji,* in 2020, featuring Basket Mouth and other stage comedians like Buchi, Senator Comedian, and Maleke, and the duo of Nedu Wazobia and Broda Shaggi renowned for their online comedy skits. In the same year, Basket Mouth released his music album, *Yabasi*, featuring song collaborations with other established Nigerian singers like Phyno, Flavour, and Umu Obiligbo. One review (of the album) exposes Basket Mouth's ingenious contributions to the Nigerian music industry through this album:

Basketmouth is not an artist, nor did he perform any song across the ten tracks and 30 minutes that form 'Yabasi.' […]. With 'Yabasi,' he shows an acumen for cohesive, progressive music formation that's so often missing from Nigerian music. 'Yabasi' is not just a surprise package because nobody ever thought Basketmouth would make an album, its quality is also a surprise package – the biggest shocker of the year. For years, people had spoken in lofty, hallowed adulation of Basketmouth's 'music head' tendencies and this is the confirmation of all that. [The album is] characterized by Highlife, Palmwine Music, Folk and Afro-Fusion. […] While horns, guitars, elements of Igbo Folk and toms collide like they moved at the prompt of an orchestra's wand, [the music producer] distinguishes those sounds with the drum arrangement they come with. (Alake 2020)

Other Nigerian comedians have diversified their online and television presences, with Ali Baba running a satirical television programme on NTA, *Strictly Speaking*, while Okey Bakassi has *The Other News*.

So many online comedians have emerged in Nigeria in recent times. Some of them have taken to the stage to perform – Josh2funny, Broda Shaggi, and Emmanuella, for example. In each of their performances, the differences between dramatic and stand-up comedy become very evident. That a performer has done creditably well in online comedy does not necessarily mean that they can translate into being equally good at live stand-up performances. As such, stage appearances for some of the aforementioned have been somewhat lacklustre in terms of performance. Nevertheless, audiences recognise them for their online work and hail them for what no doubt is their previous online successes since their stage work has not necessarily elicited the same kind of mirth as their online comedy skits. Inversely, Nigerian stage humourists also experimented with online joke performance during the COVID-19 pandemic that resulted in restrictions and shutting down of live events for most of 2020 and early 2021. For this reason, there has been a tremendous increase in online presence of stage comedians. Hence, online comedy has become more emboldened, with newer skits and personae growing increasingly popular and gaining more patronage, unlike before. Virtual performances have become the norm, with various stand-up artists embracing them to keep their arts alive. The exciting aspect of developments in online comedy is the increased participation of young, female participants who would ordinarily have found it difficult to break into mainstream stage performances. These women have found expression through the internet, deploying social media platforms to disseminate various forms of comedy and reach out to a wide range of audiences across the continent and beyond.

The youngest female comedian, Emmanuella Samuel, born in July 2010, came into the national limelight with the skit, "Not my real face" (Comedyzone 2018). Known by just her first name, "Emmanuella," this young comedian has recorded several successes to her name. After passing an audition for children, she came into comedy at the age of five playing a part in a Mark Angel Comedy production. Since then, Emmanuella has become the real face of MarkAngelComedy skits, with a YouTube page that has over 7 million subscribers and 1.3 million Instagram followers. Mark Angel has also provided opportunities for other child comedy prodigies, about Emmanuella's age to emerge, like Success Madubuike (popularly known as Aunty Success) and Success Adegor. Adegor's rise to stardom came from a viral video in which she walks home from school before school is over. The person filming asks her why she is going home early, and the quick-witted, fast-talking young child says that it is because her fees have not been paid and that the teachers can continue flogging her as much as they want but her parents do not have the money to pay the fees (Ekpu 2019). It was a desperate call for help that received serious support for both the young girl and her family from all over Nigeria. That was her entry into the Mark Angel Comedy circle. Emmanuella herself has been on several stage performances, sometimes in collaboration with Mark Angel himself, and other friends of hers – *AY Live Show* (TheBroadway TV 2019), *Funnybone Untamed* (FunnyBone Comedy TV 2017), and *Akpororo vs Akpororo* (Gemini Dreams Media 2017). These young comedians have also had several stage performances outside Nigeria – in the Gambia (Pizzy Vibes 2019), Ghana (Zion Felix 2016), and Uganda (Deejay Wilx PRO 2019), to mention a few.

Social media has opened up hitherto inaccessible opportunities for myriad artistic expressions in Nigeria. Numerous youthful female comedians now propagate their visions of society through comedy skits, mostly on Instagram and YouTube. Wilfred Okiche (2020) captures this succinctly when he avers that,

> [...] the comedy scene has historically been a boys' club, where success meant making your way up through the male-dominated world of standup gigs, headline shows, and television appearances. On the internet, there are no such gatekeepers. And for Nigerian women, that means that they are finally beginning to see their own experiences reflected back (sic) on their smartphone screens. Instead of being the butt of male comedians' jokes, female comedians like Maraji say they are flipping the script, showing that women can dish out humor too.

The coterie of Nigerian female comedians is growing by the day. It is presently led by Gloria Oloruntobi (@maraji), Maryam Apaokagi (@taaooma), and Adeyela Adebola (@iamlizzyjay), popularly called Omo Ibadan, with well over a million followers each on Instagram. Maraji and Taaooma, in their respective skits, often enact actions and respond to the same in multiple roleplays of mother-daughter, student-teacher, and many other relationships. The individual action and reaction shots are merged into one and presented as short comic videos. Maraji is also renowned for her variety of parodies of dance, religion, people, and so forth, while Taaooma has garnered a name for herself though her signature exaggerated slaps and intertextuality, where the words of characters are juxtaposed with parallels based on puns, consonance, and other similarities. Omo Ibadan performs mainly in Yoruba and pidgin English, using an Ibadan accent to punctuate her punchlines and elicit laughter.

The other aspect of the emergence of female online comedians is their representations of various ethnicities and localities in Nigeria. For example, Hafeezah Salau (i_am_feezah) and Chinaza Ezeani (miss_ezeani) take up Hausa and Igbo stereotypes, respectively, while Stephanie Isuma (@calabar_chic), Maryam Oyakhilome (@mariam_oyahkhilome), and Oluwatoyin Albert (@datwarrigirl) enact acts ascribable to folks from Calabar, Benin, and Warri areas, respectively.[1] While the stage has not been particularly receptive to female performers, online spaces have; hence, the explosive emergence of youthful women in the comedy arena.[2] A number of male comedians have also gained large social media followings and acclaim in recent times. These include Animashaun Samuel Perry (@brodashaggi), who plays the role of an *agbero* (a motor park tout, Lagos area boy), Lasisi Elenu (@lasisielenu) who makes use of a Snapchat filter to alter his face and voice for comedic effect, and Chibuike Josh Alfred (@josh2funny) who elicits humour from crossdressing and imitating women.

It is interesting to see all the successes that stand-up comedy in Nigeria has recorded as stand-alone art and the attainments it has achieved in its numerous liaisons with other genres. One foresees that – owing to its accommodative capabilities – it will remain a pervasive art form in Nigeria for some time to come. This book has illustrated the various ways it has shown its adaptability to the nation's undulating socioeconomic conditions. For that reason alone, it indubitably possesses the capacity to contract in the lean times and blossom in the times of plenty. Just prior to the COVID-19 pandemic, stand-up comedy seemed to at an all-time high in the country. Then, as the lockdown started taking its toll on live performances and close human contact, instead of withering, stand-up comedy took up virtual dissemination of its expressions, indicating its purposeful determination to survive in all conditions. The other reason stand-up comedy will continue to thrive in the perennial socioeconomic and political turmoil that the nation has been undergoing is that there is always a market for laughter in conditions of distress. Stand-up comedy forms part of the avenues for the elicitation of mirth, not just for the comedians but also the Nigerian general public who characteristically endeavour to squeeze humour out of every condition no matter how discomfiting and uncomfortable. It is not for nothing that Nigerians are referred to as one of Earth's happiest peoples. For that same reason, the music legend, Fela Anikulapo-Kuti, sang the song, "Shuffering and Shmiling," to capture the tenor of laughter in the face of unimaginable human suffering. Nigerians are survivors because they always find reasons to laugh in the face of actual and seemingly insurmountable problems, challenges, and difficulties.

Notes

1   I have concentrated on the females here because of the massive underrepresentation they have received in the stage version of comedic expressions in Nigeria. Undoubtedly, the elevation of comedians' social status enabled by stand-up comedy's successes has so empowered comedians economically that they can engage in expressions in other genres independently.

2   This list is not exhaustive as newer performers are still emerging such as: Jessica Anagor (@jessiekaey), Perpetua Chris (@perpetuachris), Ogechi Ukonu (@caramel_plugg), Amarachi Amusi (@ashmusy), Mary Grace Ogbu Chioma (@ekwutousi), and Sanni Iyabo (@paramountkomedy). They mainly use YouTube to disseminate longer comedy videos.

Bibliography

#JICF, Johannesburg International Comedy Festival. 2019. "Basketmouth (Nigeria) – Church – Johannesburg International Comedy Festival 2017." *YouTube* March 07. Accessed December 01, 2020. https://www.youtube.com/watch?v=7eB0Mfp2ciE.

AB Jokes Awhana. 2020. "AB-Jokes Insulted all the Yoruba People." *YouTube* April 25. Accessed August 14, 2020. https://www.youtube.com/watch?v=JiZYTgyviRM.

Abusidiq. 2012. "I'm Now A Billionaire; Says Comedian, Ali Baba." *Abusidiq Blog* August 24. Accessed August 13, 2020. https://www.abusidiqu.com/im-now-a-billionaire-says-comedian-ali-baba/.

AcapellaTV. 2017. "Sam and Song Goes Crazy." *YouTube* March 15. Accessed December 15, 2020. https://www.youtube.com/watch?v=_NRuLdMbero.

Achebe, Chinua. 1958. *Things Fall Apart*. London: Heinemann.

Adamu, Abdalla Uba. 2013. "Transgressing Boundaries: Reinterpretation of Nollywood Films in Muslim Northern Nigeria." In *Global Nollywood: The Transnational Dimensions of an African Video Film Industry*, edited by Matthias Krings and Onookome Okome, 287–305. Bloomington: Indiana University Press.

Adebayo, Segun. 2012. "People Should Stop Talking about My Wife and I – Ali Baba." *Modern Ghana* January 22. Accessed October 31, 2020. https://www.modernghana.com/nollywood/17131/people-should-stop-talking-about-my-wife-and-i.html.

Adebowale, Segun. 2013. "Oshiomhole Appoints Comedian Maleke as Aide." *The Eagle Online* March 31. Accessed June 23, 2020. https://theeagleonline.com.ng/oshiomhole-appoints-comedian-maleke-as-aide/.

Adedeji, Joel, and Hyginus Ekwuazi. 1998. *Nigerian Theatre: Dynamics of a Movement*. Ibadan: Caltop.

Adejunmobi, Moradewun. 1999. "Routes: Language and the Identity of African Literature." *The Journal of Modern African Studies* 37 (4): 581–596. http://www.jstor.org/stable/161427.

Adekunle, James Idowu. 2014. "Satiric Performativity of Stand-up Comedy in Nigeria." MPhil Dissertation. Department of English, University of Ibadan, Nigeria.

Adesina, Gbenro. 2011. "Why I Married 18 Wives – Elder Moses Olaya Adejumo (MON) a.k.a. Baba Sala." *Modern Ghana* May 27. Accessed April 23, 2021. https://www.modernghana.com/nollywood/14702/why-i-married-18-wives-elder-moses-olaya-adejum.html.

Adetunji, Akin. 2013. "The Interactional Context of Humor in Nigerian Stand-up Comedy." *Pragmatics* 23 (1): 1–22. doi:10.1075/prag.23.1.01ade.

African Glitz TV. 2018. "AY Live in London 2018." *YouTube* November 30. Accessed December 15, 2020. https://www.youtube.com/watch?v=JUlWkCdX9Xc.

Afroway TV. 2020. "Comedian Acapella Ask Buhari Are You Doing Well." *YouTube* March 10. Accessed August 13, 2020. https://www.youtube.com/watch?v=XZlP5Oh85rc.

Agbiboa, Daniel Egiegba. 2003. "Ethno-religious Conflicts and the Elusive Quest for National Identity in Nigeria." *Journal of Black Studies* 44 (1): 3–30. http://www.jstor.org/stable/23414701.

Agunwa, Jude C. 1997. "Religious Conflict in Nigeria: Impact on Nation Building." *Dialectical Anthropology* 22 (3/4): 335-351.

Agwu, Julius. 2013. *Jokes Apart: How Did I Get Here.* Lagos: Reel Laif Books.

Ahmad, Sa'idu Babura and Graham Furniss. 1994. "Pattern, Interaction, and the Non-Dialogic in Performance by Hausa Rap Artists." *Oral Tradition* 9 (1): 113–135.

Aigbokhaevbolo, Oris. 2018. "Nollywood, Trevor Noah, and The Comedy of Basketmouth." *The Medium* April 16. Accessed October 31, 2020. https://medium.com/@Catchoris/nollywood-trevor-noah-and-the-comedy-of-basketmouth-30e8fc7ba1cc.

Ajaye, Franklyn. 2002. *Comic Insights: The Art of Stand-up Comedy.* Beverly Hills. CA: Silman-James Press.

Ajayi-Soyinka, Omofolabo. 2011. "Performing Liberation, Performing Identity: The Theatre of Ogunde, 1944-1946." In *Les littératures africaines: Textes et terrains*, edited by Virginia Coulon and Xavier Garnier, 93–107. Paris: Karthala.

Ajumobi, Kemi. 2016. "Lepacious Bose … A Story of Commitment, Optimism and Results." *Business Day* May 20. Accessed November 02, 2020. https://businessday.ng/personality/article/lepacious-bose-a-story-of-commitment-optimism-and-results/.

Akande, Akinmade, Kofo Adedeji, and Anjola Robbin. 2019. "Language, Vulgarity and Social Critique: The Case of Nigerian Pidgin in Stand-up Comedy." *Lagos Notes and Records* 25 (1): 89–109. http://lnr.unilag.edu.ng/article/view/898.

Akinkahunsi, Timileyin. 2018. "How Depression brought out the Talent in Me – Real Warri Pikin." *Punch* November 03. Accessed May 10, 2021. https://punchng.com/how-depression-brought-out-the-talent-in-me-real-warri-pikin/

Akinrele, Akinsetan. 2019. "Opa Williams: 'Nite of A Thousand Laughs' Was Conceived at Igbobi Orthopedic Hospital." *eelive* May 29. Accessed November 01, 2020. https://www.eelive.ng/opa-williams-nite-of-a-thousand-laughs-was-conceived-at-igbobi-orthopedic-hospital/.

Akoma, Chiji. 2009. "Verbal Miscues or Cultural Agency? "Icheoku": An Introduction." *Research in African Literatures* 40 (1): 86–96. ttps://www.jstor.org/stable/30131188.

Akoni, Olasunkanmi. 2020. "Buhari appoints Ali Baba, Segun Arinze, Dare Art Alade, others into COVID-19 committee." *Vanguard* May 06. Accessed August 15, 2020. https://www.vanguardngr.com/2020/05/buhari-appoints-ali-baba-segun-arinze-others-into-covid-19-cttee/.

Alake, Motolani. 2020. "With 'Yabasi,' Basketmouth is the surprise package of 2020 in Nigerian music [Pulse Album Review]." *Pulse.ng* November 28. Accessed December 15, 2020. https://www.pulse.ng/entertainment/music/basketmouth-yabasi-album-review/m0etrfp.

Alex Muhangi Comedian. 2019. "Alex Muhangi Comedy Store July 2019 - Klint D Drunk (Part 2)." *YouTube* July 02. Accessed December 01, 2020. https://www.youtube.com/watch?v=2mcZdxqhuJw.

Alhassan, Amina. 2012. "2Face Made Me Drop My Music Career – Klint Da Drunk." *Daily Trust* January 14. Accessed November 06, 2020. https://dailytrust.com/2face-made-me-drop-my-music-career-klint-da-drunk.

Alinda, Alex. 2019. "'I Enjoy Performing in Uganda' – Says Nigerian Comedian Basketmouth." *The Tower Post* August 15. Accessed December 10, 2020. https://thetowerpost.com/2019/08/15/i-enjoy-performing-in-uganda-says-nigerian-comedian-basketmouth/.

Al Jazeera English. 2015. "My Nigeria – Basketmouth: Trash Talking." *YouTube* August 24. Accessed August 22, 2020. https://www.youtube.com/watch?v=2Kba2pzJgN0.

All Def Stand Up. 2018. "Chinedu Unaka – I Don't Speak Igbo | All Def Stand Up." *YouTube* June 14. Accessed October 01, 2020. https://www.youtube.com/watch?v=GVuyhqIOUX4.

Allure. 2019. "'The Biggest Weight Loss Secret I Know is Information' – Lepacious Bose." *Vanguard* September 02. Accessed November 02, 2020. https://allure.vanguardngr.com/2019/09/the-biggest-weight-loss-secret-i-know-is-information-lepacious-bose/.

Allure1. 2019. "Weight Loss Journey: I Can't Count How Many Tears I Shed – Lepacious Bose." *Vanguard* June 19. Accessed November 02, 2020. https://allure.vanguardngr.com/2019/06/lepacious-bose/.

Amatus, Azuh. 2005/2020. "Why I'm Not Practising as a Lawyer, Star Actress, Najite Dede." *NOMAREC* November 12. Accessed May 05, 2021. https://nomarec.com/2020/11/12/why-im-not-practising-as-a-lawyer-star-actress-najite-dede-by-azuh-amatus/.

Anitamuleya. 2010. "Klint da Drunk." *YouTube* September 21. Accessed February 24, 2011. https://www.youtube.com/watch?v=elcxD1sw-dw.

Anokam, Sam. 2011. "No comedy without me – Opa Williams." *The Nigerian Voice* July 09. Accessed November 01, 2020. https://www.thenigerianvoice.com/movie/55702/no-comedy-without-me-opa-williams.html.

Apter, Andrew. 1998. "Discourse and its Disclosures: Yoruba Women and the Sanctity of Abuse." *Africa* 68 (1): 68–97. doi:10.2307/1161148.

Apter, Andrew. 2007. *Beyond Words: Discourse and Critical Agency in Africa*. Chicago and London: University of Chicago Press.

ArseRaptor. 2010. "Andi Osho – Edinburgh Comedy Fest 2010." *YouTube* September 17. Accessed December 02, 2020. https://www.youtube.com/watch?v=ezW_4RjLPuQ&t=92s.

ArseRaptor. 2013. "Andi Osho Live at the Apollo." *YouTube* December 22. Accessed December 02, 2020. https://www.youtube.com/watch?v=5Q56ZiDDiX8.

Astil, James, and Owen Bowcott. 2002. "Fatwa is Issued on Nigerian Journalist." *The Guardian* November 27. Accessed December 31, 2020. https://www.theguardian.com/world/2002/nov/27/jamesastill.owenbowcott#:~:text=An%20Islamist%20state%20government%20in,more%20than%20220%20people%20dead.

Augoye, Jayne. 2016. "Nigerian Comedian, Gandoki." *Premium Times* October 11. Accessed November 01, 2020. https://www.premiumtimesng.com/

entertainment/212529-i-made-guiness-world-record-nigerian-comedian-gandoki.html.

Augoye, Jayne. 2019. "Basketmouth Speaks on Rape Joke that Cost him EU Slot." *Premium Times* December 03. Accessed December 28, 2019. https://www.premiumtimesng.com/entertainment/nollywood/366376-basketmouth-speaks-on-rape-joke-that-cost-him-eu-slot.html.

Auslander, Philip. 1992. "Comedy about the Failure of Comedy: Stand-up Comedy and Postmodernism." In *Critical Theory and Performance*, edited by Janelle G. Reinelt and Joseph R. Roach, 196–207. Ann Arbor: The University of Michigan Press.

Auslander, Philip. 2004. "Postmodernism and Performance." In *The Cambridge Companion to Postmodernism*, edited by Steven Connor, 97–115. Cambridge: Cambridge University Press. doi:10.1017/CCOL0521640520.006.

Awaritoma, Agoma. 2009. *Stand-up Comedy in Nigeria: A Critical Tool for Societal Development*. Abuja: Etax Printing Press.

Awaritoma, Agoma. 2015. "Laughing All the Way to The Bank: A History of Stand-up Comedy in Nigeria." *Nigeria the Goodnews*. Accessed March 15, 2016. http://nigeriathegoodnews.com/2015/01/laughing-way-bank-history-stand-comedy-nigeria/.

Awojulughe, Oluseyi. 2017. "Married a Virgin at 33, Divorced after a Year … Chigul Opens Up about Her Private Life." *The Cable Lifestyle* May 30. Accessed May 09, 2021. https://lifestyle.thecable.ng/married-virgin-divorced-chigul/

Awosiyan, Kunle. n.d. "Silverbird Man of the Year: Ali Baba Gives Accounts of How He Met Obasanjo." *Silverbird TV*. Accessed June 23, 2020. https://silverbirdtv.com/entertainment/71186/silverbird-man-of-the-year-ali-baba-gives-accounts-of-how-he-met-obasanjo/.

Ayakoroma, Barclays Foubiri. 2013. "The Rise of Stand-up Comedy Genre in Nigeria: From Nothing to Something in Artistic Entertainment." *National Institute for Cultural Orientation* July 14. Accessed October 31, 2020. https://nico.gov.ng/the-rise-of-stand-up-comedy-genre-in-nigeria/.

AY Comedian. 2013. "AY's Idol Skits – Ay Idol Skit: Omotola, Stella Damascus, Frank Edoho and Jedi." *YouTube* January 24. Accessed December 15, 2020. https://www.youtube.com/watch?v=-J1bAXxeNgo&list=UUvO4Ym5LjYTo0uZRfUvtc-w.

AY Comedian. 2014. "Okey Bakassi In Search of Who Wrote 'Things Fall Apart'."

YouTube March 18. Accessed November 12, 2020. https://www.youtube.com/watch?v=FKhs2tu9H2o.

AY Comedian. 2015. "Osama in AY Live?" *YouTube* March 31. Accessed December 24, 2020. https://www.youtube.com/watch?v=WkhSIPC9m4s.

AY Comedian. 2016a. "AY Live: Gordons takes on Princess, Mo Hits, Mode 9." *YouTube* May 12. Accessed December 15, 2020. https://www.youtube.com/watch?v=ZD29iQRG1Vc.

AY Comedian. 2016b. "Helen Paul, Gordons & I Go Dye Please, My Show is a Gospel Show Enough is Enough." *YouTube* September 05. Accessed December 24, 2020. https://www.youtube.com/watch?v=z-Pu_h-hLEY.

AY Comedian. 2017. "Emeka Smith Tearing London Audience Apart." *YouTube* September 21. Accessed November 13, 2020. https://www.youtube.com/watch?v=qP5TF_rKHIE.

AY Comedian. 2018a. "I Love Sam and Songs." *YouTube* March 14. Accessed December 15, 2020. https://www.youtube.com/watch?v=l3e0zQUk2RI.

AY Comedian. 2018b. "Klint Da Drunk Settles Beef with AY." *YouTube* January 06. Accessed December 12, 2020. https://www.youtube.com/watch?v=qNI4H37dVsY&t=304s.

AY Comedian. 2018c. "Sam & Song at AY Live London 2017." *YouTube* January 15. Accessed December 28, 2020. https://www.youtube.com/watch?v=IsZ5ya0Dd-A&pbjreload=101.

AY Comedian. 2020a. "Destalker AYLive Warri 2019." *YouTube* August 10. Accessed November 12, 2020. https://www.youtube.com/watch?v=b0Fio2SvCpg.

AY Comedian. 2020b. "Real Warri Pikin - Wetin Dey Play? (AY Live UK)." *YouTube* March 03. Accessed December 14, 2020. https://www.youtube.com/watch?v=cupmyV9LMgw.

AYL. 2011. *AY Live 2011*. VCD. Prod. Ayo Makun.

AYL2. 2007. *AY Live Volume 2*. VCD. Prod. Ayo Makun.

AYL3. n.d. *AY Live Volume 3*. VCD. Prod. Ayo Makun.

AYL5. n.d. *AY Live Volume 5*. VCD. Prod. Ayo Makun.

Azam TV. 2018. "Hatari tupu …!! Basket Mouth alivyoitikisa Tanzania – 31/12/2017." *YouTube* January 03. Accessed December 01, 2020. https://www.youtube.com/watch?v=fcIrMsAl7Cg.

Babalola, Ebun. 2009. "Comedy Now a Game for the Riffraff – Allam Bloo." *Vanguard* September 26. Accessed November 01, 2020. https://www.vanguardngr. com/2009/09/comedy-now-a-game-for-the-riffraff-allam-bloo/.

Bada, Gbenga. 2019. "Kemi Adetiba says AY is Nollywood's 'Box Office King'." *Pulse.ng* October 10. Accessed December 15, 2020. https://www.pulse.ng/ entertainment/movies/kemi-adetiba-says-ay-is-nollywoods-box-office- king/5xthbn1.

Banham, Martin, Errol Hill, and George Woodyard. 1994. *The Cambridge Guide to African and Caribbean Theatre*. Cambridge: Cambridge University Press.

Baraka, Amiri. 1968. *Blues People: Negro Music in White America*. New York: W. Morrow.

Barba, Eugenio. 1995. *The Paper Canoe: A Guide to Theatre Anthropology*. Translated by Richard Fowler. London and New York: Routledge.

Barber, Karin. 2017. *A History of African Popular Culture*. Cambridge: Cambridge University Press. doi:10.1017/9781139061766.

Barrot, Pierre, ed. 2005. *Nollywood: The Video Phenomenon in Nigeria*. Bloomington & Indianapolis: Indiana University Press.

Bellanaija. 2017. "Too Controversial? AY Makun's #BBNaija Joke at the 2017 AY Live is causing quite the Reaction on Social Media." *Bella Naija* April 17. Accessed December 26, 2020. https://www.bellanaija.com/2017/04/too- controversial-ay-makuns-bbnaija-joke-at-the-2017-ay-live-is-causing-quite- the-reaction-on-social-media/.

Betiang, Liwhu. 2013. "Global Drums and Local Masquerades: Fifty Years of Television Broadcasting in Nigeria: 1959–2009." *Sage Open* 3 (4) December 10. doi:10.1177/2158244013515685.

Bhabha, Homi K. 2004. *The Location of Culture*. London & New York: Routledge.

Billig, Michael. 2005. *Laughter and Ridicule: Towards a Social Critique of Humour*. London: Sage Publications.

Blank, Trevor J. 2016. "Giving the 'Big Ten' a Whole New Meaning: Tasteless Humor and the Response to the Penn State Sexual Abuse Scandal." In *The Folkloresque: Reframing Folklore in a Popular Culture World*, edited by Michael Dylan Foster and Jeffrey A. Tolbert, 179–204. Logan: Utah State University Press.

BMU2. 2007. *Basket Mouth Uncensored Volume 2*. VCD. Prod. Bright Okpocha. CN Media.

BMU3. 2009. *Basket Mouth Uncensored Volume 3*. VCD. Prod. Bright Okpocha. CN Media.

Bodunde, Charles. 2001. *Oral Traditions and Aesthetic Transfer: Creativity and Social Vision in Contemporary Black Poetry*. Bayreuth: Bayreuth African Studies.

Boricua, Orgullo. 2018. "Gina Yashere Stand Up Comedy." *YouTube* May 26. Accessed January 24, 2020. https://www.youtube.com/watch?v=HYegKkfJ65k.

Boss Blaze. 2015. "How Reggae Music Is Made According to Klint The Drunk … Hilarious!!" *YouTube* October 15. Accessed November 15, 2020. https://www.youtube.com/watch?v=PWWVPhDcro8.

Buckman-Owoo, Jayne. 2018. "Comedy was the Last Thing on My Mind – Heiress Jacinta." *Graphic Showbiz* January 18. Accessed December 10, 2020. https://www.graphic.com.gh/entertainment/celebrity/comedy-was-the-last-thing-on-my-mind-heiress-jacinta.html.

Bunkley, Nick. 2012. "Would-Be Plane Bomber Is Sentenced to Life in Prison." *The New York Times* February 16. Accessed December 02, 2020. https://www.nytimes.com/2012/02/17/us/would-be-plane-bomber-sentenced-to-life.html.

Channels Television. 2015. "EN: Imitating Children Has Been Helping Me in Comedy – Helen Paul." *YouTube* October 21. Accessed December 24, 2020. https://www.youtube.com/watch?v=WogRjcp50a4.

Channels Television. 2018. "Faceoff: President Buhari Watches as Comedian MC Tagwaye Mimics Him." *YouTube* June 23. Accessed December 24, 2020. https://www.youtube.com/watch?v=VvPvX4JWZ0Q.

Chima, Chudi. 2016. "Gandoki Breaks World Record, Sets New One with 48 Hours Stand-up Comedy." *The Cable Lifestyle* October 02. Accessed November 01, 2020. https://lifestyle.thecable.ng/gandoki-stand-up-comedy-record/.

Chima, Francis U. 2017. "Satire in Traditional African Oral Poetry: The Edda Igbo Example." *Ethnosensitive Dimensions of African Oral Literature: Igbo Perspectives*, edited by Afam Ebeogu, 105–137. New York: African Heritage Press.

Chimezie, Amuzia. 1976. "The Dozens: An African-Heritage Theory." *Journal of Black Studies* 6 (4): 401–420. doi:10.1177/002193477600600407.

ChortleUK. 2011. "Andi Osho on Dave's One Night Stand." *YouTube* April 18. Accessed December 02, 2020. https://www.youtube.com/watch?v=nFAW5d-FG3k&t=70s.

Churchill Show. 2017a. "Basketmouth Performance at Laugh Festival 2." *YouTube* December 17. Accessed December 01, 2020. https://www.youtube.com/watch?v=fs_eF49kaok.

Churchill Show. 2017b. "Nigerian Men Compliment in Capital Letters – Salvado." *YouTube* December 24. Accessed December 01, 2020. https://www.youtube.com/watch?v=H6wEHlHiooY&list=RDmuLhHKlcwLI&index=12.

Chreist, Fred M. 1969. *Foreign Accent.* Princeton: Prentice-Hall.

Clark, Ebun. 1980. *Hubert Ogunde: The Making of Nigerian Theatre.* Oxford: Oxford University Press.

Coates, Oliver. 2017. "Hubert Ogunde's *Strike and Hunger* and the 1945 General Strike in Lagos: Labor and Reciprocity in the Kingdom of Ọba Yẹ́jídé." *Research in African Literatures* 48 (2): 166–184. doi:10.2979/reseafrilite.48.2.12.

Comedy Central Stand-Up. 2020. "The Weirdly Racial Undertones of 'Willy Wonka' – Opey Olagbaju – Stand-Up Featuring." *YouTube* January 28. Accessed December 26, 2020. https://www.youtube.com/watch?v=262-t-kgw6M.

Comics News. 2009b. "'How I get My Jokes' – Mandy Uzonitsha." *The Nigerian Voice* November 09. Accessed November 03, 2020. https://www.thenigerianvoice.com/news/7642/how-i-get-my-jokes-mandy-uzonitsha.html.

Comics News. n.d. "I'm Single 'cos I Don't Want Just any Relationship – Lepacious Bose." *Nigeria Film.com.* Accessed November 02, 2020. https://www.nigeriafilms.com/more/88-comics-news/8255-i-m-single-cos-i-don-t-want-just-any-relationship-lepacious-bose.

Comics News. 2009a. "Unveiling Nigeria's Female Comedians." *The Nigerian Voice* July 10. Accessed November 03, 2020. https://www.thenigerianvoice.com/lifestyle/7024/unveiling-nigerias-female-comedians.html.

Coetzee, Marié-Heleen. 2018. "Embodied Knowledge(s), Embodied Pedagogies and Performance." *South African Theatre Journal* 31 (1): 1–4. doi:10.1080/10137548.2018.1425527.

Comedyzone. 2018. "Not My Real Face Emmanuella Mark Angel Comedy." *YouTube* June 15. Accessed December 15, 2020. https://www.youtube.com/watch?v=OxFVejKzl-c.

COZATV. 2015. "Akpororo in COZA [COZA at 16]." *YouTube* April 06. Accessed December 14, 2020. https://www.youtube.com/watch?v=2J2-bz7fi4I.

CreatedbyKelz. 2018. "BasketMouth Live in Antwerp Belgium | Comedy | Lord of the Ribs | The Son of Peter." *YouTube* February 21. Accessed December 02, 2020. https://www.youtube.com/watch?v=CLF3PVRnvMI.

Culler, Jonathan. 1981. *The Pursuit of Signs: Semiotics, Literature, Deconstruction.* Ithaca: Cornell University Press.

Cybertechproduction. 2011. "Gina Yashere Live DVD – Produced by Paul M Green." *YouTube* January 26. Accessed January 29, 2020. https://www.youtube.com/watch?v=LQFTQRIWtdE.

CYR4. 2008. *Crack Ya Ribs: Julius d'Genius Agwu Live Series 4.* VCD. Prod. Julius Agwu.

Daddyface Tv. 2018. "Basketmouth Katika Jukwaa La Wasakkatonge Comedy Gala Tanzania." *YouTube* January 02. Accessed December 01, 2020. https://www.youtube.com/watch?v=ZJieotaqBN0.

Dan-Inna, Chaibou, and Ousmane Tandina. 1997. "Niger." In *The World Encyclopedia of Contemporary Theatre: Africa*, edited by Don Rubin, Ousmane Diakhaté and Hansel Ndumbe Eyoh, 212–218. London: Routledge.

Davies, Christie. 1982. "Ethnic Jokes, Moral Values and Social Boundaries." *The British Journal of Sociology* 33 (3): 383–403. doi:10.2307/589483.

David-Adegboye, Temitope. 2010. "I Get Rejected as A Comedian Because I'm Female –Lepacious Bose." *Gists Nollywood* July 24. Accessed November 02, 2020. https://www.nollywoodgists.com/news/8387/i-get-rejected-as-a-comedian-because-im-female-lep.html.

De-9ja Music Ent. 2017a. "Ali Baba vs Akpororo Comedy." *YouTube* February 18. Accessed December 24, 2020. https://www.youtube.com/watch?v=PjL03WQPc-c.

De-9ja Music Ent. 2017b. "Seyi Law Most Outstanding Comedy Performance." *YouTube* February 23. Accessed December 12, 2020. https://www.youtube.com/watch?v=zhwOgFuHbR0.

De-9ja Music Ent. 2017c. "Ali Baba Latest Comedy Performance 2017 @ Njoy 13.0." *YouTube* June 13. Accessed December 20, 2020. https://www.youtube.com/watch?v=NFedpFgUD0U.

Deejay Wilx PRO. 2019. "Emmanuella Live on Stage at Freedom City in Uganda." *YouTube* September 09. Accessed December 16, 2020. https://www.youtube.com/watch?v=LKwM2wJCL4o.

Deuber, Dagmar. 2006. "Aspects of Variation in Educated Nigerian Pidgin: Verbal

Structures." In *Structure and Variation in Language Contact*, edited by Ana Deumert and Stefanie Durrleman, 243–261. Amsterdam: Benjamins.

Deuber, Dagmar. 2005. *Nigerian Pidgin in Lagos: Language Contact, Variation and Change in an African Urban Setting*. London: Battlebridge.

Dibie, Godfrey Atunu, and Odey Simon Robert. 2018. "Pidgin English and the Attrition of Indigenous Languages in South–Southern Nigeria." *International Journal of Language, Literature and Culture* 5 (2): 16–26. http://www.openscienceonline.com/journal/archive2?journalId=701&paperId=4571.

Diallo, Youssouf. 2006. "Joking Relationships in Western Burkina Faso." *Zeitschrift für Ethnologie* 131 (2): 183–196. Accessed June 19, 2020. https://www.jstor.org/stable/25843051.

Directory Nigeria. 2010. "Atuyota Akporobomeriere a.k.a Ali Baba." December 22. Accessed 09 December 2011. directory-nigeria.org/atuyota-akporobomeriere-a-k-a-ali-baba.html.

Dobrow, Julia R., and Calvin L. Gidney. 1998. "The Good, the Bad, and the Foreign: The Use of Dialect in Children's Animated Television." *The Annals of the American Academy of Political and Social Science* 557: 105–119.

Dollard, John. 1973. "The Dozens: Dialectic of Insult." In *Mother Wit from the Laughing Barrel*, edited by Alan Dundes, 277–294. Jackson: University Press of Mississippi.

Drewal, Henry John. 1974. "Gelede Masquerade: Imagery and Motif." *African Arts* 7 (4): 8–19+62–63+95–96. doi:10.2307/3334883.

Drewal, Henry John, and Margret Thompson Drewal. 1983. *Gẹlẹdẹ: Art and Female Power among the Yoruba*. Bloomington: Indiana University Press.

Eagleton, Terry. 2019. *Humour*. New Haven and London: Yale University Press.

Ebeogu, Afam. 1991. "Njakiri: The Quintessence of the Traditional Igbo Sense of Satire." In *Spoken in Jest*, edited by Gillian Bennett, 29–46. Sheffield: Academic Press.

Ebewo, Patrick. 2001. "Satire and the Performing Arts: The African Heritage." In *Pre-colonial and Post-colonial Drama and Theatre in Africa*, edited by Lokangaka Losambe and Devi Sarinjeive, 48–58. Claremont, South Africa: New Africa Books.

EbonyLifeTV. 2017. "AY Live 2017 – Big Brother Naija contestants, Davido and others Live on Stage." *YouTube* April 28. Accessed December 26, 2019. https://www.youtube.com/watch?v=ysTNu0hv5VU.

Ego-Alowes, Jimanze. 2017. *Minorities as Competitive Overlords*. Ibadan: Safari Books Ltd.

Ekpang, Juliet Nkane, and Victor Bassey. 2014. "Calabar Humaphors: An Analysis of Selected Jokes in Nigerian Stand Up Comedy." *LWATI: A Journal of Contemporary Research* 11 (2): 176–184. https://www.researchgate.net/publication/342917726_Calabar_Humaphors_An_analysis_of_selected_jokes_in_Nigerian_stand_up_comedy.

Ekpu, Patrick. 2019. "Six Years on Air! Basketmouth Celebrates 565th Episode of 'My Flatmates'." *Newspeak* May 31. Accessed December 15, 2020. https://newspeakonline.com/six-years-basketmouth-celebrates-565th-episode-my-flatmates/.

Ekpu, Ray. 2019. "The Success Adegor Story." *The Guardian* March 26. Accessed December 16, 2020. https://guardian.ng/opinion/the-success-adegor-story/.

Ekwuazi, Hyginus. 1991. *Film in Nigeria*. Jos: Nigerian Film Corporation.

Elugbe, Ben Ohiọmamhẹ, and Augusta Phil Omamor. 1991. *Nigerian Pidgin: Background and Prospects*. Ibadan: Heinemann Educational Books.

Empire Entertainment Smile. 2019. "Forever Comedian Performing on Stage | Alibaba Jan 1st concert |." *YouTube* January 09. Accessed December 24, 2020. https://www.youtube.com/watch?v=2AQyu0VuSz4.

Encomium. 2015. "'Comedy has Done Almost Everything for Me' – Tee A." *Encomium* September 03. Accessed August 14, 2020. http://encomium.ng/comedy-has-done-almost-everything-for-me-tee-a-2/.

Erhariefe, Tony Ogaga, and Rummy Chukwuma. 2016. "My Regrets – Ali Baba." *The Citizen*. February 20. Accessed August 15, 2020. https://thecitizenng.com/my-regrets-ali-baba/.

Escandon, Rosa. 2019. "24-Year-Old Ayo Edebiri Takes Comedy Seriously." *Forbes* October 29. Accessed October 07, 2020. https://www.forbes.com/sites/rosaescandon/2019/10/28/24-year-old-ayo-edebiri-takes-comedy-seriously/#32b58a60525d.

Eseoghene, Enyoyi. 2017. "Mandy Uzonitsha's 15 Years Journey as Nigeria's First Female Comedian." *Glam & Essence* March 08. Accessed August 15, 2020. https://www.glamandessence.com/mandy-uzonitshas-25years-journey-as-nigerias-first-female-comedienne/#.XzuuAOgzbIU.

Ezenwa-Ohaeto. 1996. *The Voice of the Night Masquerade: Poems*. Ibadan: Kraft Books.

Ezenwa-Ohaeto. 1999. *Contemporary Nigerian Poetry and the Poetics of Orality.* Bayreuth: Bayreuth African Studies.

Faraclas, Nicholas G. 1996. *Nigerian Pidgin.* London: Routledge.

Filani, Ibukun. 2015a. "Discourse Types in Stand-up Comedy Performances: An Example of Nigerian Stand-up Comedy." *European Journal of Humour Research* 3 (1): 41–60. doi:10.7592/EJHR2015.3.1.filani.

Fiebach, Joachim. 1996. "Cultural Identities, Interculturalism, and Theatre: On the Popular Yoruba Travelling Theatre." *Theatre Research International* 21 (1): 52–58. doi:10.1017/S0307883300012700.

Fiebach, Joachim. 2015b. "Stand-up Comedy as an Activity Type." *Israeli Journal of Humor Research* 4 (1): 73–97. http://sfile-pull.f-static.com/image/users/122789/ftp/my_files/International%204-1/5-Stand-up%20Comedy%20as%20an%20Activity%20Type.pdf?id=26329032.

Fiebach, Joachim. 2016. "The Use of Mimicry in Nigerian Stand-up Comedy." *Comedy Studies* 7 (1): 89–102. doi:10.1080/2040610X.2016.1139810.

Fiebach, Joachim. 2017. "On Joking Contexts: An Example of Stand-Up Comedy." *Humor* 30 (4): 439–461. doi:10.1515/humor-2016-0107.

Fiebach, Joachim. 2020. "A Discourse Analysis of National Identity in Nigerian Stand-up Humour." *Discourse Studies* 22 (3): 319–338. doi:10.1177/1461445620906035.

Filani, Ibukun, and Temitope Michael Ajayi. 2019. "Ideologies in Nigerian Stand-up Comedy." *Linguistik Online* 100 (7): 141–158. doi:10.13092/lo.100.6023.

Finnegan, Ruth. 1970/2012. *Oral Literature in Africa.* Cambridge: Open Book Publishers.

Fiofori, Tam. 2010. "Is it Funny?" *Next* May 01. Accessed 09 December 2011. http://234next.com/csp/cms/sites/Next/ArtsandCulture/Art/5526748-147/story.csp.

Flax, Jane. 1990. *Thinking Fragments: Psychoanalysis, Feminism, and Postmodernism in the Contemporary West.* Berkeley: University of California Press.

FlipTV. 2016. "Video: Chigul Will Crack You Up (Nigerian Lifestyle & Entertainment)." *YouTube* August 12. Accessed December 24, 2020. https://www.youtube.com/watch?v=pn8x9bJR_jc.

Flow Entertainment. 2017. "Sam and Song Special Birthday Present for Apostle Suleiman." *YouTube* March 30. Accessed December 15, 2020. https://www.youtube.com/watch?v=zip5dpMr04A.

Fosudo, Sola. 2009/2010. "Stand-up Comedy as Popular Art and Theatrical Entertainment in Nigeria." *IJOTA: Ibadan Journal of Theatre Arts* (5 & 6): 1–18. https://www.lasu.edu.ng/publications/arts/olusola_fosudo_ja_09.pdf.

FunnyBone Comedy TV. 2017. "Emmanuella @ FunnyBone Untamed (Nigerian Comedy & Entertainment)." *YouTube* August 29. Accessed December 15, 2020. https://www.youtube.com/watch?v=gJzPBJ6z0U0.

Furniss, Graham. 1996. *Poetry, Prose and Popular Culture in Hausa*. Edinburgh: Edinburgh University Press.

Gaudio, Rudolf Pell. 2009. *Allah Made Us: Sexual Outlaws in an Islamic African City*. Chichester: Wiley-Blackwell.

Gaudio, Rudolf Pell. 2011. "The Blackness of 'Broken English'." *Journal of Linguistic Anthropology* 23 (2): 230–246.

Gbedu Magazine. 2016. "Ace Comedian, Ali Baba Misses his Comedy Counterpart: Late Comedian, Mohammed Danjuma." *Gbedu Magazine* May 17. Accessed August 15, 2020. https://www.gbedumagazine.com/ace-comedian-ali-baba-misses-his-comedy-counterpart-late-comedian-mohammed-danjuma/.

Gemini Dreams Media. 2017. "Emanuella Performs at Akpororo vs Akpororo PH." *YouTube* May 19. Accessed December 15, 2020. https://www.youtube.com/watch?v=O-8UQNbKht0.

Girls Killing It. 2016. "Mandy Uzonitsha – Nigeria." *Girls Killing It* January 18. Accessed August 14, 2020. https://girlskillingitfoundation.weebly.com/news/mandy-uzonitsha.

Globacomlimited. 2010. "Basket Mouth Performing Live @ Glo Laffta Fest." *YouTube* June 01. Accessed August 28, 2020. https://www.youtube.com/watch?v=IvuGmlG86OY.

Gluckman, Max. 1963. *Order and Rebellion in Tribal Africa*. New York: Free Press.

Godfreychi. 2018. "Godfrey's 'Regular Black' One Hour Showtime Comedy Special." *YouTube* October 10. Accessed September 30, 2020. https://www.youtube.com/watch?v=XylEzaQ7Fx0.

Gold Edge TV. 2020. "Desktalker the Best Comedian for this Generation." *YouTube* May 04. Accessed November 16, 2020. https://www.youtube.com/watch?v=WVQ_TEiS2MU.

Grainger, Roger. 2010. *The Uses of Chaos*. Oxford: Peter Lang.

Hamada, Rachel. 2014. "Nigerians turn on comic for rape 'joke'." *The Guardian*.

08 January. Accessed December 26, 2020. https://www.theguardian.com/world/2014/jan/08/nigeria-basketmouth-rape-joke.

Hamzia. 2015. "Throwback: Nigeria's Comedy Fore-fathers We Cannot Forget Too Soon – Education – Nairaland." *Nairaland Forum* August 18. Accessed August 13, 2020. https://www.nairaland.com/2534587/throwback-nigerias-comedy-fore-fathers-cannot.

Handel, Ducor. 2015. "Why Is Buhari After Dasuki?" *The Guardian* September 19. Accessed April 13, 2020. https://guardian.ng/opinion/why-is-buhari-after-dasuki/.

Haynes, Jonathan. 1994. "Structural Adjustments of Nigerian Comedy: Baba Sala." *Institute for Advanced Study and Research in the African Humanities: Media, Popular Culture, and 'the Public' in Africa* 8: 17–18, 20. Accessed 23 June 2020. http://hdl.handle.net/2027/spo.4761530.0008.010.

Haynes, Jonathan. 2016. *Nollywood: The Creation of Nigerian Film Genres*. Chicago: The University of Chicago Press.

Haynes, Jonathan, and Onookome Okome. 2000. "Evolving Popular Media: Nigerian Video Films." In *Nigerian Video Films*, edited by Jonathan Haynes, 51–88. Athens, Ohio: Ohio University Centre for International Studies.

Heyd, Theresa. 2015. "The Metacommunicative Lexicon of Nigerian Pidgin." *World Englishes* 34 (4): 669–687. doi:10.1111/weng.12164.

Hiphopdivas100. 2012. "Basket Mouth 00." *YouTube* July 30. Accessed November 18, 2020. https://www.youtube.com/watch?v=EfyCEEdRWd8.

Hirsch, Lily E. 2020. *Weird Al: Seriously*. Lanham, MD: Rowman & Littlefield.

Hron, Madelaine. 2016. "From 'Tutsi Crush' to 'FWP': Satire, Sentiment, and Rights in African Texts and Contexts." In *The Routledge Companion to Literature and Human Rights*, edited by Sophia A. McClennen and Alexandra Schultheis Moore, 215–223. Oxon: Routledge.

Hutchison, Marc. 2017. "Andi Osho Dealing with Political Correctness." *YouTube* August 16. Accessed December 27, 2019. https://www.youtube.com/watch?v=CbXTSRDLsqw.

Ibrahim, Muhammad Muhsin. 2019. *Kannywood: Unveiling the Overlooked Hausa Film Industry*. Century Research and Publishing Limited.

Igihe. 2018. "The Best of Klint Da Drunk at Seka Festival/Kigali-Rwanda." *YouTube* March 26. Accessed December 01, 2020. https://www.youtube.com/watch?v=n6NB49nsXfE.

Igomu, Samuel O. 2018. "Severity in Hilarity: Appraising the Satirical Value of Stand-up Comedy in Nigeria." In *Joke-Performance in Africa: Mode, Media and Meaning*, edited by Ignatius Chukwumah, 245–266. London and New York: Routledge.

Ijalana, Esther. 2010. "I have a different history of Nigerian Comedy – Gbenga Adeyinka." *TNV: The Nigerian Voice* May 16. Accessed August 23, 2019. https://www.thenigerianvoice.com/movie/24097/i-have-a-different-history-of-nigerian-comedy-gbenga-adeyi.html.

In Allure. 2010. "Our Father taught us to Respect Everyone"â€" Najite & Mitchelle Dede." *Vanguard* July 04. Accessed October 25, 2020. https://www.vanguardngr.com/2010/07/our-father-taught-us-to-respect-everyone%E2%80%94-najite-mitchelle-dede/.

Itewo, Obaro. 2010. "Night of Thousand Laughs made me popular, left me poor – MC Basketmouth." *Modern Ghana* October 13. Accessed August 17, 2020. https://www.modernghana.com/nollywood/9154/night-of-thousand-laughs-made-me-popular-left.html.

Iwenjora, Fred. 2018. "How 'A Night of Thousand Laughs' died and resurrected – Opa Williams." *Vanguard* July 14. Accessed 01 November 2020. https://www.vanguardngr.com/2018/07/how-a-night-of-thousand-laughs-died-and-resurrected-opa-williams/.

Jacob, Ray Ikechukwu. 2012. "A Historical Survey of Ethnic Conflict in Nigeria." *Asian Social Science* 8 (4): 13–29. doi:10.5539/ass.v8n4p13.

Jaguda. 2012. "Julius Agwu Takes Crack Ya Ribs to New York & Glasgow." *Jaguda* July 31. Accessed December 15, 2020. https://jaguda.com/events/julius-agwu-takes-crack-ya-ribs-to-new-york-glasgow/.

Jebose. 2014. "I am tired of America – Jude Away Away." *The Punch* November 21. Accessed November 02, 2020. https://jebose1.rssing.com/chan-29429548/all_p2.html.

Jekins, Akinlolu. 2020. Interview on Nigerian Stand-up Practise in the Diaspora by Izuu Nwankwo (September 19).

Jenner, Bryan R. A. 1976. "Interlanguage and Foreign Accent." *Interlanguage Studies Bulletin* 1 (2/3): 166–195.

Jeyifo, Biodun. 1984. *The Yoruba Popular Theatre of Nigeria*. Lagos: Nigeria Magazine.

Joe, Audu Yusuf. 1984. "Hausa Folktheatre and Occupational Groups: Some Examples in Zaria, Kaduna State." MA Thesis in Drama. Ahmadu Bello University, Zaria, Nigeria.

Jowitt, David. 1991. *Nigerian English Usage: An Introduction*. Lagos: Longman.

Just for Laughs. 2018. "Gina Yashere – Air Cubana." *YouTube* December 26. Accessed January 29, 2020. https://www.youtube.com/watch?v=ZUtUAmU9ylk.

JusticeCrack. 2020. "How Depression Brought Out the Talent in Me – Anita Alaire Afoke Asuoha Real Warri Pikin." *YouTube* April 21. Accessed December 14, 2020. https://www.youtube.com/watch?v=CQvr3hbe3Ak.

Juvenis TV. 2016a. "Gordons Tackles Sex and Orgasm (Nigerian Music & Entertainment)." *YouTube* February 25. Accessed December 15, 2020. https://www.youtube.com/watch?v=DtA7pOKlWI4.

Juvenis TV. 2016b. "Helen Paul Reveals How Ladies Get Husbands in Church (Nigerian Music & Entertainment)." *YouTube* May 02. Accessed August 14, 2020. https://www.youtube.com/watch?v=ViPVgVC9mQM.

Juvenis TV. 2016c. "Osama on Bombings in Nigeria (Nigerian Music & Entertainment)." *YouTube* May 07. Accessed December 14, 2020. https://www.youtube.com/watch?v=oEv9aIq0IDs.

Juvenis TV. 2020. "I Go Dye Attacks President Buhari on Corruption; Says Give Us Money." *YouTube* July 23. Accessed November 13, 2020. https://www.youtube.com/watch?v=bt2rsu3YyV8.

Kagire, Linda M. 2019. "Basketmouth to Perform in Kigali." *The New Times* February 22. Accessed December 10, 2020. https://www.newtimes.co.rw/entertainment/basketmouth-perform-kigali.

Kehinde, Oyebola Folajimi. 2016. "A Night of a Thousand Laughs: A Pragmatic Study of Humour in Nigeria." *International Journal of Scientific and Research Publications* 6 (6): 433–437. http://www.ijsrp.org/research-paper-0616/ijsrp-p5460.pdf.

Kenny Blaq. 2017. "Kenny Blaq stops Music Comedy (Nigerian Comedy)." *YouTube* October 26. Accessed December 26, 2020. https://www.youtube.com/watch?v=EsJ_JExYqCE.

Kenny Blaq. 2019. "The African Praise Experience 2019." *YouTube* August 06. Accessed December 24, 2020. https://www.youtube.com/watch?v=HTQP43ty6N4.

Kenny Blaq. 2020. "The Oxymoron of Kennyblaq (The Rush) Full Video." *YouTube* April 21. Accessed December 24, 2020. https://www.youtube.com/watch?v=x_IVdYbmbl0.

Khaleel, Ibrahim. 1996. "The Hausa." In *Ethnic and Cultural Diversity in Nigeria*, edited by Marcellina Ulunma Okehie-Offoha and Matthew N. O. Sadiku, 37–62. Trenton, NJ: African World Press.

Kilarigbo Live. 2015. "Helen Paul Battle with Gordons on Stage (Nigerian Entertainment)." *YouTube* October 12. Accessed December 24, 2020. https://www.youtube.com/watch?v=6FXKwjt-ly8.

Kilarigbo Live. 2018. "Comedian Klint D Drunk makes Gov. Rochas Okorocha burst into Laughter." *YouTube* January 21. Accessed October 15, 2020. https://www.youtube.com/watch?v=1BlcGN8Us2k.

Kofoworola, Kayode Gboyega. 2007. "The Court Jester in Nigerian Drama." In *Clowns, Fools and Picaros: Popular Forms in Theatre, Fiction and Film*, edited by David Robb, 101–114. Amsterdam and New York: Brill-Rodopi. doi:10.1163/9789401205399_009.

Krefting, Rebecca. 2014. *All Joking Aside: American Humor and Its Discontents*. Baltimore: Johns Hopkins University Press.

Krings, Matthias, and Onookome Okome, eds. 2013. *Global Nollywood: The Transnational Dimensions of an African Video Film Industry*. Bloomington: Indiana University Press.

Lakoju, Tunde. 1984. "Popular (Travelling) Theatre in Nigeria: The Example of Moses Olaiya Adejumo." *Nigeria Magazine* 149: 35–46.

Lamidi, Mufutau Temitayo. 2017. "Multimodal Code-pairing and Switching of Visual-verbal Texts in Selected Nigerian Stand-up Comedy Performances." *Legon Journal of Humanities* 28 (2): 195–129. doi:10.4314/ljh.v28i2.5.

Laugh Angle. 2017. "Alibaba's Funniest Jokes #4, On Laugh Angles." *YouTube*. July 04. Accessed December 20, 2020. https://www.youtube.com/watch?v=6rR7X9y7TUw.

Lawal, Ayodele. 2011. "Top Comediennes Making Waves." *PM News* October 14. Accessed August 19, 2020. https://www.pmnewsnigeria.com/2011/10/14/top-comediennes-making-waves/.

Lawal, Babatunde. 1996. *The Gelede Spectacle: Arts, Gender, and Social Harmony in an African Culture*. Seattle: University of Washington Press.

Lee, Ashley. 2020. "Yvonne Orji Knows it's Hard to Laugh Right Now. But 'Black Joy is an Act of Defiance'." *Los Angeles Times* June 05. Accessed December 26, 2020. https://www.latimes.com/entertainment-arts/tv/story/2020-06-05/hbo-yvonne-orji-insecure-momma-i-made-it.

Lequarrk. 2008. "Basket Mouth Stand Up Part 1." *YouTube* June 17. Accessed December 01, 2020. https://www.youtube.com/watch?v=u2FJAGOrh5o.

Leveen, Lois. 1996. "Only When I Laugh: Textual Dynamics of Ethnic Humor." *MELUS* 21 (4): 29–55. doi:10.2307/467641.

Liberation TV. 2019. "Klint Da Drunk & Aboki 4 Christ Live @ Grace Nation." *YouTube* April 09. Accessed December 14, 2020. https://www.youtube.com/watch?v=rIkCZ21x6fY.

Limon, John. 2000. *Stand-up Comedy in Theory, or, Abjection in America*. Durham, NC: Duke University Press.

Lindfors, Bernth. 1976. "Ogunde on Ogunde: Two Autobiographical Statements." *Educational Theatre Journal* 28 (2): 239–246. doi:10.2307/3206666.

Lippi-Green, Rosina. 2011. *English With an Accent: Language, Ideology, and Discrimination in the United States*. New York, NY: Routledge.

Living in Bondage. 1992. Directed by Chris Obi Rapu.

Locke, John. 2014. "The Late Late Show – [2014.03.07] – Andi Osho." *YouTube* March 10. Accessed January 29, 2020. https://www.youtube.com/watch?v=UNqsgaZh7bM.

Mann, Charles. 1993. "The Sociolinguistic Status of Anglo-Nigerian Pidgin: An Overview." *International Journal of the Sociology of Language* 100/101: 167–178.

MC Mbakara TV. 2019. "Mimicko Mimicks Nigerian Actors to Audience Delight: MC Mbakara Concert 2019." *YouTube* August 18. Accessed December 24, 2020. https://www.youtube.com/watch?v=axEK-iPpWFk.

Meek, Charles Kingsley. 1937. *Law and Authority in a Nigerian Tribe*. London: Oxford University Press.

Mensah, Eya Offiong. 2011. "Lexicalization in Nigerian Pidgin." *Concentric: Studies in Linguistics* 37 (2): 209–240.

Mike, Lawrence. 2020. "Before Stardom with … Lepacious Bose." *Punch* April 18. Accessed August 19, 2020. https://punchng.com/before-stardom-with-lepacious-bose/.

Miller, B. 2010. *The Art of Stand-up: Basic Joke Structure* October 13. Accessed January 15, 2012. www.m.examiner.com/comedy-in-hartford/the-art-ofstand-up-basic-joke-structure.

Molue Talk. 2007. *Julius Agwu Beaten in London* August 27. Accessed December 03, 2020. https://molue.blogspot.com/2007/08/julius-agwu-beaten-in-london.html.

Moreau, R. E. 1944. "Joking Relationships in Tanganyika." *Africa* 14 (7): 386–400. doi:10.2307/1157006.

MrCokoBar. 2010. "Basketmouth's Sellout Show at the indigO2 London Feb 21st 2010 – Cokobar.com." *YouTube* April 21. Accessed December 03, 2020. https://www.youtube.com/watch?v=vrC3w6pi0Ag.

Muendo, Stevens. 2015. "Basket Mouth Rocks Nairobi Comedy Lovers." *The Standard.* Accessed December 10, 2020. https://www.standardmedia.co.ke/entertainment/thestandard/2000124103/basket-mouth-rocks-nairobi-comedy-lovers.

Muomah, Onyinye. (2014). "The Rise and Rise of Chigul." *Premium News* August 3. Accessed May 09, 2021. https://www.premiumtimesng.com/entertainment/165963-the-rise-and-rise-of-chigul.html.

Musa, Rasheed Adeoye. 2005. "Sustaining the Development of Theatre Practice in Nigeria: Options for Theatre Workers." *Nigerian Theatre Journal* 8 (1): 16–37.

Musasizi, Simon. 2014. "Nigeria's Gordons Cracks up Kampala." *The Observer* February 23. Accessed December 02, 2020. https://www.observer.ug/component/content/article?id=30305:-nigerias-gordons-cracks-up-kampala.

Na'Allah, Abdul-Rasheed, and عبد الرشيد نا الله. 1997. "Interpretation of African Orature: Oral Specificity and Literary Analysis / تفسير الأدب الأفريقي الشفوي." *Alif: Journal of Comparative Poetics* 17: 125–142. doi:10.2307/521610.

Naija Live Comedy. 2012. "Koffi Live 1 – Nigerian Stand-up Comedy." *YouTube* February 15. Accessed November 12, 2020. https://www.youtube.com/watch?v=tzBFIt_zXaM.

Naija Live Comedy. n.d. "Koffi Live 2 – Nigerian Stand-up Comedy." *YouTube.* Accessed November 12, 2020. https://www.youtube.com/watch?v=OcbO4vRb6ns.

Ndinda, Jacque. 2019. "A Night of a Thousand Laughs." *Chicamod.* Accessed December 01, 2020. http://www.chicamod.com/2011/09/10/a-night-of-a-thousand-laughs/.

Ndolo, Ike S. 1989. "The Case for Promoting the Nigerian Pidgin Language." *The Journal of Modern African Studies* 27 (4): 679–684. doi:10.1017/S0022278X00020504.

News. 2017. "Full List of All 371 Tribes in Nigeria, States Where They Originate." *Vanguard* May 10. Accessed November 11, 2020. https://www.vanguardngr.com/2017/05/full-list-of-all-371-tribes-in-nigeria-states-where-they-originate/.

NFC. n.d. "My Man Impregnated Another Woman – Comedian, Princess." *Nigeria Films.com.* Accessed August 14, 2020. https://www.nigeriafilms.com/more/88-commics-news/9040-my-man-impregnated-another-woman-comedian-princess.

Nigerian Films. 2009. "Francis Agoda." *Nigerian films.com* February 23. Accessed December 09, 2011. nigeriafilms.com/artists_profile_derails.asp?user_id=1929.

Nigeria Galleria. 2017a. "Nigerian Comedians." *Nigeria Galleria.* Accessed October 27, 2020. https://www.nigeriagalleria.com/Nigeria/Personality-Profiles/Comedians/Basketmouth.html#:~:text=His%201st%20standup%20comedy%20was,the%20world%20of%20standup%20comedy.

Nigeria Galleria. 2017b. "Nigerian Comedians." *Nigeria Galleria.* Accessed November 04, 2020. https://www.nigeriagalleria.com/Nigeria/Personality-Profiles/Comedians/Helen-Paul.html.

Njoku, Benjamin. 2017. "Lepacious Bose opens up on her past." *Vanguard* December 13. Accessed November 02, 2020. https://www.vanguardngr.com/2017/12/lepacious-bose-opens-past/.

NML. n.d. *Nigeria Must Laugh.* VCD. Prod. Uche Ogbuagu.

Nneji, Ogechukwu Miracle. 2013. "Nigerian Jokes as Humour Construction: A Sematico-Pragmatic Study." *International Journal of Research in Arts and Social Sciences* 4: 111–123.

Nnenyelike, N. 2005. "First time I earned N500, I felt as if it was a million naira." *The Sun* April 22. Accessed 09 December 2011. http://www.eslnetworld.com/webpages/features/showtime/2005/April/22/showtime-22-04-2005-003.htm.

NTL1. 2002. *Nite of a Thousand Laughs Volume 1.* VCD. Opa Williams.

NTL2. 2003. *Nite of a Thousand Laughs Volume 2.* VCD. Prod. Opa Williams.

NTL3. 2004. *Nite of a Thousand Laughs Volume 3.* VCD. Prod. Opa Williams.

NTL4. 2004. *Nite of a Thousand Laughs Volume 4.* VCD. Prod. Opa Williams.

NTL5. n.d. *Nite of a Thousand Laughs Volume 5.* VCD. Prod. Opa Williams.

NTL6. n.d. *Nite of a Thousand Laughs Volume 6.* VCD. Prod. Opa Williams.

NTL7. 2005. *Nite of a Thousand Laughs Volume 7.* VCD. Prod. Opa Williams.

NTL8. n.d. *Nite of a Thousand Laughs Volume 8.* VCD. Prod. Opa Williams.

NTL9. 2006. *Nite of a Thousand Laughs Volume 9.* VCD. Prod. Opa William.

NTL11. 2007. *Nite of a Thousand Laughs Volume 11.* VCD. Prod. Opa Williams.

NTL12. n.d. Nite of a Thousand Laughs Volume 12. VCD. Prod. Opa Williams.

NTL13. n.d. *Nite of Thousand Laughs Volume 13.* VCD. Prod. Opa Williams.

NTL14. 2008. *Nite of a Thousand Laughs Volume 14.* VCD. Prod. Opa Williams.

NTL15. 2008. *Nite of a Thousand Laughs Volume 15.* VCD. Prod. Opa Williams.

NTL16. n.d. *Nite of a Thousand Laughs Volume 16.* VCD. Prod. Opa Williams.

NTL17. 2009. *Nite of a Thousand Laughs Volume 17.* VCD. Prod. Opa Williams.

NTL19. n.d. *Nite of a Thousand Laughs Volume 19.* VCD. Prod. Opa Williams.

NTL20. n.d. *Nite of a Thousand Laughs Volume 20.* VCD. Prod. Opa Williams.

Nwachukwu-Agbada, J. O. J. 2004. "Igbo Humor in the Novels of Chinua Achebe." In *Emerging Perspectives on Chinua Achebe Volume II: Isinka, The Artistic Purpose: Chinua Achebe and the Theory of African Literature,* edited by Ernest N. Emenyonu and Iniobong I. Uko, 151–168. Trenton, NJ: African World Press, Inc.

Nwachukwu-Agbada, J. O. J. 2006. "Ezenwa-Ohaeto: Poet of the Njakiri Genre." In *Of Minstrelsy and Masks: The Legacy of Ezenwa-Ohaeto in Nigerian Writing,* edited by Christine Matzke, Aderemi Raji-Oyelade and Geoffrey V. Davis, 153–177. Amsterdam: Editions Rodopi.

Nwachukwu-Agbada, J. O. J. 2014. "Igbo Humor." In *Encyclopedia of Humor Studies,* edited by Salvatore Attardo, 379–381. Thousand Oaks: SAGE Publications, Inc. doi:10.4135/9781483346175.n175.

Nwaubani, Adaobi Tricia. 2018. "Letter from Africa: Why Nigeria's Hate Speech Bill us a Jokes Killer." *BBC News* March 15. Accessed August 14, 2020. https://www.bbc.com/news/world-africa-43386636.

Nwankwọ, Izuu E. 2010. "On the Difference of the Same: Theatre, Performance and the Tortuous Path of a Nation's Development." *Nigerian Theatre Journal* 10 (1): 22–35.

Nwankwọ, Izuu E. 2015. "From Court Jesting to Microphone Comedy: Towards a History of Nigeria's Stand-up Comedy." *ANSU Journal of Theatre and Humanities* 1 (1): 48–67.

Nwankwọ, Izuu E. 2019. "Incongruous Liaisons: Routes of Humour, Insult and Political (In)correctness in Nigerian Stand-up Jokes." *European Journal of Humour Research* 2: 100–115. doi:10.7592/EJHR2019.7.2.nwankwo.

Nwankwọ, Izuu E. 2021. "Shifting Cognitions of Offence: Self-censorship in the Stand-up Acts of Basket Mouth and Trevor Noah." *Journal of African Cultural Studies.* Advance online publication. doi:10.1080/13696815.2021.1968806.

Nwankwọ, Izuu E. Forthcoming. "Taboo, Censorship and the Limits of Humor in African (Diaspora) Stand-up Comedy."

Nwanne, Chuks. 2010. "Ali Baba Yesterday, Today and 20 Years After." *The Guardian Life Magazine* January 16. Accessed August 13, 2020. http://theguardianlifemagazine.blogspot.com/2010/01/ali-baba-yesterday-today-and-20-years.html.

Obadare, Ebenezer. 2016. *Humor, Silence and Civil Society in Nigeria.* Rochester, NY: University of Rochester Press.

Obafemi, Olu. 1996. *Contemporary Nigerian Theatre: Cultural Heritage and Social Vision.* Bayreuth: African Studies Series.

Obiozo, Okey. 2019. "John Chukwu: Reminiscence of a Legendary Showbiz Impresario." *Prime Pointers* November 19. Accessed August 14, 2020. http://primepointers.com/2019/11/19/john-chukwu-reminiscence-of-a-legendary-showbiz-impresario/.

Odegbami, Segun. 2014. "Behind the Prison Walls: Climax Magazine, October 20 & 27, 1988." In *Me, Football and More: A Selection of the Media Writings of 'Mathematical' Segun Odegbami Volume One,* by Segun Odegbami, 30–33. Bloomington, IN: Author House.

Odeh, N. 2011. "How I discovered Ali Baba." *The News* March 01. Accessed December 09, 2011. http://thenewsafrica.com/2011/03/01/how-i-discovered-ali-baba/.

Odeyemi, Joshua. 2012. "It's now I Want To Start Comedy, Says Klint Da Drunk." *Daily Trust* September 29. Accessed November 06, 2020. https://dailytrust.com/its-now-i-want-to-start-comedy-says-klint-da-drunk.

Ogoanah, Felix N., and Fredrick O. Ojo. 2018. "A Multimodal Generic Perspective on Nigerian Stand- up Comedy." *European Journal of Humour Research* 6 (4): 39–59. doi:10.7592/EJHR2018.6.4.ogoanah.

Ogunbiyi, Yemi, ed. 1981. *Drama and Theatre in Nigeria: A Critical Source Book.* Lagos: Nigeria Magazine.

Ogunjimi, Opeoluwani. 2012. "Why I'm not rich – TEE A." *Vanguard* July 28.

Accessed November 01, 2020. https://www.vanguardngr.com/2012/07/why-im-not-rich-tee-a/.

Ogunsuyi, S. 1999. "Style and Medium in African Folk Film." *The Performer* 3 (1): 32–40.

Ohai, Chux. 2016. "Many Comedians Copy my Jokes – Gandoki." *The Punch* October 07. Accessed November 01, 2020. https://punchng.com/many-comedians-copy-jokes-gandoki/.

Ohai, Chux. 2015. "Okey Bakassi started stand-up comedy, not me 'Opa Williams." *Punch* May 22. Accessed November 01, 2020. https://punchng.com/entertainment/e-punch/okey-bakassi-started-stand-up-comedy-not-me-opa-williams/.

Ohiri, Innocent C. 2006. "The Role of the Theatre in a Depressed Economy: A Study of the Nigerian Situation." *Nigerian Theatre Journal* 9 (1): 127–139.

Ojaide, Tanure, and Enajite Eseoghene Ojaruega. 2020. "Tradition and subjectivities: Warri-related Comedians and Their Art." *Tydskrif Vir Letterkunde* 57 (2): 81–91.

Ojaide, Tanure. 2006. *The Activist*. Lagos: Farafina.

Ojoye, Taiwo. 2017. "Queen of Comedy." *Punch* August 13. Accessed May 08, 2021. https://punchng.com/queens-of-comedy/.

Ojoye, Taiwo. 2019. "Depression Pushed me into Comedy – Anita Asuoha (Real Warri Pikin)." *Punch* August 25. Accessed May 19, 2021. https://punchng.com/depression-pushed-me-into-comedy-anita-asuoha-real-warri-pikin/

Okagbue, Osita. 2007. *African Theatres and Performances*. London: Routledge.

Okanlawon, Taiwo. 2020. "I Had to Smile through Performance while I Cry Myself to Sleep – Chigul Opens on Depression." *PM News* December 16. Accessed May 09, 2021. https://www.pmnewsnigeria.com/2020/12/16/i-had-to-smile-through-performance-while-i-cry-myself-to-sleep-chigul/.

Oke-Hortons, Laurence. 2020. "Kudos! See The Amazing Weight Loss Transformation Of Chigul." *Koko* June 16. Accessed May 09, 2021. https://koko.ng/see-the-amazing-weight-loss-transformation-of-chigul/.

Okiche, Wilfred. 2020. "How Two Nigerian Women are Breaking into Comedy's Boys Club." *The Christian Science Monitor* August 10. Accessed December 15, 2020. https://www.csmonitor.com/World/Africa/2020/0810/How-two-Nigerian-women-are-breaking-into-comedy-s-boys-club.

Okigbo, Charles. 1986. "Television in the Lives of Nigerian Youths." Paper presented at the International Television Studies Conference at London, July 10–12. https://files.eric.ed.gov/fulltext/ED294530.pdf.

Okoh, Julie. 2005. "Theatre Practice in Nigeria: Problems and Prospects." *Nigerian Theatre Journal* 8 (2): 402–421.

Okome, Onookome. 2019. "Nollywood: A Cinema of Stories." In *Transnational Media: Concepts and Cases*, edited by Suman Mishra and Rebecca Kern-Stone, 73–80. Hoboken, NJ: John Blackwell.

Okon, Augusta. 2010. "Stand Up Comedy – A Thriving Platform in Nigerian Entertainment." *News Viral* April 28. Accessed January 25, 2011. https://ezinearticles.com/?Stand-Up-Comedy---A-Thriving-Platform-in-Nigerian-Entertainment&id=4192292.

Okon-Ekong, Nseobong, and Vanessa Obioha. 2016. "The Transformation of Yibo Koko." *This Day* December 18. Accessed October 31, 2020. https://www.thisdaylive.com/index.php/2016/12/18/the-transformation-of-yibo-koko/.

Okon-Ekong, Nseobong. 2016. "The Gentleman of Comedy." *This Day* October 23. Accessed August 13, 2020. https://www.thisdaylive.com/index.php/2016/10/23/the-gentleman-of-comedy/.

Okon-Ekong, Nseobong. 2017a. "At Launch of Secrets of the Streets, Teju Babyface Discloses Why He Stepped Away from Comedy." *This Day* May 28. Accessed August 13, 2020. https://www.thisdaylive.com/index.php/2017/05/28/at-launch-of-secrets-of-the-streets-teju-babyface-discloses-why-he-stepped-away-from-comedy/.

Okon-Ekong, Nseobong. 2017b. "Taking Comedy as Serious Business." *This Day* June 04. Accessed August 13, 2020. https://www.thisdaylive.com/index.php/2017/06/04/taking-comedy-as-serious-business/.

Okpewho, Isidore. 1992. *African Oral Literature: Backgrounds, Character, and Continuity*. Bloomington and Indianapolis: Indiana University Press.

Okunola, Akindare. 2020. "How Anita Alaire Afoke Asuoha (realwarripikin) Became Warri's Biggest Female Export." *NET: Nigerian Entertainment Today* February 12. Accessed November 06, 2020. https://thenet.ng/how-realwarripikin-became-warris-biggest-female-export/.

Olaniyan, Tejumola. 2004. *Arrest the Music!: Fela and His Rebel Art and Politics*. Bloomington and Indianapolis: Indiana University Press.

Olayiwola, Abiodun. 2007. "From Celluloid to Video: The Tragedy of the Nigerian

Film Industry." *Journal of Film and Video* 59 (3): 58–61. https://www.jstor.org/stable/20688569.

Olayiwola, Abiodun. 2011. "Nollywood at the Borders of History: Yoruba Travelling Theatre and Video Film Development in Nigeria." *The Journal of Pan African Studies* 4 (5): 183–195. https://go.gale.com/ps/anonymous?id=GALE%7CA306754344&sid=googleScholar&v=2.1&it=r&linkaccess=abs&issn=08886601&p=LitRC&sw=w

Olonilua, Ademola. 2011. "Pillars of Stand-up Comedy." *NBF General Topics* December 03. Accessed 09 December 2011. http://www.nigerianbestforum.com/generaltopics/?p=110004.

Olonilua, Ademola. 2018. "I Died but Woke up on My Way to Mortuary – Julius Agwu." *Punch* February 10. Accessed December 02, 2020. https://punchng.com/i-died-but-woke-up-on-my-way-to-mortuary-julius-agwu/.

Olorunyomi, Sola. 2003. *Afrobeat! Fela and the Imagined Continent*. Ibadan and Trenton, NJ: IFRA and Africa World Press.

Olorunyomi, Sola. 2003. "On Whose Side are the Orisa (Gods)?" In *Fela: From West Africa to West Broadway*, edited by Trevor Schoonmaker, 157–171. New York: Palgrave Macmillan.

Olukole, Tope. 2010. "How Obasanjo Yabbed Me on My First Encounter with Him – Ali Baba." *Modern Ghana* March 20. Accessed June 23, 2020. https://www.modernghana.com/nollywood/6540/how-obasanjo-yabbed-me-on-my-first-encounter-with.html.

Omeruah, Theonlychigul. 2020. "Chigul Entertains." *YouTube* October 31. Accessed December 15, 2020. https://www.youtube.com/watch?v=PrIXVvFygvM.

Omoniyi, Tope. 2009. "So I Choose to Do am Naija Style: Hip hop, Language, and Postcolonial Identities." In *Global Linguistic Flows: Hip hop Cultures, Youth Identities, and the Politics of Language*, edited by H. Samy Alim, Awad Ibrahim and Alastair Pennycook, 113–135. London: Routledge.

Onifade, Mufu. 2011. "Living Legends Series: Celebrating the Doyen of Comedy." *National Mirror* September 21. Accessed 09 December 2011. nationalmirroronline.net/arts_culture/arts_culture_news/21076.html.web.

Onishi, Norimitsu. 2015. "Nigeria's Comics Pull Punch Lines from Deeper Social Ills." *The New York Times* December 05. Accessed June 23, 2020. https://www.nytimes.com/2015/12/06/world/africa/nigerias-comics-pull-punch-lines-from-deeper-social-ills.html.

Onogu, William Sunday. 2013. "Quality Assurance and Stand-up Comedy in Nigeria." *Nigerian Theatre Journal* 13 (1). http://sonta.org/wp-content/uploads/2019/02/NTJ-Vol-13-1.pdf.

Onyenankeya, O. M., K. U. Onyenankeya, and O. Osunkunle. 2017. "The Persuasive Influence of Nollywood Film in Cultural Transmission: Negotiating Nigerian Culture in a South African Environment." *Journal of Intercultural Communication Research* 46 (4): 297–313. doi:10.1080/17475759.2017.1329158.

Onyerionwu, Ezechi. 2007. "Stand-up Comedy and Dead-end of Theatre Tradition." *The Vanguard* May 27. Accessed April 14, 2009. http://allafrica.com/stories/200705280772.html.

Onyerionwu, Ezechi. 2010. "Stand up Comedy as a Pop Art." *Vanguard Online*. 16 May. Accessed January 25, 2011. www.vanguardngr.com/2010/05/stand-up-comedy-as-a-pop-art/.

Onwuanum, Ada. 2009. "Comedy is no funny matter – Opa Williams." *The Nigerian Voice* February 21. Accessed November 01, 2020. https://www.thenigerianvoice.com/news/5918/comedy-is-no-funny-matter-opa-williams.html.

Onyeche, Joseph. 2004. As Naija Pipo dey Tok: A Preliminary Analysis of the Role of Nigerian Pidgin in the Nigerian Community in Sweden. *Africa & Asia* 4 (1): 48–56.

Opejobi, Seun. 2017. "Dasuki speaks on Buhari's Arrest after 1985 Coup." *Daily Post* July 19. Accessed April 13, 2020. https://dailypost.ng/2017/07/19/dasuki-speaks-buharis-arrest-1985-coup/.

Orhiunu, Wilson. 2007. "Tribal Stereotypes in Nigerian Comedy: The Calabar Example." *iNigerian.com* July 25. Accessed August 14, 2020. https://www.inigerian.com/tribal-stereotypes-in-nigerian-comedy-the-calabar-example/.

Orji, Bernard Eze. 2018. "Humour, Satire and the Emergent Stand-up Comedy: A Diachronic Appraisal of the Contributions of the Masking Tradition." *European Journal of Humour Research* 6 (4): 24–38. doi:10.7592/EJHR2018.6.4.orji.

Osadola, Samuel Oluwaseun. 2012. "A Historical Analysis of Ethnic Conflict in Nigeria." *Research Paper (Postgraduate)*. Accessed November 12, 2020. https://www.grin.com/document/202626.

Osho, Andi. 2020. *Andi Osho*. Accessed December 02, 2020. https://www.andiosho.co.uk/about/#:~:text=Andi%20is%20an%20award%2Dwinning,and%20Never%20Mind%20The%20Buzzcocks.

Osofisan, Femi. 2008. "Theatrical Life after the Generals: Or Nigerian Theatre in

Search of a Lifeline." In *Trends in the Theory and Practice of Theatre in Nigeria*, edited by Duro Oni and Ahmed Yerima, xiii–xxv. Lagos: Society for Nigerian Theatre Artists.

Osuolale-Ajayi, Ibukun. 2022. "Discourse and Humour Strategies in Two-Person Stand-up Art in Nigeria." In *Stand-up Comedy in Africa: Humour in Popular Languages and Media*, edited by Izuu Nwankwọ, 127–148. Stuttgart: Ibidem Verlag.

Oti, Sonny. 2009. *Highlife Music in West Africa: Down Memory Lane ...* Lagos: Malthouse Press Limited.

Owojaiye, Mayowa. 2019. "The Metamorphosis of Nigerian Comedy and DStv as a Platform for Exposure." *Business Day* April 09. Accessed August 14, 2020. https://businessday.ng/opinion/article/the-metamorphosis-of-nigerian-comedy-and-dstv-as-a-platform-for-exposure/.

Oyatogun, 'Funmi. 2017. "The Fascinating True Story of a Man, His Seventeen Wives and the Beginning of Nollywood." *Medium* November 21. Accessed April 23, 2021. https://medium.com/@funmi.oyatogun/the-fascinating-true-story-of-a-man-his-seventeen-wives-and-the-beginning-of-nollywood-6c06863bd8c

Pablo Live TV. 2016a. "Enjoy Nigeria's comedian Gordons @ Pablo Live." *YouTube* April 04. Accessed December 02, 2020. https://www.youtube.com/watch?v=YdaQ4Yzq2Gc.

Pablo Live TV. 2016b. "Pablo Live Comedy Show ft Nigeria's Gordons." *YouTube* May 23. Accessed December 02, 2020. https://www.youtube.com/watch?v=WjPhiVdoJIA.

Paul, Helen. 2020. "Helenpaul on Fire at Warri Again." *YouTube* January 18. Accessed August 15, 2020. https://www.youtube.com/watch?v=7UfTqO6a3uk.

Phiri, Sam. 2012. "Zambia: Two Things Involved Comes to Country." *Times of Zambia* December 14. Accessed December 01, 2020. https://allafrica.com/stories/201212170545.html.

Pius, Aramide. 2008. "A Great Mum I am, a Good Wife ... I Doubt – Mandy." *TNV: The Nigerian Voice* December 27. Accessed August 14, 2020. https://www.thenigerianvoice.com/movie/5543/a-great-mum-i-am-a-good-wife-i-doubt-mandy.html.

Pizzy Vibes. 2019. "Watch Emmanuella And Mark Angel Best Comedy Performance On Stage." *YouTube* August 06. Accessed December 15, 2020. https://www.youtube.com/watch?v=pr6ZNQ7cvAY.

PM Entertainment. 2012. "I Love Beautiful Girls." *PM News* January 06. Accessed August 14, 2020. https://www.pmnewsnigeria.com/2012/01/06/i-love-beautiful-girls/.

Proudly Nigerian. 2016. "John Chukwu (JC)." *Proudly Nigerian* May 27. Accessed August 13, 2020. http://iamproudlynigerian.com/library/john-chukwu-jc/.

Pulse Nigeria. 2014. "Basketmouth Apologises for Offensive Joke | Pulse TV." *YouTube* January 07. Accessed December 26, 2019. https://www.youtube.com/watch?v=6u1Co-mT4qE.

Radcliffe-Brown, Alfred. 1940. "On Joking Relationships." *Africa: Journal of the International African Institute* 13 (3) July: 195–210. doi:10.2307/1156093.

Radiopalmwine. 2009. "Mrs Stella Obasanjo & Clink The Drunk." *YouTube* June 10. Accessed May 24, 2021. https://www.youtube.com/watch?v=M83-T7zUH3U/.

Raheem, Saheed. 2018. "A Sociolinguistic Study of Social-Political Activism and Non-Violent Resistance in Stand-Up Comedy Performances in Nigeria." *Africology: The Journal of Pan African Studies* 12 (6): 75–92.

Reel Nolly Studios. 2017. "Klint Da Drunk. 'Don't Worry Be Happy' Rib Cracker." *YouTube* August 11. Accessed August 12, 2020. https://www.youtube.com/watch?v=KZkKBYUc368.

Resuss TV. 2019. "Chigul Entertains – Funny Exclusive Highlights." *YouTube* November 22. Accessed December 15, 2020. https://www.youtube.com/watch?v=x6Y6jm2DzHo.

Riemenschneider, Dieter. 1984. "Ngugi wa Thiong'o and the Question of Language and Literature in Kenya." *World Literature Written in English* 24 (1): 78–87. doi:10.1080/17449858408588872.

Rutter, Jason. 1997. Stand-up as Interaction: Performance and Audience in Comedy Venues. PhD Thesis, Department of Sociology, University of Salford, Manchester, UK. http://usir.salford.ac.uk/id/eprint/14688.

Ryan, Connor. 2015. "New Nollywood: A Sketch of Nollywood's Metropolitan New Style." *African Studies Review* 58 (3): 55–76. doi:10.1017/asr.2015.75.

Sahara TV. 2013. "Comedian BasketMouth's Joke on President Jonathan's Achievements." *YouTube* January 26. Accessed November 12, 2020. https://www.youtube.com/watch?v=GoiDbucqcc0.

Sam and SongTV. 2020. "Herdsmen/Farmers Clash: Sam and Song Speaks on the

Consequences of Attack2020." *YouTube* December 31. Accessed January 15, 2021. https://www.youtube.com/watch?v=iddz3scTjyA.

SamTV 360. 2018. "Sam & Song @ Stars in Worship 2017." *YouTube* February 26. Accessed December 15, 2020. https://www.youtube.com/watch?v=G2DjBM0oAK0.

Sangala, Tom. 2015. "Basket Mouth Leaves BICC in Stitches." *The Times* December 08. Accessed December 10, 2020. https://times.mw/basketmouth-leaves-bicc-in-stitches/.

Şaul, Mahir, and Ralph A. Austen. 2010. *Viewing African Cinema in the Twenty-first Century: Art Films and the Nollywood Video Revolution.* Athens: Ohio University Press.

Schegloff, Emanuel A., and Harvey Sacks. 1973. "Opening Up Closings." *Semiotica – Journal of the International Association for Semiotic Studies / Revue de l'Association Internationale de Sémiotique* 8 (4): 289–327.

Schermerhorn, Richard A. 1978. *Comparative Ethnic Relations: A Framework for Theory and Research.* Chicago and London: University of Chicago Press.

Scovel, Tom. 1969. "Foreign Accents, Language Acquisition and Cerebral Dominance." *Language Learning* 20: 245–253.

Seki. 2018. "Seki." 14 October. Accessed October 31, 2020. https://sekidance.org/sekirivers/.

Showtime People. 2009. "Nite of a 1000 laughs holds at the Muson." *Vanguard* September 25. Accessed 01 November 2020. https://www.vanguardngr.com/2009/09/nite-of-a-1000-laughs-holds-at-the-muson/.

Showtime People. 2010. "Opa Repackages a Nite of 1000 Laughs." *Vanguard* April 23. Accessed November 01, 2020. https://www.vanguardngr.com/2010/04/opa-repackages-a-nite-of-1000-laughs/.

Showtime People. 2014. "Fabulous Life of Rich Nigerian Comedians." *Vanguard* February 22. Accessed August 14, 2020. https://www.vanguardngr.com/2014/02/fabulous-life-rich-nigerian-comedians/.

Siderz Entertainment TV. 2019. "Gordons De Berlusconi shares his poverty story in church and the congregation erupts in Laughter." *YouTube.* 18 September. Accessed December 14, 2020. https://www.youtube.com/watch?v=nJtGQ8zC5wE.

Sokunbi, Wale and Sam Nwanze. 1990. "When Humour Died." *National Concord* Lagos, October 26.

StreamComLive. 2016. "Best of Still Ringing Comedian." *YouTube* November 2. Accessed December 15, 2019. https://youtu.be//tCaVCC0hWnw.

Stuart, Mikayla. 2018. "Who's Laughing Now: The Gender Gap in Stand-Up Comedy." *Spec Magazine* December 04. Accessed November 05, 2020. https://www.specmag.org/read-us/2018/11/26/whos-laughing-now-the-gender-gap-in-stand-up-comedy.

Sunday, Adesina B., and Ibukun Filani. 2019. "Playing with Culture: Nigerian Stand-up Comedians Joking with Cultural Beliefs and Representations." *Humor* 32 (1): 97–124. doi:10.1515/humor-2017-0085.

TA Media. 2020. "Aproko Best Mimic of Olu Jacobs." *YouTube* July 07. Accessed December 14, 2020. https://www.youtube.com/watch?v=bUCNIWyOheU.

TheBroadway TV. 2019. "AY Brings Out Success On Stage At AY LIVE 2019." *YouTube* April 24. Accessed December 16, 2020. https://www.youtube.com/watch?app=desktop&v=DPIOhmT389M.

This Day. 2016. "The Transformation of Yibo Koko." *This Day* December 18. Accessed August 14, 2020. https://www.thisdaylive.com/index.php/2016/12/18/the-transformation-of-yibo-koko/.

Tidi, Michael. 2018. "Warri Economic Summit: Reviving Africa's Humour Capital." *Vanguard* May 13. Accessed November 01, 2020. https://www.vanguardngr.com/2018/05/warrri-economic-summit-reviving-africas-humour-capital/.

Times Reporter. 2014. "It was a Night of a Thousand Laughs at Car Wash Gardens." *The New Times* August 04. Accessed December 01, 2020. https://www.newtimes.co.rw/section/read/77352.

Timothy-Asobele, S. J. (2003). *Nigerian Top TV Comedians and Soap Opera*. Lagos: Upper Standard Publications.

TNC Reporter. 2016. "My beef with Princess –Lolo 1." *The News Chronicle* January 31. Accessed November 04, 2020. https://thenews-chronicle.com/my-beef-with-princess-lolo-1/.

Tolbert, Jeffrey A. 2016. "Introduction." In *The Folkloresque: Reframing Folklore in a Popular Culture*, 175–178. Logan: Utah State University Press.

Tolu. 2013. "'I was a Comedy Apprentice for 3 Years' – Bovi." *Information Nigeria* February 09. Accessed August 13, 2020. https://www.informationnigeria.com/2013/02/i-was-a-comedy-apprentice-for-3-years-bovi.html.

Trendtv Entertainment. 2020. "Kenny Blaq Thrill Wizkid, D'banj, Tekno, Omotola,

Mercy and Ike At Laugh Fest." *YouTube* June 14. Accessed December 24, 2020. https://www.youtube.com/watch?v=k7yeknKEfAU.

Turner, Victor. 1969. *The Ritual Process: Structure and Anti-Structure*. Chicago: Akline.

Udodiong, Inemesit. 2019. "Top 5 Nollywood Movies that Won at the Box Office in 2019." *Pulse.ng.* December 31. Accessed December 15, 2020. https://www.pulse.ng/bi/lifestyle/top-5-nollywood-movies-that-won-at-the-box-office-in-2019/20kjlsk.

Udoye, Edwin Anaegboka. 2011. *Resolving the Prevailing Conflicts Between Christianity and African (Igbo) Traditional Religion through Inculturation.* (Beiträge zue Missionswissenschaft und Interkulturellen Theologie Band) Zurich: Lit Verlag.

Ugboma, Bovi. 2020. "Bovi and His Billionaire Friends (Stand up Comedy)." *YouTube* April 05. Accessed December 14, 2020. https://www.youtube.com/watch?v=hwDo3aMyBTU.

Ukiwo, Ukoha. 2003. "Politics, Ethno-Religious Conflicts and Democratic Consolidation in Nigeria." *The Journal of Modern African Studies* 41 (1): 115–138. http://www.jstor.org/stable/3876192.

Umeh, Charles C. 1989. "The Advent and Growth of Television Broadcasting in Nigeria: Its Political and Educational Overtones." *Africa Media Review* 3 (2): 54–66.

Umukoro, Sam. 2013. "'I was Paid N50 for My First Show': Ali Baba tells Sam Umukoro in New Interview (Part 1)." March 07. Accessed August 14, 2020. https://ynaija.com/i-was-paid-n50-for-my-first-show-ali-baba-tells-sam-umukoro-in-new-interview-part-1/.

Uzoatu, Uzor Maxim. 2019. "Nigerians should talk on how to co-exist." *The Sun* May 15. Accessed August 14, 2020. https://www.sunnewsonline.com/nigerians-should-talk-on-how-to-co-exist/?fbclid=IwAR2biNCKocWKBUmUsKUTg-eICLNL5JW-ibw2ixH15PLNo28gItRrOCz2Ge0.

Wali, Obiajunwa. 1963. "The Dead End of African Literature?" *Transition* (10): 13–15. doi:10.2307/2934441.

Wegru, Joseph Yelepuo. 2000. "The Dagaaba-Frafra Joking Relationship." *Folklore* 14: 86–97. doi:10.7592/FEJF2000.14.dagaaba.

Wilkinson, Jane. 1986. "Nigerian Pidgin and Comedy." *Africa: Rivista Trimestrale Di Studi E Documentazione Dell'Istituto Italiano per L'Africa E L'Oriente* 41 (4): 616–626. https://www.jstor.org/stable/40760062.

Yashere, Gina. 2014. "Gotham Comedy Club NY Live on AXS TV." *YouTube.* April 30. Accessed December 02, 2020. https://www.youtube.com/watch?v=mPdLCC3S5zw.

Yaw Naija Entertainment. 2017. "Mimicko mimics Olu Jacobs, Sam Loco, Pete Edochie, Others at Funny Enough with MC Prince." *YouTube.* June 30. Accessed December 24, 2020. https://www.youtube.com/watch?v=mphkoo-Az7s.

Yékú, James. 2016. "Akpos Don Come Again: Nigerian Cyberpop Hero as Trickster." *Journal of African Cultural Studies* 28 (3): 245–261. http://www.jstor.org/stable/24758691.

Zion Felix. 2016. "Emanuella & Kalybos Concert In Ghana – Full Performance." *YouTube.* August 14. Accessed December 15, 2020. https://www.youtube.com/watch?v=FD6jKQctRFI.

Zulu-Okafor, Zik. 2010. "Opa Williams: Father of Modern Comedy." *Naija Rules* January 22. Accessed May 06, 2021. https://www.naijarules.com/threads/opa-williams-father-of-modern-comedy.36007/.

Index